Pr...

'There are too ... new edition of Blainey's excellent history of our winter sport is especially welcome. The beauty of Blainey's book is not just his clear writing, but his ability to marry fine detail with broad and thematic sweeps. It's an accessible and diverting picture of how football evolved ... He has assembled footy's causes, origins, problems and solutions into such a coherent and credible whole that everything has a role to play in the evolution of our national game.'—*Herald Sun*

'Geoffrey Blainey can really write and he has a nose for the forgotten details that make you sit up, such as early games being played on oblong grounds, sides of forty, goals rare and round balls."—*The Age*

'*A Game of Our Own* will bring rich enjoyment to readers with a deep interest in the history of Australian sport and popular culture.'—*JAS Review of Books*

'ground-breaking, lucidly written'—*The Age*

'a definitive work on the subject'—*Australian Book Review*

'an enjoyable and informative read'—*The Mercury*

'an exhilarating account'—*Australian Financial Review*

'beautifully written'—*The West Australian*

A Game *of* Our Own
The Origins of Australian Football

A GAME *of* OUR OWN
The Origins of Australian Football

Geoffrey Blainey

Football Commences

Published by Black Inc.,
an imprint of Schwartz Media Pty Ltd
Level 4, 289 Flinders Lane
Melbourne Victoria 3000 Australia
email: enquiries@blackincbooks.com
http://www.blackincbooks.com

Copyright © Geoffrey Blainey 2010

First edition 1990
Second edition 2003

ALL RIGHTS RESERVED.
No part of this publication may be reproduced, stored in a retrieval system, or transmitted in any form or by any means electronic, mechanical, photocopying, recording or otherwise without the prior consent of the publishers.

Sources of Illustrations: The owners' names are followed by the page numbers on which their material appears: A Brace Esq. 200 / Australian Gallery of Sport 43, 80, 205 / John Oxley Library 154 / Mead & Beckett Publishing, *S T Gill's Australia* 34 / Radio Times Hulton Picture Gallery 28 / South Australian Archives 133,136 / State Library of Victoria 6, 23, 39, 65, 72, 76, 83, 86, 89, 93, 95, 102, 111, 127, 140, 147, 149, 158, 191, 202 / T W Cooke collection 4, 69 / Jeff Busby 19 / Ebes collection, Tivoli Cards & Paper 162, 171 / Library Council of Victoria xi.

National Library of Australia Cataloguing-in-Publication entry

Blainey, Geoffrey, 1930-

A game of our own : the origins of Australian football

ISBN: 9781863954853 (pbk.)

Previously published: 2003.

Australian football--History.

796.336

Index by Michael Ramsden
Printed in Australia by Griffin Press

Contents

Preface ix

1. The Man in the Zingari Stripe 1
2. Football in the Paddock 11
3. To the Goldfields 31
4. The Day of the Round Ball and the Oblong Ground 46
5. When Harrison Grabbed the Ball and Ran 68
6. Rise of the Barrackers and Hissers 82
7. High Marks, Little Marks and Goal Sneaks 98
8. 'Victorian – perish the thought!' 132
9. The Hidden Money 157
10. The Tribulations of the Man in White 176
11. Myths: Gaelic and Aboriginal 187

Acknowledgements and Sources 213
Early Rules of Football 221

Index 241

Preface

This book traces the origins and the early growth of the game of Australian football, alias Australian Rules. Some of the game's early history is lost in the mists of the past, but most of the salient landmarks and changes can be pieced together. Indeed, since the first edition of this book was published in 1990, some of the lost pieces of the jigsaw have come to light through the ransacking of old newspapers and the discovery of forgotten letters, diaries and notebooks. More evidence will be found, and new deductions drawn from that evidence, over the next twenty years.

The game is essentially an Australian invention. It arose in the late 1850s, when the various kinds of English football were still in flux, and at first it borrowed extensively from games played mainly in English public schools and especially at Rugby School. Almost at once it was a distinctive game. So quickly did it move in its own direction under its own momentum, and so often did it devise or adapt rules and tactics that, within twenty years, it was far removed from the older rugby and the new soccer, and was still changing. By the late 1870s, when for the first time a few Melbourne and Adelaide and Sydney clubs made the coastal voyage to play against each other, it had become a very distinctive code of football. The game probably changed even more over the next hundred years. It will continue to change.

On some of the features of the early game, the evidence is sparse. The game had few rules in its first years, and many important matters, such as the shape of the playing field, were not even mentioned. Thus, until the first edition of this book appeared, it was assumed that originally the game must have been played on an oval-shaped playing field. It is easy to see how this idea gained credence because the evidence was meagre. I did not find clues that Australian football was commenced on a rectangular field until – nearly a year after I had begun my research – I came across a description of a match played between Melbourne and Carlton on 9 June 1877. That day, they were allowed the privilege of playing on the Melbourne Cricket Ground, and the sporting reporter noted their difficulty in adjusting to the wide wings of a circular arena. About the same time I found a diagram of a playing field in the 1877 edition of the annual Victorian magazine *The Footballer*; the field was oblong. Other clues favour the hypothesis that Australian football began on a rectangular ground and then, when it moved to the various cricket grounds, adapted itself to their round or oval arena.

As it is not easy to investigate a question as elementary as the shape of the early arenas, we cannot be fully confident about several other important facets of the early game. One of the crucial questions is why Australian football did not adopt a sending-off rule. As the arena was huge and as the play sometimes moved with high speed from one end of the arena to the other, it was very difficult for an umpire. There were acts of violence which an umpire could not see: they took place behind the play or were too far ahead of him to be seen clearly. By 1900 violence was all too frequent in Melbourne matches. Other major football codes permitted an umpire or referee to ban an offending player from the field for the remainder of the game, but Australian football refused to adopt that harsh form of discipline. Why it refused is not clear. Only in recent years has Australian football, at its senior level, adopted a policy of appointing two – and now three – central umpires. That policy of course leads to inconsistencies, for the game has a cavalcade of rules, some of which depend heavily on personal judgement rather than simple facts.

The first edition of this book ended the story in or around 1880 – soon after the forming of the Victorian Football Association, and soon after the playing of the first matches against teams from other colonies. The second edition extended the story for twenty or more years and added new sections to the old while also, here and there, making verbal alterations for the sake of accuracy, clarity or pithiness. Furthermore the early Victorian, South Australian and Gaelic rules printed at the end of the book were augmented by additional rules, as indicators of how the game evolved.

Before and after the first edition of this book appeared, the idea was widespread that Australian football was simply an offshoot of Gaelic football, a rather similar game played in Ireland. Indeed, this book was initially sponsored by the National Australian Football Council and its general manager, Ed Biggs, partly to investigate whether that Gaelic theory was valid. The theory seemed plausible because the two games had much in common. On the other hand, several earlier historians of the Australian game had pointed out that they could find little or no direct evidence in favour of a Gaelic origin. Their conclusions tended to be ignored. Eventually I realised that it was not enough to point to the lack of concrete evidence in favour of the Gaelic interpretation. It was vital to produce evidence positively refuting a Gaelic interpretation. Slowly that evidence came to hand, and it can be found in Chapter 11 of this edition.

In the last twenty years the Gaelic theory has declined dramatically in popularity, only to be challenged by another. There is now support, especially in some academic and football circles and a section of the media, for the theory that Australian football is really an

*An artist stood in the Botanical Gardens in 1889 and sketched, taking a few liberties, the football grounds on the other side of the Yarra. Towards the horizon can be seen, from left to right, the East Melbourne ground (with the Exhibition Building above it), the Melbourne Cricket Ground and the Richmond ground. The arena nearest the river was the Friendly Societies' Gardens (*The Australasian Sketcher, *26 December 1889).*

old Aboriginal game, adopted in the 1850s by white newcomers to Melbourne. So far there is even less evidence, actual or circumstantial, for the Aboriginal theory than for the Gaelic theory.

At present the evidence is overwhelming that the Australian game in its first years was a deliberately chosen mixture of English rules, to which were added a stream of Australian innovations. The innovations, now nation-wide in origin, continue at such a fast pace that the present game would not be recognisable to the players of 1860.

The Australian Football League, the present guardian of the game, has become a good friend to Aboriginal footballers, and they have more than repaid the debt. They are one of the ornaments of the game: perhaps nothing has done more to enrich football in the last half-century than the increasing role of Aboriginal champions.

But the idea that they invented the game seems to be fanciful. Two recent investigators – Greg de Moore and Gillian Hibbins – having surveyed the wide range of evidence from the 1850s, wrote books which affirmed without hesitation that the theory of an Aboriginal origin is weak or even 'ludicrous'. Unfortunately the Australian Football League prefers to support or tolerate the Aboriginal theory rather than to investigate it seriously.

In telling this story, I had to make decisions about time and distance. In describing past games, I prefer yards and feet and the old imperial measurements. If a footballer in the 1870s was said by a newspaper to have kicked the ball 60 yards, it is unwise to translate this, as we might do now, into 60 metres. A yard is not a metre: such a translation inflates unduly the length of a long kick. To convert '60 yards' precisely into 54.9 metres (or even 55) is to convey an impression of accuracy which the original newspaper account did not really intend. Likewise, when the early rule-makers decided to define a ground as not more than 200 yards in length, we would be silly to write, without an explanation, that they fixed the maximum length of a ground at no more than 182.88 metres or, say, 183 metres. Immediately we lose sight of the rough-and-ready but practical way in which the early rules were made and the early matches reported in the newspapers.

Time also creates a difficulty. In 1895 all clocks in Victoria were permanently advanced by twenty minutes and six seconds in order to create the present Australian Eastern Standard Time. This means that a Melbourne football match which was reported to have commenced at, say, 3.00 pm on a Saturday before 1895 really began at about 3.20 pm, if translated into modern time. This was a very late start, especially in mid-winter, but the late start was unavoidable because most players and spectators worked on Saturday morning. As matches often came to an end towards 5.30 or 6.00 pm by the old Victorian time, or some twenty minutes later by our time, we glimpse the darkness in which many games must have ended. I have retained the old measurement of time in the narrative.

In describing the development of the game, I usually prefer the newer phrase 'Australian football'. Originally it was just called football. Later it was usually called 'Victorian Rules', especially from the late 1870s. Later came 'Australian Rules' and 'Aussie Rules'.

Geoffrey Blainey
Melbourne
June 2010

CHAPTER ONE

The Man in the Zingari Stripe

In the parkland outside the Melbourne Cricket Ground stand three old and ghost-like gum trees. Though two have been dead for decades, they are protected by fences made of iron pickets. A long and neat scar in the trunk of the trees is still visible, and a plaque near the foot of one tree proclaims that long ago it was scarred by Aboriginals when they cut away the bark with their stone axes to make a simple canoe or other receptacle. Those spectators who park their cars near these trees in the football season scarcely notice them, let alone their significance. But the football they come to watch was largely invented in that parkland, and some of the first matches were played around those trees when they were flourishing in the 1850s.

The parkland was then dotted with large redgums, and occasionally the football was kicked into the upper branches while underneath the players waited, ready to grab the ball after it fell. The trees were an accepted obstacle in those first experimental years and we have the report of one match in which the ball, kicked by a player, hit the trunk of a tree and was then deflected between the goalposts. The goal was actually allowed. The rules of this new game were not only very different from those of today, but were also different from those of any other football game in the world. The game was, from the start, a new recipe with old ingredients.

Of the main codes of football played in the world, Australian Rules is one of the oldest. By the normal definition of age, it is older than American football or gridiron, older than Rugby League, older than the modern version of Gaelic football from which it is widely said to have been descended, a little older than Association football or soccer, but younger than Rugby.

In Britain are very old Rugby clubs and teams. Football at the Rugby School began to take on its distinctive form in 1823. In London the still-active Guy's and St Thomas' Hospitals Rugby Football Club, on one line of descent, goes back to 1843. But Rugby Union, in view of its proud amateur tradition, did not attract large crowds during its early decades. Its clubs did not attract a band of followers as large as those watching the famous English soccer and Australian football teams.

Few of the senior football clubs in the world, irrespective of the specific code they play, can be as old as the senior Australian football clubs. No famous soccer club is as old as the senior football clubs in Victoria. When I tried to place the football clubs in the Australian Football League and the English Football League in order of seniority, I assumed that the list would be led by English teams such as Manchester United or Blackburn Rovers or another famous long-standing club. It surprised me to discover that even the English Football League, the oldest of all the national leagues in the dominant international code of soccer, has no club that matches the antiquity of the early Victorian clubs. According to my investigations, that combined list of old senior clubs in the two codes runs in this sequence:

1858 Melbourne
1859 Geelong
1862 Notts County
1863 Stoke City
1864 Carlton
1865 Nottingham Forest

Essendon and St Kilda and some of the middle-aged clubs in the Australian Football League have a longer history than the oldest senior clubs in such famous football nations as Germany and Argentina. Even Collingwood, which is a young club by Australian standards, being founded in 1892, is as old as the oldest of the senior Italian clubs, Genoa. Similarly, Port Adelaide, founded in 1870, goes back much further than the oldest senior club in that wonderful footballing nation Brazil.

The Australian brand of football, though old, is sometimes seen as young and even as an imported game in those Australian cities in which today it has an immense following. How it arose, and how it was shaped, is a strange story.

The new game was influenced not only by those who sat on committees and drew up rules, but by those who actually played. Thomas Wills filled all roles. He played, captained, umpired and helped to shape the rules of the new game that soon attracted spectators to the parklands only a mile from the heart of goldrush Melbourne. Sometimes he even claimed that he had initiated it. He once recalled that 'this manly game was first introduced into the Colony by the writer in 1857, but it was not taken too kindly until the following year'. His assertion cannot be accepted literally but he did as much as anybody in the first years to make it an attractive sport, though, when he ceased playing, it was still far from the game we know.

Tom Wills was brought up with a silver spoon in his mouth: his father was a rich sheepowner. He was also brought up with a spoon of vinegar, the bitter taste of which he was careful to conceal. His grandfather, Edward Wills, was an English criminal who at Kingston on Thames had been sentenced to death for highway robbery, the sentence being commuted to transportation for life. Reaching Sydney in 1799 this convict and his free wife eventually began to do well as the owners of a general store and tavern. Tom Wills' father, Horatio Spencer Wills, was born in Sydney and eventually became a printer and publisher. He also took up land on the

Thomas Wentworth Wills, who did more than any other man to sponsor the new game. This photo (from the T Wills Cooke collection) was probably taken after Wills returned from school in England. Dapper and sensitive here, he wears a 'couldn't care less' look in photos of fifteen years later.

Molonglo Plains, not too far from the present Canberra, and involved himself in that remarkable overland movement of sheep and cattle which occupied the vast areas of the Port Phillip District, later to become the Colony of Victoria. Tom Wills, the earliest hero of Australian football, was born on 19 August 1835. He was aged four when in April 1840 he set out with his parents from the upper Murrumbidgee on that long journey, camping each night beside a large fire, travelling each day with the straggling flock, and crossing the wider rivers – for there were no bridges – on the body of a cart or dray which, modified, served as a slow-moving boat. The family eventually settled at Lexington, near the present Ararat in western Victoria, where they built a slab hut and then a substantial homestead far from the nearest church, police station and shop. Aboriginals were still living in the district, their numbers cut down by disease, and young Tom Wills played with them. One of his cousins once recalled that, to the delight of the local Aboriginals, Tom learned to speak their language with some fluency. He was also 'very clever at picking up their songs, which he delivered with a very amusing imitation of their voice and gestures'.

The family longed for the precious items of the cities and eventually bought a cottage piano which was carried by sailing ship from London and by dray from Port Phillip Bay. They also believed in educating their children. Tom, at about the age of ten, went to Melbourne, to Brickwood's Academy, where he won a little notice at a cricket match on Batman's Hill, near Spencer Street and the Yarra River. He made two 'ducks', or spectacles as they were then called, and also suffered one black eye when he missed a catch.

When he was about fourteen Tom made the long voyage by sailing ship past Cape Horn and across the Atlantic to England where he was enrolled at the Rugby School in the Midlands. The venture was a triumph for the grandson of a convict. The Rugby School might have viewed it as less of a triumph had it known of the new boy's background, for the biblical phrase that the sins of the fathers were visited on the children generation after generation was held in high regard as a kind of mixed law of morality and genetics, meaning that 'bad blood' was not easily changed. The English boarding school at first must have been a lonely and dislocating experience. Though Tom was initially behind most boys in his studies, he compensated in sport, and in a letter to his father in August 1851 he recounted not only the sermons he heard in the school chapel but also the impressive scores he had made in cricket that summer. His aunt, the widow of a famous Australian convict, Dr Redfern, and now remarried and living in London, visited Tom at Rugby in 1853 and declared him 'a fine youth – sensible, well-looking and gentlemanly'. He was not, however, as

Horatio Spencer Wills, Australian-born squatter who played a part in founding Australian football by his decision to send his son Tom all the way from Melbourne to boarding school in England. There Tom developed his obsession with cricket, football and other sports.

ambitious as his father had hoped. The father, to whom he wrote regularly and whose replies arrived some six or eight months later, asked himself, with much exaggeration, whether he had produced a dunce. Such scrawling hand-writing, he complained, with errors in spelling and mistakes in grammar such as no educated lad should make!

Tom's school work improved markedly, but it could not match his brilliance at games. At the age of sixteen he captured ten wickets in a game against the Westminster School, and in a match against an All England Eleven he scored a total of 51 runs which in the low scoring of that era was almost equal to 200 runs today. Playing for Kent with the famous 'Lion of Kent', the bowler Alfred Mynn, he captured nine of the wickets of the Gentlemen of Sussex. Playing at Lords against the Marylebone Cricket Club, he captured another long list of wickets. He was one of England's most promising cricketers and was pointed out – to a man who later emigrated to Melbourne and became one of the makers of

Australian Rules – as 'that young fellow from Rugby, who plays with a 4 lb. bat, and hits terrific'.

Tom Wills returned with his heavy bat to Australia, reaching Melbourne at Christmas 1856. He found the town transformed. The wool port of 25,000 people was now a city of some 80,000

Leading Victorian cricketers of 1859, elegant in their coloured cravats. Many of the best Victorian cricketers had played in the first games of Australian football in the winter of the previous year.

people and the world's richest shipper of gold. With a new university, houses of parliament and the continent's first steam trains and telegraph line, it seemed at last to be part of Britain.

Wills appeared, soon after landing, at the regular afternoon practice at the Melbourne Cricket Ground, just a mile from the main streets of the city. His reputation came ahead of him and the other players watched him eagerly, and maybe enviously, for he was conspicuous in his 'somewhat flashy getup' and his Zingari stripe or sash. Zingari was the Italian word for gypsies, and Wills was about to become the dashing gypsy of the sportsfield, always playing and always capturing the public eye.

He was then aged twenty-one. Highly athletic and strong in stamina and determination, he was already an outstanding cricketer.

Strength and timing rather than conspicuous style were his characteristics and he later suggested that he was more the rough-and-ready player who achieved results than one of those 'pretty showy players who have been puffed up to the skies'.

Dashing in his appearance, he was careful to groom himself in the latest fashion. One photograph of him – not fully clear, because photography was in its infancy – shows him with long wavy hair worn half-way down the ears, the hair parted on the right-hand side, clipped chin-whiskers of darkish colour and a short moustache. In contrast the expression on the face is withdrawn rather than assertive. The noticeable part of his physique is his hands: they are unusually large.

Wills was dour and sensitive, and even introverted at times. He could also be kind and companionable. 'Taciturn' was the word sometimes applied to him, but he did not extend his silence to the printed page. He enjoyed writing letters and he wrote them rather in the manner of a speaker declaiming forcefully from a platform. A long letter he wrote in 1858 to a Melbourne sporting paper is a landmark in the history of Australian football.

Wills quickly became one of Victoria's finest cricketers. For the Melbourne Cricket Club he was a big hitter, a fine fieldsman, a clever tactician and a foxy bowler who could send down either fast or slow balls. It was still an era mainly of under-arm bowling, and he was to be accused a few seasons later of 'throwing' by raising his bowling arm above the height of the shoulder when delivering the ball.

An innovator, he is said to have introduced Australia to the idea that the captains should toss a coin in order to determine which team had the first choice of batting or bowling. For the season 1857–58 he became secretary of the Melbourne Cricket Club, a part-time position, and when his own club had no fixture on a Saturday afternoon, he gladly offered to play for any other side.

Other clubs were happy to select him, and in his second season as Melbourne cricketer he was recorded as playing twice for St Kilda against Richmond and once for Collingwood against Richmond,

The Melbourne Cricket Ground on New Year's Day, 1864, when tents and temporary pavilions were built to cater for the large crowd. In this Charles Toedel print the white smoke from the passing steam train can be seen though the gum-tree boughs on the left. Footballers were no more welcome than locomotives on the arena.

and no doubt he made appearances for an even wider variety of clubs. In January 1858 he helped Victoria to defeat New South Wales in one of the first intercolonial matches, and he was to play sixteen times for Victoria and captain the team on eight occasions. A total of sixteen appearances for Victoria, in a period when only one appearance was possible in the normal year, was perhaps the equivalent of a career covering say 200 Test and interstate cricket matches today. He was to leave the Melbourne club in November 1858 and to play for Richmond which he was to captain in cricket on and off for many years.

He was attracted to virtually every sport except horse-racing. His work at the office of a Collingwood solicitor was apparently not arduous; nor did he wish it to be so, for games appear to have pleased him more than work. His worry was that Melbourne did not yet provide him and his friends with sufficient sport for every available Saturday. The cricket season ended in May: what game could he play next? He decided to arouse public interest in football – another of the games he had played at Rugby School.

CHAPTER TWO

Football in the Paddock

Football was already being played in Melbourne. It is likely that in every year since at least 1840 one match – and in certain years perhaps up to five matches – was played in Melbourne. As newspapers were confined to a few pages, most of which were filled by advertisements, and as they rarely printed news about sports, they would have noticed only a few of such football matches as were played on public holidays in the paddocks and parklands that were close to the young town.

Near Batman's Hill, long since flattened to make way for the shunting yards and goods sheds of the Spencer Street railway station, the Irish sport of hurling was played in July 1844 between teams owing allegiance to Clare and Tipperary, and on the same day a game of football was a lesser attraction. During the Christmas celebrations of 1845, reported *The Port Phillip Herald*, a football was kicked while the greasy pole was being climbed. At the end of 1849 the Old White Hart Inn in Bourke Street advertised a holiday sports meeting at which goat racing and skittles and other games would be played, the fun-fair ending with a 'Grand Match at the old English Game of Football'. In March 1850, a month which seemed too hot for football, another match was arranged in Melbourne for a trophy of a silver pocket watch. How the winning players would apportion the silver watch between themselves was not made clear. In August of the same year the Victorian Gymnastic Games staged a football match that went on for two and a half hours. In November at Geelong a football match with six men on each side was played for a wager. These early tussles must have followed a variety of rules, some of which were home-made.

Compared to horse-racing and hunting and cricket, football did not yet appeal to the general public. The majority of its followers were probably workingmen and so it was played only on public holidays, for most men normally worked six days a week. Sunday, of course, was not available for sports.

In Melbourne, football made its first jump forward when it became the game of people possessing more leisure. Schoolboys then formed the main leisure class: their relatively short working week allowed them some time for sports, especially on Saturday. Moreover, by the late 1850s, some of those headmasters fresh from England were eager to encourage that emphasis on 'manly games' which was now visible in many English boarding schools.

Dr John E Bromby was one headmaster who, almost as soon as he landed in Melbourne, was willing to foster football amongst older boys at the new Church of England Grammar School. Athletic and energetic, he displayed his fitness in front of the students by chopping wood or digging in his garden. Educated at the grammar school in Hull and at the well-known Uppingham School, he had shone in classics and mathematics at St John's College, Cambridge, before teaching in his own small school in Bristol. In 1847 he began a term of five years as principal of Elizabeth College at Guernsey in the Channel Islands before returning to Hull to help his old father, a clergyman.

In retrospect, the highlight of Bromby's English career was when he competed at Cambridge with Alfred Tennyson for the poetry medal, the subject of their poems being that exotic African city of Timbuctoo. Late in 1857 Bromby found himself attracted to a more southerly Timbuctoo; he packed his possessions and set sail for Melbourne where in April 1858 he opened the new school on St Kilda Road. He attracted about eighty students and within a few months many were playing football.

The first bluestone buildings of Melbourne Grammar then stood near an expanse of tree-dotted wasteland. Not a building stood between the school and the shores of what we call the Albert Park Lake but which was then called 'the swamp' or lagoon. Bullocks, moving slowly in pairs, drew the loaded drays past the school on their way to outlying villages and sheep stations, and for a mile or more their straight route towards St Kilda passed through wasteland with not a building on either side of the road. Plentiful parklands within a mile of the city were a hallmark of Melbourne, and these surrounding open lands strongly affected the rise of football and the type of game that was preferred. The first characteristic of Australian football to a foreigner is the exceptionally large arena on which it is played. The game was born on the sweeping parklands. Most of the early matches – as far as we know – were played on expanses that make the present football grounds seem tiny.

Across the long lagoon and the parklike wastelands, the village of St Kilda stood on its low hill overlooking the bay. There, in Acland Street, just above the present site of Luna Park, William C Northcott conducted his own school in the hope, he told fond parents, that their boys could become officers in the army or navy, members of the bar or civil service, or students at the university which had been opened on the other side of Melbourne two years previously. His St Kilda Grammar School occupied the former Pembroke Hotel, a brick building of twenty-one rooms, many of which had a commanding view of the bay. The salt breeze was believed to make the site healthy, and Northcott encouraged his boys to play various sports and do physical exercises.

His school was two or three years older than the Melbourne Grammar School and football might well have been played there even before Dr Bromby reached the colony. Whatever may be the facts, Mr Northcott soon met Bromby – both were Cambridge graduates – and they agreed that their two grammar schools should play a match of football at the start of the winter of 1858. It is the earliest football game on record between two Victorian schools or clubs. Played either on the wastelands near St Kilda Road or on the government reserve which ran along the St Kilda seafront within sight of Northcott's school, the match's duration and rules are not known. But Dr Bromby recorded in his journal of 5 June 1858 that his school won the match.*

Closer to the city, the Scotch College was also eager to play. Older than the rival schools, it was possibly playing football before Mr Northcott and Dr Bromby encouraged their boys to play the game. It is on record at Scotch College that one of its masters, Harvey, imported six footballs from England and taught some of his students to play football in the school yard: their code was probably Rugby, from which school he is said to have come. As Scotch College had recently moved to new stone buildings in East Melbourne, on a site now occupied by St Andrew's Hospital, it held an ideal position for football, and its boys could walk to the parklands near the Melbourne Cricket Ground in only five minutes.

Scotch's new headmaster, Alexander Morrison, had been until 1857 the rector of Hamilton Academy in Lanarkshire, Scotland.

---

* The match was not rediscovered until the late 1980s when Anne Mancini and Gillian Hibbins found a brief note in Bromby's journal. Evidence of other early matches between schools could well be found in years to come.

It is significant that the three Melbourne schools which in 1858 played football were governed by new headmasters from differing backgrounds in England, Scotland and the Channel Islands. The three heads were conscious of the quickening emphasis on sport in many English public schools, but they had not come from schools which happened to play the same code of football. If in the British Isles they all had fallen within the Rugby influence, that particular code would have made quick headway in Victoria, not only in the schools but in the clubs which the senior boys joined when they left school. Instead, Victoria's schools inherited no favourite code. They were free to develop – they had to develop – their own code of football.

Two months after Melbourne Grammar had defeated the St Kilda school it agreed to play the Scotch College. In the city of Melbourne these were the two best-known secondary schools and taught the sons of many of the leading merchants, bankers, lawyers and other men of property and the professions. News of the proposed match actually reached the newspapers and, on Saturday, 7 August 1858, *The Melbourne Morning Herald* reported:

> A grand football match will be played this day, between the Scotch College and the Church of England Grammar School, near the Melbourne Cricket Club ground. Luncheon at the pavilion. Forty a side. The game to commence at twelve o'clock.

The pavilion was almost certainly the Melbourne Cricket Club's low bungalow-type club house, but the cricket ground itself was not opened for the schoolboy footballers. Its strip of turf, if it could be called turf, was considered precious. The cricket ground was declared out of bounds to the footballers, less because it was like a lawn than because it was so patchy that the cricket club was reluctant to allow it to deteriorate further.

The Saturday chosen for the football match was sunny but cool. Around noon the two teams – a few masters playing with the boys – gathered on the stretch of park that sloped up from the cricket ground. The available playing field was enormous and, as far as we know, extended from the fence of the Richmond Cricket Ground almost across to where the Hilton Hotel now stands. The present railway line to Jolimont and Clifton Hill was parkland in the 1850s and so the footballers had a vast expanse from which they could choose. If the teams had used the maximum length of parkland, their arena could have stretched about 800 metres from goal to goal, or four times the length of today's Australian football ground. As the 'Yarra Park' attracted many strollers and perhaps clusters of playing children, the schoolboys were unlikely to have seized the entire parkland for their match. If they concentrated on the middle stretch of parkland which sloped less steeply and had the advantage of closeness to the luncheon tables at the pavilion of the Melbourne Cricket Ground, they could have played along a goal-to-goal line of nearly 600 metres, stretching from the western fence of the Richmond cricket ground to the Jolimont Terrace. The Melbourne Cricket Ground in those years lacked a wide perimeter of grandstands, but at some time on this merry afternoon the footballers chasing the ball were near the walls of the present western and northern grandstands.

Almost no part of the park was flat and some stretches were littered with pebbles. The park was also studded with small trees, and several times the football must have bounced off a trunk of a tree or perched in a branch. Some of the gum trees were so large and spreading that at no one viewing point could a spectator – and perhaps several hundred were present for part of the afternoon – possess a view of the whole arena. Play was sometimes out of sight, even for those spectators who sat high in a horse-drawn vehicle near the boundary.

It is almost certain that the goal at one end of the arena must have been out of sight of the goal at the other end, because then, as now, a ridge or spur makes it impossible for those standing near the fence of the Richmond ground to see the Jolimont houses which front the park. The goals themselves were probably two pairs of well-marked trees, roughly the same distance apart, but we cannot rule out the possibility that posts were placed in the soil to mark the goals.

Each team selected its own central umpire, after the fashion of cricket. Melbourne Grammar chose Tom Wills; his presence suggests that he might have also been an umpire of that school's previous game in June. The Scotch College chose a distinctive umpire whose long red hair and beard must have been conspicuous as he followed the play amongst the gum trees. John Macadam was aged thirty-one, had lived for three years in Melbourne, and for most of that time had taught chemistry and natural history at the Scotch College. A doctor of medicine from Glasgow, he was probably overqualified for his teaching post and was soon to make a new career as Melbourne's health officer, the first lecturer in chemistry at the university's medical school, member of parliament for Castlemaine, for eight months the colony's postmaster general and the secretary of the committee which despatched the explorers Burke and Wills to central Australia. What experience of football, if any, this strong-voiced redhead possessed we do not know. Almost forgotten today, Dr Macadam figured prominently in two important events of our social history, neither of which was linked to his main career. He was not only an umpire of this historic game of Australian football, but his name survives in the only Australian indigenous food to be found in American supermarkets, the macadamia nut.

For much of the afternoon the game lurched back and forth. The play was probably congested, with a big pack hovering near the ball and preventing it from breaking loose. After nearly three hours of play, Scotch College was on the brink of scoring. *The Melbourne Morning Herald*, reporting in its Monday edition, wrote that 'most jubilant were the cheers that rang among the gum trees and the she oaks of the park when Scotch College obtained a goal'. Even the redheaded umpire probably joined in the cheers, for this was a game to enjoy.

After the scoring of the first goal there was probably a pause and even the wolfing down of refreshments in the pavilion. Melbourne Grammar players then snatched the initiative and before long they goaled. The hope that another goal would decide who was the winner was frustrated by failing light or what the press called 'Evening's anxious shades'. As the printed calendar tells us that the sun, on that afternoon, set at eight minutes past five, the light was probably dim enough in that tree-studded arena to have terminated the game some fifteen minutes earlier. The match therefore must have been almost five hours in length, with perhaps one major and one minor interval reducing the actual playing time to just over four hours. That was twice as long as the present Australian game.

The teams played again two Saturdays later, and neither could score. Another two Saturdays passed and they played again. Neither side goaled, and so the match was declared a draw, the football season having ended.

The match between the schools has become a legend, but this was not the first game of Australian football played that year in Melbourne. Nor was it Australian football as we know it. Australian football was not a once-only invention, recognisable from the outset, but a game that evolved during many decades. Nonetheless, this match, spread over three separate Saturdays in 1858, was a vital step in that evolution. Football in Victoria was moving from that phase of the 1840s and early 1850s when it was essentially a game played only at carnivals and holidays, a game played according to a

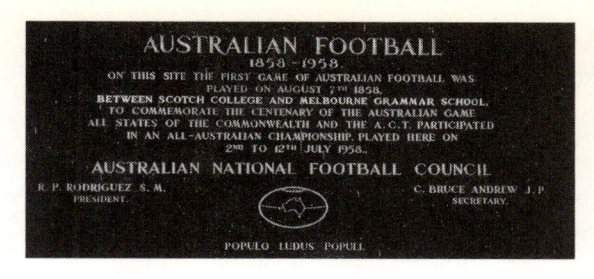

> AUSTRALIAN FOOTBALL
> 1858–1958
> ON THIS SITE THE FIRST GAME OF AUSTRALIAN FOOTBALL WAS
> PLAYED ON AUGUST 7TH 1858,
> BETWEEN SCOTCH COLLEGE AND MELBOURNE GRAMMAR SCHOOL.
> TO COMMEMORATE THE CENTENARY OF THE AUSTRALIAN GAME
> ALL STATES OF THE COMMONWEALTH AND THE A.C.T. PARTICIPATED
> IN AN ALL-AUSTRALIAN CHAMPIONSHIP, PLAYED HERE ON
> 2ND TO 12TH JULY 1958.
> AUSTRALIAN NATIONAL FOOTBALL COUNCIL
> R. P. RODRIGUEZ, S. M.   C. BRUCE ANDREW, J.P.
> PRESIDENT   SECRETARY
> POPULO LUDUS POPULI

'The match between the schools has become a legend.' The tablet sits on the outer wall of the Melbourne Cricket Ground.

variety of rules, to a new phase in which it was played regularly according to a new set of rules. It was ceasing to be a sideshow. It was becoming, like cricket, a game in its own right.

While the schoolboys and a few of the schoolmasters were chasing the football around the park on Saturdays, other matches of football – overlooked by history – were taking place in the same park. Football in Melbourne in 1858 was making a two-pronged advance. Just when secondary schools were becoming absorbed in football, young men and late teenagers were organising matches which were to have stronger effects on the development of Australian football.

Exactly one month before Scotch College met Melbourne Grammar at football for the first time, Tom Wills launched his own plan. He wrote a letter – he liked to write public letters – to the new sporting weekly, *Bell's Life in Victoria*, suggesting that a football club be formed. What was in his mind was not fully clear, but at least we have the letter in which he followed his zig-zag route:

> Sir – Now that cricket has been put aside for some months to come, and cricketers have assumed somewhat of the chrysalis nature (for a time only 'tis sure), but at length will burst forth in all their varied hues,

Here he paused for breath. For some reason he was determined to mention the butterfly – the chrysalis – and the way in which it vanished in winter and reappeared in summer in garish colours rather like a cricketer's cap and sash. Although Tom's sentence was now almost out of hand, he pressed on with some special advice for cricketers:

> rather than allow this state of torpor to creep over them, and stifle their now supple limbs, why can they not, I say, form a foot-ball club, and form a committee of three or more to draw up a code of laws? If a club of this sort were got up, it would be of vast benefit to any cricket-ground to be trampled upon, and would make the turf quite firm and durable; besides which, it would keep those who are inclined to become stout from having joints encased in useless superabundant flesh.

A careful scanning of this sentence suggests that, contrary to a view sometimes expressed, Wills was not writing primarily on behalf of the Melbourne Cricket Club. There is no evidence that the cricket club then or in any year of the following decade wished to see its turf trampled upon by footballers. Indeed, if Wills was expressing views of the Melbourne Cricket Club, he would have expressed those views primarily at a meeting of the club's committee rather than in a personal letter to the press. He was simply a sports-lover who, feeling at a loose end when the winter came, hoped that a new activity could keep together those who played cricket with him in the long summer. He was not even certain that football would be the most appropriate winter game, as the last half of this letter indicated:

> If it is not possible to form a foot-ball club, why should not these young men who have adopted this new-born country for their mother land, why I say, do they not form themselves into a rifle club, so as at any-rate they may some day be called upon to aid

their adopted land against a tyrant's band, that may some day 'pop' upon us when we least expect a foe at our very doors.

Wills did not have to tell his readers that defence was a matter of urgency. The war in the Crimea, in which Britain and France and Sardinia fought on the side of Turkey against the Russian Czar, had ended only two years ago; and during the war there was widespread fear that a Russian warship would suddenly appear at Port Phillip Heads and capture ships about to carry away the new-mined gold to England. As no telegraph line then ran between Australia and Europe, a Russian raider could quietly sail across the equator towards the British colonies without a word of her whereabouts reaching Australia. Moreover, Britain's sense of her own might had suddenly been jolted by another war, for only the previous year the British troops in India had been taken by surprise in the Sepoy mutiny and British garrisons had been besieged and even massacred. Tom Wills was therefore using a powerful argument which we, knowing little about the war fears of that time, are inclined to view less seriously than his pleas for a new football club. On the defence argument, his letter elaborated. He said that firing a rifle at a target was less hazardous than a batsman facing a fast bowler:

> Surely, our young cricketers are not afraid of the crack of the rifle, when they face so courageously the leathern sphere, and it would disgrace no one to learn in time how to defend his country and his hearth. A firm heart, a steady hand, a quick eye, are all that are requisite, and, with practice, all these may be attained.

Wills rounded off his letter with the hope that someone would form a football or rifle club or, failing that, organise athletic games.

Whether the letter had influence on football is uncertain. Wills himself must have been inclined to think his letter had achieved little, because in the following year he wrote again in *Bell's Life* calling on cricket clubs to stage athletics meetings in winter. Of course, such meetings would compete with football games.

Tom Wills' letter of 10 July 1858 is the most celebrated document in the early history of Australian football and deservedly so. Curiously, the first part of the letter on football is quoted far more frequently than the important second part on defence and rifle-shooting. His first love was not football, and that game would merely be the winter gymnasium for the cricketers. He would have been almost as happy belonging to a rifle club, though his letter does not suggest that he saw rifle-shooting as an aid to the eye of the batsman or the aim of the bowler. Essentially the letter reveals a young man seeking the companionship and camaraderie of the sporting contest. He also had an underlying seriousness. As we will see, many of the early makers of Australian football had a mission that went beyond leisure and laughter. In their eyes sport built character and thereby built the nation.

The letter from Tom Wills drew no prompt response. No doubt a few of his cricketing friends commented privately, telling him that they were keen to play the game. A few others might well have asked themselves why, if a new football or rifle club was so important, Wills did not stir himself and organise one. But Wills was not a very methodical organiser. That was the main reason why he served for only one cricket season as secretary of the Melbourne Cricket Club. When his term ran out he is said to have left the club with its amenities – cigars, cricket balls, cricket boots, Zingari flannels and the club's correspondence – all stuffed higgledy-piggledy in a large tin box in the pavilion. Though this untidy scene was described long after the event by one of Wills' critics, it has the ring of truth.

So far as we know, Wills did not directly invite his cricketing friends to meet him one Saturday afternoon in the park for a game of football. That important task seems to have been taken up by an East Melbourne publican. James or 'Jerry' Bryant ran Bryant's Parade Hotel which stood on Wellington Parade, just across the

An artist employed by The Melbourne Post *of 1866 depicted a game in the Richmond Paddock. In the middle background is the pavilion of the Melbourne Cricket Ground. Spectators can be seen sheltering beneath the gum tree inside the playing arena.*

wide road from the Yarra Park where most of the early football matches were played: as there was no railway line to Clifton Hill then, his customers had merely to cross the wide road in order to enter the park. Bryant was a former Surrey cricketer, the first professional cricketer to be hired by the Melbourne Cricket Club and an occasional member of the Victorian cricket eleven, and he was eager to make his hotel a place where sportsmen met. On Saturday, 31 July 1858, *Bell's Life* informed its readers that Bryant on that same afternoon would provide a football for those who wished to play the game in the adjacent park. Bryant's hope, apart from fostering games, was presumably that the thirsty players would drink in his hotel when they brought back his football at the end of the afternoon.

The publican Bryant was supported in his plan by 'a number of gentlemen interested in keeping the muscles in full vigour during the winter, and also anxious for an occasional afternoon's outdoor exercise'. Intending players were invited by the sporting journal *Bell's Life* to meet at one o'clock either on the cricket ground or in the adjacent park. In fact it was in the park that they played. This was possibly the scratch match remembered long after because nearly every imaginable code of scratch football was imitated in the one afternoon. The English players tried a version of Rugby and the Scots played a game that defied description while the Irishmen yelled and punted the ball straight up into the air. While that day some players followed the rules they had learned in the British Isles, other footballers followed 'no rules at all'.

It was expected that at the end of the day a committee would be formed to draw up a few simple rules. Possibly they did draw up rough rules based on that afternoon's experience, but no copy of the rules has survived. Perhaps the only copy was written on the minds of players rather than on paper. Nonetheless, during the anarchy of these first games, when the loose rules were varied from match to match, certain ways of playing became more legitimate. The footballers were groping towards effective rules that suited the mixture of players and the distinctive open spaces and climate of Melbourne.

The footballers again played in the parkland, just outside the low fence of the Melbourne Cricket Ground, on the last three Saturdays in August according to the brief notices in Melbourne newspapers. It is even possible that they also played on the first Saturday. In a small city where so much news travelled effectively by word of mouth, newspapers tended to report events only when a modicum of public interest was already aroused. There was no reason why the press should have reported the early kickabouts by footballers. They were not yet worthy of news. Accordingly, the early records of the new code of football remain meagre.

Wills had gained publicity because, possessing a quiet sense of drama, he viewed the letters column of a newspaper as a public arena, like the cricket pitch. His publicised contribution to the new code of football was vital but so too was the unrecorded work of those organisers of scratch matches and kickabouts – young men who pegged out a spacious stretch of parkland for the afternoon, enlisted a few dozen players, borrowed or bought a football and designated a pair of trees at each end of the arena as goalposts. Various unrecorded games of football were probably played in Melbourne's parks in the later weeks of the winter and early spring of 1858, without a hint of them reaching the newspapers.

Parkland near St Kilda was one resort for footballers. On Saturday, 31 July, one week before the first of the celebrated trio of schoolboy matches at the Richmond Park, 'a football match against the St Kilda Club came to an untimely end'. Apparently a team consisting mainly of schoolboy players, including a few from Melbourne Grammar, were St Kilda's opponents, but the 'grown men' of St Kilda felt thwarted by the tactics and tenacity of the schoolboys. After a long spell of scoreless football a few of the men 'began to fisticuff'. We only have the schoolboys' version of the episode as told in a pithy entry in the diary of the Rev. Dr Bromby, but they themselves could well have added to the frustration by insisting on rules with which the men were not familiar. Indeed, Bromby's diary hints as much, noting that the older St Kilda players were 'irritated that after an hour and a half's struggle they were unable to kick'. This suggests that St Kilda wished to play a more kicking style of football (closer to soccer) whereas the other team made full use of the scrummages and brawny play of the Rugby game. To reach an agreement on rules was the formidable task facing the football enthusiasts in Melbourne.

In this mounting excitement about football, the Melbourne Cricket Club had a part. How important was its part we shall never know. The club, following the English practice, did not yet allow footballers to use the cricket turf. Its main aim was to promote and play cricket. It is true that the club's secretary, Wills, was an advocate of football, but he did not advocate it in the formal name of the club; moreover, he was about to resign from its own cricket team and play cricket for Richmond in the season beginning late in 1858. That the Melbourne Cricket Club's professional, Jerry Bryant, made available the leather football for the scratch match at the end of July may partly reflect the club's interest but his own interest was more as a publican. And yet there can be little doubt that most of the keenest players and supporters of the game of football were members of the Melbourne Cricket Club. Indeed, there is evidence that the Melbourne Football Club, which was tentatively formed late in the winter of 1858, was at first confined to members of the cricket club.

South Yarra was another oasis of football during the opening season. It was then a rural village with large mansions and their gardens standing on the higher ground and with the cottages of gardeners, grooms, coachmen, blacksmiths and tradesmen nestling in the narrow lanes and streets. The young botanical gardens already occupied a large area, and nearby the rows of grape vines ran neatly down the north-sloping hill towards the Yarra. At Punt Road the river was regularly crossed on a wooden punt with tall post-and-rail sides to prevent the travelling livestock and drays from falling into the river, while nearby a few watermen rested in their small rowing boats, ready to scull passengers who could not be bothered waiting for the slow punt.

The South Yarra footballers met in Fawkner Park, which was

larger then. No rows of houses trimmed the park's size along Punt Road and St Kilda Road. South Yarra's footballers were mostly gentlemen and white-collar workers, many of whom had played football at well-known English public schools, especially Rugby and Winchester, each of which played its own code of football. A few of the players were older boys from Melbourne Grammar School, which stood near the edge of the park.

The South Yarra team was confident enough to arrange a game of football with Melbourne – the first recorded match between two clubs or suburban teams – and the prospect of such a match aroused excitement in the city. *Bell's Life* offered a brief forecast of the game on the morning of Saturday, 25 September, observing that the Melbourne team had practised more but that South Yarra possessed footballers who had played at English public schools as well as the incalculable asset of 'perfect discipline'. Perfect discipline would certainly be needed to blend, in the one team, footballers who were reared on such contrasting styles as the Rugby and Winchester codes. On the chosen Saturday afternoon, twenty-six players represented each side at the Yarra Park. Whether the entire fifty-two played on the rough ground at the same time is not certain. The only certainty is that Melbourne won with a goal kicked at about 5.30 pm.

That was probably the last match of the season. The days were now longer, the cricket clubs were preparing their wickets for the new season, and the footballers themselves probably still preferred cricket as a game. But the first football season had provided enough enthusiasm to suggest that when the next winter came, those players who had not gone to the latest gold rush or moved to another city or even to England would be there again, kicking the ball about and arguing about the rules.

They had to argue about the rules, for the rules were still being shaped. There were no rules governing a host of minor matters, and even on the big questions – such as whether the ball could be picked up with the hands or merely kicked – agreement was not easily achieved. The matches played in 1858 are described with such meagre detail that it is impossible to know the main rules, but there survives an account of the first match of the following year, and it describes utter confusion. While some of the footballers insisted on picking up the ball or catching it or holding on to it, other players thought too much ball-handling was outrageous.

Football at the Rugby School in England in 1870. The shape of the ball, if the artist drew accurately, was somewhere between the present soccer ball and Rugby ball.

They said that a player should never touch the ball with hands and that football (it was usually called 'Foot Ball') should be simply a game for the foot rather than the hand.

In the contest between competing kinds of football the Rugby game had the benefit of a coincidence. Soon after Tom Wills returned to Melbourne there appeared a best-seller extolling life and sport at the Rugby School. Perhaps the most influential book ever written about school days in the English-speaking world, *Tom Brown's School Days* was published in London just four months after Wills had returned to Melbourne. The anonymous author of the book was Thomas Hughes, a London barrister aged thirty-four, himself a former student of the school and rather like Wills in his obsession with sport.

The novel described life at the school in the days of the famous headmaster, Dr Thomas Arnold. It gloried in the games, especially the football, and rather exaggeratedly – to the vexation of *The Edinburgh Review* – made the late Dr Arnold seem like a 'patron saint of athleticism'. The book was Christian in tone: its aim was not merely to entertain but to do good. While *Tom Brown's School Days* now gives the impression of extolling a way of life that seems fusty, it was as exciting and magnetic to schoolboy readers in 1857 as were the first songs of the Beatles just over a century later.

The book held a message for educational reformers, arguing that team games moulded character. Appearing a few months after the end of the Crimean War, the book also caught the mood of the time with its implicit message that a nation's schools would contribute to the nation's defences if they produced courageous, energetic, wholesome young men.

The story of Tom Brown reached a huge audience. Copies of the book must have reached Melbourne in the second half of 1857, box after box packed in the hold of sailing ships. How many were sold in Victoria we have no means of ascertaining, but the book was often mentioned or praised in newspapers and journals of the following three years. The headmaster of the new Melbourne Grammar School wrote in his diary how much he was moved by reading that 'noble work'. *The Argus* within a year of the arrival of the book paid tribute to its power in promoting a love of sport or what it called 'violent exercise' in Victoria, while the main sporting journal, *Bell's Life in Victoria*, considered that the book was one of the moulders of a remarkable change in public attitudes. As far as we can tell, young men in Melbourne did not play organised football in 1857 but did in 1858, and this book on life at Rugby School possibly did as much as Tom Wills to spread early enthusiasm for football, and especially the courageous football played at Rugby School.

In Victoria the supporters of Rugby football were almost certainly outnumbered by those migrants who in England had played a different kind of football. Thus Eton and Harrow, Winchester and Marlborough and each of the well-known public schools of England played football according to its own rules. At Cambridge University the students arrived from such a diversity of footballing backgrounds that in the 1840s hockey was the more popular game largely because its rules could be agreed upon.

In essence the game in both England and Victoria in the late 1850s was like a set of football bladders, each capable of being blown into many different shapes. It was still possible to reconcile conflicting rules and invent new ways of playing. Fifteen years later the game of football was no longer so easily shaped. If Melbourne sportsmen had begun to play regular football not in 1858 but fifteen years later, they would probably not have invented their own game but instead have borrowed either Rugby or soccer, ready-made from England.

CHAPTER THREE

To the Goldfields

More and more football clubs were formed. At huddles beneath trees in the parklands or meetings in the rooms of cricket clubs and hotels, young men came together and put in a few shillings each to buy the football, goalposts and boundary flags. At first their games were rarely reported in the press, and a club could briefly flourish and die with only a whispered record that it had ever existed. Some clubs were playing scratch matches before they formally existed. A game of fun and leisure, football still served the players rather than the spectators.

Clubs did not yet insist on loyalty, and in the first years of Melbourne football a player was happy to run onto the field for three different clubs in the course of the year and pledge temporary loyalty to each. The early accounts of matches are puzzling until one realises that a particular surname denotes not two brothers but the same man playing for different clubs in quick succession. We view the fickleness of today's players as unprecedented, but it is as old as Australian football. Even the captain of a team was appointed only for one match at a time during the initial years of Australian football.

At the end of the first season, 1858, there were at least three informal clubs – Melbourne, South Yarra and St Kilda – as well as several school teams in the city and nearer suburbs. Emerald Hill (South Melbourne) and Prahran teams appeared in 1859, the year in which football's first rules were printed. Richmond, University and Collingwood took the field in 1860, though the Collingwood and Richmond clubs eventually dissolved and have no apparent connection with the present clubs. By 1862 Royal Park and Essendon fielded teams, though the Essendon team was soon to scatter, to be reformed in the early 1870s. By 1864 there was the first of the teams named Fitzroy. In the same year Carlton was born and thereafter remained very much alive. Warehousemen took to the field in 1865: the warehousemen were a gentlemanly version of the present Storemen and Packers and worked for importing firms whose warehouses full of English hardware and textiles stood in Flinders Lane or near the riverside wharves. The Albert Ground in St Kilda Road – in 1908 the scene of the first final of the Davis Cup to be held in Australia – was long known as The Warehousemen's Cricket Ground. All these teams and others long forgotten played each other irregularly, their captain or secretary simply arranging the match and venue and kick-off time a few weeks in advance of the chosen Saturday. There were no regular fixtures of games, no premiership ladder and no list of leading goalkickers, but the game was thriving.

    Outside Melbourne the fever for football first infected Geelong. Linked to Melbourne by railway – the longest railway in the land – as well as by steamships with cheap fares, Geelong's population of about 25,000 included enough athletic men of leisure to form a team. Indeed, an early historian of Australian football, C C Mullen, insisted that Geelong was the birthplace of the code and that Tom Wills had formed six football clubs in Geelong as early as 1856. Early newspapers, however, reveal no evidence for this claim. If as many as six clubs existed, they must have played mainly on concealed grounds far from the eyes of the press. Moreover, Wills could not have founded football clubs in Geelong in the winter of 1856 because he was still playing cricket in England; he returned to Australia only at Christmas-time that year.

The first football club in Geelong was probably formed in April 1859 when Stitt Jenkins, an advocate of the new cult of total abstinence from alcohol, called a meeting with the aim of forming a Saturday afternoon football club. He was eager to cultivate morality amongst young men at a time when the consumption of alcohol in Victoria was high. *The Geelong Advertiser* applauded his football venture: 'The game is one of the healthiest and easiest that could be adopted by persons cramped during the week by desk or counter service and standing in need of a little bracing exercise'. Whether Mr Jenkins' venture was successful is not clear. Three months later, another meeting of what were called 'admirers' of football was held at the Victoria Hotel in Geelong to plan a match for the following Saturday. *The Geelong Advertiser*, reporting the meeting, advised admirers of the game that the ball would be ready at the ground and that after the game a committee would be elected at a meeting at the nearby Portarlington Hotel.

Soon Geelong was playing its matches not far from the new railway station, on the Argyle ground in Aberdeen Street. It was a very sloping ground with a wonderful view of the bay and the You Yangs. When a south wind blew strongly, play must have been hopelessly bottled up at the downhill end. The north wind was ideal because it counterbalanced the law of gravity.

Tom Wills, having moved to the family's rural estate near Geelong, captained the Geelong footballers in several matches in 1860, and his skills and zest fostered the game. His step-cousin, H C A Harrison, who was variously captain of the Richmond and Melbourne teams, moved to Geelong in his employment in the

Customs Department and he captained Geelong in 1862. As well as the stimulus from these two champion footballers, Geelong had local players eager to excel in the new game. The rivalry between Geelong and Melbourne in the early 1860s, and their emphasis on different styles of play, helped to shape a distinctive kind of football, unknown elsewhere in the world. Then, as in the modern post-war era, Geelong was the exponent of open rather than congested football.

When the enthusiasm for football reached the Victorian goldfields is not certain. Several historians argue that it did not have to reach the goldfields because it was born there. It would be interesting to learn where their theory originated. It is probably modern,

A new digger arrives at a Victorian goldfield in the 1850s when Victoria and California were rivals for the title of greatest gold producer in the history of the world (a sketch by S T Gill, goldfields artist).

and has crept into currency more through folklore than through research. It seems that writers of advertising copy, television scripts and tourist brochures, seeking one sentence which depicted the birth of Australian football as colourful, singled out the goldfields for that colour. Certainly the new game did arise when Victoria was the main gold colony, and a small army of fit young men was following the gold rushes, but the new theory is accompanied by scant evidence. If the new game definitely arose on the goldfields, it should be easy to designate the particular goldfield where it was first recorded. Was it Fiery Creek or Beechworth, or was it California Gully or Redan? The theory is silent. Did it arise in the early 1850s? The theory again is silent. It would be surprising if football matches were not played on a public holiday at several of the hundreds of goldfields, but it would be equally surprising if young men who were excitedly digging for gold or travelling across the country to the latest rush should begin to play regularly a game that required energy and time and involved the risk of injuries that could prevent them from digging for gold. Above all, there is so far no evidence that football in the early goldfields differed from the variety of games played in Victoria in the previous decade.

Serious sports in this period were more for young men who worked at desks or sat on high stools in offices than for those who did hard physical labour. The big goldfields of Ballarat and Bendigo each possessed by the mid-1850s several dozen young men who worked in banks and schools, mercantile or government offices, but so far no evidence indicates that either of those cities fathered the new game of football.

The new code of football reached the Bendigo goldfield in 1861. J B Thompson, who had been secretary of the committee that drew up the first football rules in Melbourne in May 1859, moved to Bendigo and became secretary and captain of its first football club, called Sandhurst. Formed on 3 June 1861, it promptly organised a practice match in the Lower Reserve, now Rosalind Park. There the ball was 'well kicked and hunted' until an argument broke out, bringing the game to an end. On Saturday, 15 June, Sandhurst played a formal match against Volunteers, a team consisting of the part-time volunteer soldiers. On that day a goal was kicked by Sandhurst, but when the game was resumed on the second day no goal was scored. On the third Saturday the footballers arrived at the ground only to find a large crowd assembling to celebrate St Peter's and St Paul's Day and completely occupying the arena. This unfinished match was presumably played according to Melbourne rules. Ultimately, football was to become very popular in the Bendigo district which, at times in the twentieth century, was to field the strongest competition outside any capital city.

Ballarat was the fourth-largest city in Australia in 1860 and the second-largest in Victoria, and if the new game was to capture the people it had to capture them in Ballarat. As early as January 1860 it was possible to buy a brand-new football at John Little's shop in Main Street, the busy zigzag street in East Ballarat. Whether he stocked footballs because a customer had ordered them or whether he had imported them from England at his own risk we do not know. Presumably it was one of his footballs which was kicked about at the Ballarat Athletic Club's sports meeting on Friday, 27 April 1860, when football was the eighteenth item on the long programme of events. Late in this autumn afternoon two teams, each with six players, played a match of football. Two years later, on the same sports ground in Sturt Street, football was listed as one of many contests at the sports meeting organised by the Eight Hours and Early Closing Association. There the spectators no longer saw teams with six on each side, but a crowd of players for whom the football 'furnished amusement and exercise'.

In Ballarat even the children must have been playing football in the open spaces around the tall poppet-heads of the mines, for on New Year's Day in 1862 the Wesleyan Sabbath School from Brown Hill held its annual picnic and 100 children took part in three cricket games while another group – in the quaint phrase of the newspaper – 'employed themselves at football'. As a leather football was expensive, home-made footballs must have been used.

The football made of tightly rolled newspaper, favoured by children for kick to kick some half-century ago, was unlikely to have been kicked on that New Year's Day because newspapers then ran to only four or six pages and, after being read, were avidly saved as wrapping paper.

Ballarat possessed a senior football club in 1862 and perhaps even a year earlier. Its players were eager, and almost every winter afternoon at around four o'clock they arrived at Mr Greene's private paddock near the cemetery and kicked the ball and scrummaged and charged. Sometimes they were too strenuous and in a ten-a-side match between bankers and others, two players in pursuit of the ball 'cannoned against each other'. One player dislocated his shoulder, and the dislocation with much difficulty was reduced by a doctor until the footballer eventually walked home. After the accident the game was not resumed. The Melbourne football club's rules were used as a basis for drawing up Ballarat's own rules, but so long as Ballarat did not play against other towns it mattered little which rules it adopted. In fact, each isolated club was like a railway with its own distinct gauge or width of rail, and only when the separate railways seemed likely to meet each other at a new junction was a common gauge and a common list of rules essential. The new railway linking Ballarat and Geelong in April 1862 enabled isolated Ballarat to play football against another city for the first time, and by then Ballarat footballers must have seen the advantage of adopting all the rules currently followed by footballers in Geelong and Melbourne.

On Friday, 18 July 1862, the Ballarat players went in the morning's steam train to Geelong, the first time some had travelled in a train. At the railway station in Geelong they were welcomed by the rival footballers, were served what in those days was called a 'liberal repast' or hearty meal, and were toasted with drinks. In fine weather the two teams went 'in high spirits' to the ground where 300 to 400 spectators were waiting. The spectators, however, had to watch two and a half hours of football before Mr O'Dwyer of 'the Geelongers' scored the first goal amidst deafening cheers. After a brief spell the match was resumed and Harrison of Geelong showed what could be achieved, even on soft ground full of moisture, by virtually playing the whole field. Once he ran with the ball to the forward-line, where Mr Timms scored another Geelong goal.

The prospect of a return match aroused intense interest in Ballarat, for no outside team had ever played there; indeed Wayne Hankin, who has read every early Ballarat newspaper in search of scraps of football history, observes that a visit by Melbourne or Geelong teams to Ballarat was to remain a rarity during the 1860s. Seven weeks after the match in Geelong, the Ballarat footballers were ready for their own special day. They met the Geelong team at the ornate railway station, welcomed them with enthusiasm, and escorted them along the street to the George Hotel, still standing with its elegant cast-iron balconies like a grand wedding cake. There, in front of 'a first-rate spread', the Ballarat hosts busied themselves with their hospitality, quietly hoping that the Geelong players would eat until they burst. Then the teams walked down the hill to the new cricket ground to find what for those days was a large crowd of 800 to 1,000 spectators, even including women. Alas for Ballarat, it lost the match easily. The only consolation was that Geelong had to wait two and a half hours before scoring its second goal.

Meanwhile football spread to a few of the remote Victorian towns. Warrnambool, a port town of about 1,500 people, was linked to Melbourne by small ships that were tossed about in Bass Strait in winter storms. By 1861 some of the young men of the town tried the new game, and *The Warrnambool Examiner* on 4 June predicted that the 'good old English game of football' would become popular and reported that on the previous Saturday afternoon about twenty players were 'kicking with all their might' – until suddenly 'bang burst the ball'. Before long a club was formed, a subscription of five shillings was collected from each member, and pig-skin bladders were ordered so that the game could continue

The new game spread to hundreds of country towns. Readers of **The Australasian Sketcher** *of 28 July 1884 found a series of cartoons describing the kind of episode that happened when a football team went by horse-drawn coach to a neighbouring town.*

even when the football burst. Special matches were organised – married players versus bachelors, and country players versus townsmen – but on the chosen days many players were absent and scratch matches had to be substituted. Nonetheless, the play usually went on with vigour until dusk. On one Wednesday afternoon the ball was still 'flying to and fro in all directions', though the players could no longer be identified in the dim light.

What rules they played we do not know. It would be rash to suggest that they were necessarily playing by the new Melbourne rules. After one season the game seemed to fade away and for some years the annual ploughing match, embracing many farmers and their strong pairs of horses, become a more regular fixture than football.

Far beyond the extending railway lines, other country towns tried the new game. Maryborough, a flourishing goldfield, played football in 1862. At the gold town of Heathcote, standing amongst the hills between Kilmore and Bendigo, two hotels organised a team which on 15 June 1862 played the rest of the town. In some towns, only two or three matches took place during the short season, which normally did not commence until June.

Most of the smaller towns and some of the largest in Victoria knew no football. Nearly all men, whether miners or shopkeepers or farmers, worked on Saturday afternoon, and it was not easy for employees to obtain leave merely to play football. Even then they usually lost part of their salary or wages if they gained permission to leave work early on Saturday afternoon in order to go to the football ground. Only a large town possessed a sufficient number of those bank clerks, school teachers, self-employed tradesmen, owners of gold claims and other men of property who had the freedom on Saturday afternoon to chase a football. It was slightly easier for cricket to flourish because that game could take advantage of the public holidays at Christmas and Easter. Today, Easter normally falls within the football season, but in those days it normally occurred towards the end of the cricket season.

The upcountry enthusiasm for the new game came partly from the newspapers in Melbourne. A few dozen matches were described briefly during each football season of the early 1860s, and some of the excitement of the afternoon was conveyed by the newspaper reports. Already it was the custom, a little unfair, to shower more honour on the forwards than the defenders, and schoolboys with one eye on a little glory must have hoped to be goalkickers rather than backmen. As goals were rare they were a highlight and worth recording. Thus on 16 August 1862 the report in *The Illustrated Melbourne Post* typically noted the only goal scored in the course of the afternoon:

> One of the best contested matches was played on Saturday last, between the Royal Park and the Essendon clubs, the superior skill of the latter being balanced by the great physical ability of the former. One goal was kicked by McHaig for the Essendon but from that time the tide of battle rolled from one end to the other, without a victory being declared to either party.

Sheer physical strength was an important asset in that era when Australian football was much closer to Rugby than it is today. A reporter sent to describe a football match was careful to notice which side seemed to be the heaviest. Falls and 'spills' were frequent, and the reports in newspapers gave to such falls and tumbles an emphasis which has almost vanished from descriptions. If the ground was wet and the players who hit the ground became muddy, the reporters announced in their flowery prose that 'it was difficult to distinguish those who had embraced mother earth'. The indignity of mud, bruises and somersaults was stressed partly because most players were men of visible dignity who were always referred to as Mister by the newspapers.

The emerging code of football spread with remarkable speed, and its crowd-pleasing ingredients made a few observers predict that it would continue to spread. In 1862, however, came signs that the new game was no longer so attractive. In Melbourne's parklands, compared to the previous year, fewer spectators stood around the boundaries and fewer boys were perched on the lower branches of the gum trees. The check to the game's popularity in Melbourne was also noticed in 1863, though football continued to spread into the goldfields and larger towns.

There was now slightly less prosperity in Victoria, and perhaps more footballers and spectators were working on Saturday afternoons. These were the years of the exodus of thousands of Victorians in small steamships to the new goldfields on the South Island of New Zealand; and many business-houses in Melbourne, Ballarat and Bendigo felt the strain. Moreover, on Saturday afternoons of the early 1860s, young men of leisure had another distraction. The volunteer movement, in which militiamen engaged in military manoeuvres and paraded in magnificent uniforms, was gaining strength. In 1863 Ballarat had to refuse an invitation to play football against Geelong on the Queen's Birthday holiday, one of the few public holidays of the year, because several of its footballers were to visit Melbourne to take part in a military parade.

Victoria's vogue for martial display in the early 1860s even affected the footballers' new uniforms. Almost from the birth of Australian football the players had worn coloured caps, a practice borrowed from England. Thus the rules of the Sheffield football club in 1857 insisted that each player provide himself with a cap of dark blue or red, depending on the team for which he was chosen. As football was not yet a spectator sport, a distinctive cap was sufficient to distinguish the players in the eyes of the only people who counted – the other players and the umpire. In Melbourne, as the spectators multiplied, a coloured cap and shirt along with the customary long white trousers enabled a footballer running with the ball to be recognised easily from a distance, and by September 1862 most of the football clubs had chosen such distinctive shirts and caps that the weekly sporting paper *Bell's Life* exulted in the 'gorgeous colours' of the teams as they hunted the ball across the grass.

The colours themselves reflected the temporary enthusiasm for martial display. Thus Geelong in 1862 sported a cap of red, white and blue and a flannel shirt of solferino. The name solferino has virtually vanished from colour charts, but it was then a new dye of bright crimson, named after a recent battle fought in north Italy in 1859 between the French and Austrian armies. Equally significant is the fact that in 1861 Melbourne's colour was no longer its original white but the bold magenta. That colour, still on the colour charts, was also brand new, having been devised from coal tar and named after a famous battle in north Italy during that same war of 1859. The enthusiasm for these new colours with their strong tints of war was short-lived, like Victoria's volunteer rifle corps and volunteer cavalry regiments. Within three years the Melbourne team had abandoned its perky cap with the magenta stripe on the white background, while Geelong by the mid-1870s was wearing a version of its present blue and white stripes rather than the warlike solferino.

In the inaugural two or three seasons, there were strong competing influences on the distinctive style of game which was emerging. The first was Rugby; and the daily newspapers which reported football noted the initial importance of Rugby-type rules and the way in which they were being altered or erased in Victoria. The second influence was those English immigrants who preferred a soccer type of football, and they quickly succeeded in preventing too much congestion and too much ball-handling in the Rugby

Sandhurst v Bendigo: *Silver cups, not premiership flags, were the customary trophies in the first decades of Australian football. The silversmiths of Victoria made scores of cups, some of them elaborate with emu's eggs and other adornments, for competition amongst city and country football teams.*
This trophy was presented to the winners of the Bendigo match played before a crowd of 2,000 on Wednesday 4 July 1883. Wednesday was a popular afternoon for football because Bendigo shops were closed then but open all day on Saturday.s Sandhurst defeated Bendigo to win this cup, now held in the Australian Gallery of Sport in Melbourne. The Sandhurst team included such evergreen footballing names as Cordner and Sheldon.

tradition. The third powerful influence was those individual players who by their own football skills and their willingness to find compromises between conflicting English rules began to impose new skills and rules on the game they played: in that era the stronger and more articulate players made the rules and, being human, made rules which protected their own distinctive skills and preferences. The fourth influence was the open parklands of Melbourne that allowed very spacious arenas and so facilitated from time to time a more mobile game and permitted an unusually large number of footballers to play in each match.

Finally, there was one unusual influence. It is vital to ask whether Australian football was launched in a relatively wet or dry season. Were the playing fields within a couple of miles of the city as soft in the late 1850s as in a normal Melbourne winter, or were they exceptionally hard? The evidence suggests that the ground was unusually hard in those months when the first games were played. Melbourne, in the winter of 1858, experienced a little rain on every second day, but the showers were light and merely wetted the grass. The total rainfall for the late autumn and the winter was exceptionally low. Between 1 April and 31 August only 6.43 inches of rain (or about 164 millimetres) were recorded in Melbourne.

The detailed measuring of rain in the city was initiated only in 1855, but thereafter we have accurate figures which enable us to confirm that the inaugural football season had the lowest rainfall of any April–August period during the first quarter century of the keeping of records. It is therefore almost certain that in the year when the first regular football was played in Melbourne, the ground must have been unusually hard. As the main football arena consisted of sloping and gravelly ground, the topsoil had little chance of retaining moisture. Accordingly, there was a strong danger of serious injury if the unmodified Rugby rules were adopted in Melbourne. For example, tripping was an essential part of Rugby and several other English codes, so much so that even on the hard ground of Melbourne the practice of tripping players was not abandoned without a struggle; but it was soon abandoned during that early attempt to find practical rules.

After only two seasons of regular football, several of the leaders of the new code of football were congratulating themselves that they had banished much of the roughness. J B Thompson, who had studied at Cambridge University and knew the various English school codes, told *Argus* readers that it was almost as if the Humane Society had taken over football. The rough game of the English schoolgrounds had been partly tamed. Most Victorian footballers, a few hours after the match was over, could no longer be identified by their limp or their stiff movements. Nor did spectators who stood by the flags on the boundary line now so often see 'a dozen players rolling on the ground together'. Thompson was to say more than once that football rules which suited schoolboys in England did not necessarily suit Australian men who on the Monday morning had to return to work and earn their living in a respectable occupation. 'Black eyes don't look so well in Collins Street', he wrote.

It is commonly said that Australians learned their games from England and then made them more aggressive. Here was a new game which for a brief time moved in the reverse direction, prompting a few English immigrants of the 1860s to write home to tell their friends that here at last was the football for true gentlemen.

CHAPTER FOUR

The Day of the Round Ball and the Oblong Ground

The first rules of Australian football were so brief that they were printed on one sheet of paper. Those country sportsmen who wished to learn the new rules could – in those days before the typewriter and copying machine – simply borrow them and spend five minutes in writing them out by hand. Occasionally the rules were printed, and *The Cricketer's Guide* printed them so that cricketers could take up the game in winter. Interestingly, they were less often called the rules than the laws of the Melbourne Football Club 'as played in Richmond Paddock, 1859'.

An athlete living at a distance from Melbourne and wishing to take up the game could not have played it simply on the knowledge gained by reading the ten rules. Many important matters were not mentioned in the first rules: what kind of football to use, the number of players in a team, the duration of a match, the width of the goal, the length of the ground, and even such crucial matters as whether a version of the offside rule applied or whether umpires should be appointed. Several of these questions were not clarified for the simple reason that the players could not yet agree. A few rules were not deemed important enough to write down, and some facets of the game were considered by the rule-makers to be still in a fluid state and wisely left fluid by a gap in the rule book. The rule book was full of gaps and omissions. Some of the unwritten rules can be gleaned from early descriptions of games or be fitted together like a jigsaw puzzle. Some will remain the subject of dispute.

The first formal rules were the outcome of a meeting of a small committee of players held at the Parade Hotel in Wellington Parade, East Melbourne, only one or two kicks away from the football ground in the park. Selected by the footballers themselves after the first practice match of the season, the committee of rule-makers met on Tuesday, 17 May 1859 and discussed rules which for the most part had been found to work well during the preceding season. Tom Wills was probably the foremost in this discussion. While the list of seven committee men included a secretary and treasurer, it included no president, and it can be assumed that Wills, as the first name listed on the committee, took the chair. Two of his more articulate colleagues were William J Hammersley and James B Thompson, who had been fellow-students at Cambridge's Trinity College before migrating to Victoria during the gold rushes. They were knowledgeable about English football. Another graduate from a British university was Thomas Henry Smith who, leaving Trinity College, Dublin, came to Melbourne to teach classics at the Scotch College and actually played in the well-known schoolboys' match against Melbourne Grammar in the previous season. At least four of the seven had played or watched one or another version of football at British schools or universities, and they were probably the more forceful members of the committee that drew up the rules.

It remains unclear how many members of the committee supported the Rugby School's rules. Certainly they were divided in their opinions and for that reason they consulted copies of the Eton, Harrow and Winchester rules. In designing the rules for football in Melbourne, they were not merely plucking rules from here and there and combining them. The games played the previous season on the capacious grounds of Melbourne must already have brought certain rules and styles of play into prominence, and on behalf of the existing players the new committee had to confirm those rules which most footballers were likely to accept.

Mainly they were setting down simple rules which had already been tested, but they were also devising or selecting new rules which might solve some of the recent disputes that had occurred during play. By the end of the meeting they had moved a long way from the more Rugby-style rules which possibly prevailed in most matches played in the previous season. They were content with far fewer rules than Rugby imposed. They also tried to eliminate some of the vigour and roughness of the Rugby game, though even then they probably sensed that the rough play arose more from the mood of the players and the urgings of the crowd than the rules set down on paper.

Of their first code of ten rules, three lasted only a short period. They were vital rules on the contentious issues of how a goal should be scored, what degree of roughness was allowable, and how much the ball could be handled. As a reading of the first ten rules will indicate, there was one remarkable omission, soon remedied. A new eleventh rule specified a free kick for infringement of the rules and formally appointed umpires to interpret the rules.

With these first written rules, the Melbourne footballers stood on their own, sponsoring a game that was neither like Rugby nor soccer, though blending some of the skills and rules of both codes. Financially they were also alone, for they seemed to have severed any formal connection with the Melbourne Cricket Club. Although most of the seven committee men were also excellent cricketers and were members of the Melbourne Cricket Club, and although four were serving or had served on that club's committee, their new football club was independent. Known as the Melbourne Football Club, it played nearly all its games on the paddock outside the cricket ground rather than on the cricket turf. The fact that its

'A Run for Goal': Melbourne versus Carlton in The Australian Pictorial Weekly *of 12 June 1880.*

committee met in a hotel rather than the cricket pavilion was a clear sign of its independence. Significantly, the new secretary of the Melbourne Cricket Club, Thomas Wray, after being elected to the committee of rule-makers, apparently took no part in its discussion and did not affix his name to the rules.

Most of the early football grounds in Melbourne had straight and not curved boundaries. In the first fifteen years most football matches in Victoria were played on a rectangular field, like the present Rugby or soccer field but much larger. This fact comes as a surprise. It has been assumed that all games were played on an oval-shaped ground, as they are today, and everything in history books or reminiscences implies that the oval ground was used from the outset. Possibly the prominence of cricketers and the Melbourne Cricket Club in the early years of football erroneously helped to suggest that the round boundaries of a cricket field rather than the rectangular English football field were normal.

The rectangular grounds mostly used for senior football in Melbourne were very large. Some could have been 400 yards long, depending on the actual ground available, on the slopes and tree-clusters of the park where the game was played, and on the wishes of the captains. In the first three years of the game the length of the typical arena was probably closer to 300 yards, or half as long again as the typical football ground today. While the captains decided how long the ground should be, there existed as early as 1859 a rule limiting the ground's width. It must not be more than 200 yards wide. The length and width of the present football ground had almost arrived, but the ground's oval shape lay in the future.

Australian football remains the only major code in the English-speaking world which is not played on grounds of standard size. Soccer, American football and the two Rugby codes are played on grounds that are measured exactly. They reflect the influence of the industrial revolution and its emphasis on exact measurement, uniformity and precision. They also reflect, in their relatively cramped playing arenas, the high price of land in the cities of the northern hemisphere where these games at first became popular. In contrast, Australian football was born in a continent where open land even in the new cities remained plentiful, and so the playing arena could be large. Moreover, the game developed in the tree-studded parklands of Melbourne, where it was possible to specify the rough width of the playing field but unwise to specify the length. As the goals at each end of the ground were all-important for the playing of football, the position of the large gum trees with their overhanging branches often determined the exact site for the goals.

The Day of the Round Ball and the Oblong Ground

In some of the early matches, two trees not far apart must have served as the goalposts. A football field was then the longish distance between two isolated pairs of suitable trees.

More often, though, the trees and their low branches were in such a position that they could not serve as goals, and so special hand-made goalposts had to be erected. It was sensible to erect the posts where the approach to goal was not completely obscured by large trees standing close together. Such humdrum factors helped to decide the best place for the goals and therefore the length of the playing arena. In a few parks the sedimentary rocks came very close to the grass, and the position of those rocky patches also influenced the decision where not to erect the goals. Eventually, in the 1870s, the sheer number of spectators and the difficulty of preventing them in their excitement from invading the arena helped to transfer the game of football to the main cricket grounds, most of which had a low wooden fence along the boundary. It was to prove easy for a football code which did not play on exactly measured grounds to move to cricket fields, for they were not standardised in England or Australia.

Few of the early football matches were played on the main cricket grounds. The footballers were seen as a nuisance because they trampled on the grass, leaving muddy patches and creating potholes. When a player caught the ball and called out 'Mark!', he actually drew a line on the ground with his boot. If he decided to use the place kick, he scuffed a small hole in the grass before placing the ball on the ground. If the congested play hovered over the same tiny square of ground for ten minutes, as sometimes happened, the ground was likely to suffer, especially in wet winter. As it was more difficult in an Australian than an English summer to maintain a turf wicket and a grassy outfield, curators of the cricket grounds were naturally wary of preparing, for the opening cricket matches, a ground that had been scarred by the footballers.

In July 1859, in the second season of organised football, trial matches were actually played on the Melbourne Cricket Ground. Both matches were played between the Melbourne team, dressed in white, and South Yarra, dressed in blue. A large part of the ground was roped off and the oblong boundary clearly marked with flags. As only a part of the playing surface was selected, it must have been one of the smaller football arenas used in Victoria during that year. The afternoon was windy, and heavy rain halted the match for a short time, but 2,000 spectators including large numbers of women were watching when Melbourne kicked the only goal. As the game began at about 2 pm and went on until the light began to fail, not all spectators waited until the end. Three weeks later another match between these teams, each fielding twenty-five players, was again marred by wind and rain. The damage to the turf must have been visible. Few other matches were played on the Melbourne Cricket Ground during the 1860s.

On the grassy slopes between the later Jolimont railway station and the Melbourne Cricket Ground, was the first playing arena of Australian football. A rectangle, it slowly changed shape. Gradually the rectangle, while still appearing huge to newcomers from England, became narrower and shorter. Part of the pressure for change possibly came from the caretaker of the park who saw grand old trees damaged because they were too close to one goal or because they became a crowded perch for small boys gathering like cockatoos. Moreover, a smaller arena allowed a second football ground to be fitted into the park or permitted more space for the children who skipped or played ball, or the women who wheeled prams, or the older people who strolled on a sunny winter afternoon. The rectangular ground did not have completely straight boundaries; big trees probably dictated a curve or detour here and there.

Before long the football ground had an unmistakeable appearance. At each end were the goalposts, rather short and not yet painted white. By 1866 a rule declared that the goalposts must be 7 yards apart. The boundary lines were also marked by lower posts, hammered into the ground before the start of the match and then pulled out and carried home. These posts were maybe 20 yards apart. So that they could be seen clearly by fast-running players or distant spectators, they often carried a pennant or flag on the top. On a windy day the fluttering flags added a gaiety to the occasion.

Each match was commenced in the manner of present-day Rugby and soccer games, with a kick-off from the centre of the ground. The captains tossed a coin for the choice of goal and the one who lost the toss handed the ball to his best kicker. The match then began with a version of the offside rule dictating where the players placed themselves. All the players of one side gathered near their team mate who was about to kick the ball, while the opposing team, standing well apart towards the opposing goal, waited to gather in that first long place kick and carry or kick the ball back towards the centre of the ground. Undoubtedly the players hunted in packs in the early years and fought and wrestled like bears. The heaving, pushing and charging were probably restrained compared to Rugby, but it was still a congested game by modern standards.

The earliest rules allowed a goal to be scored when the ball was forced between the goalposts in the course of a scrummage. It seems likely that for many years the ball while in the scrummage could legally be pushed between the goalposts so long as the hands, arms or knees of the attacking team propelled the ball. Most goals, however, came from definite kicks, attempted while the player was close to the goalposts. If the ball was touched by the hands or body of an opposing player, the score was not allowed. If the ball grazed the side of the goalpost, the score was not allowed. The official rules gave no guidance for the occasional episode when a player made his kick, the ball hit a tree and then was deflected – to the player's delight – between the goalposts. In the Yarra Park in June 1864, a combined team from Eastern Hill and Royal Park were playing Melbourne, and Neil of the combined team picked up the ball in what we would now call the forward-pocket and kicked it towards the goal. With much force the ball hit the stump of a tree, rebounded at right angles and sailed between the goalposts. The goal was allowed.

Disputes about goals were frequent, especially if the two captains served as umpires. If there was any doubt about the way the goal had been scored, the outcry was loud. When Geelong came to

While there was not yet a football magazine or Record published during each week of the football season, a journal called The Footballer *appeared from 1875 to cover the year's results.*

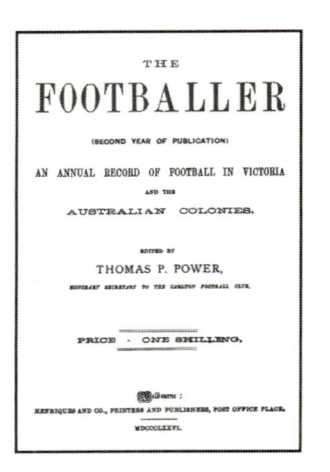

THE
FOOTBALLER
(SECOND YEAR OF PUBLICATION)

AN ANNUAL RECORD OF FOOTBALL IN VICTORIA
AND THE
AUSTRALIAN COLONIES.

EDITED BY
THOMAS P. POWER,
HONORARY SECRETARY TO THE CARLTON FOOTBALL CLUB.

PRICE - ONE SHILLING.

HENRIQUES AND CO., PRINTERS AND PUBLISHERS, POST OFFICE PLACE.
MDCCCLXXVI.

play in the Richmond Paddock in August 1862 and Melbourne kicked a goal, the celebrated Harrison who was then the Geelong captain claimed the goal had been kicked unfairly. The Melbourne team disagreed, and the game was abandoned.

If a goal was kicked late in the afternoon, when darkness was setting in, the game was promptly declared 'over'. If the light was still clear, the ball was returned to the centre of the ground, and the players took up their positions in two clusters, well apart, and the ball was kicked off again. In 1866 the new drafting of the rules stipulated that, after one goal had been scored, the teams should change ends so that the losing side gained the advantage of any wind. This rule, however, was not always enforced. Many rules seemed to hold an opting-out clause.

Determination, cunning and a confident voice often served as a substitute for firm rules. Thus there was no written rule on the question of when a game should end, and even the 1866 rules do not specify how long a game should continue. H C A Harrison recalled that in the early years the first team to score two goals was the winner. A match could therefore be spread over several Saturdays until at last a team kicked its second goal. As the same match could go on and on, Saturday after Saturday, the setting of regular fixtures for a whole season was impossible.

In 1862 the Caledonian Society offered a challenge cup for the best football team; and when the challenger won, it in turn had to face new challengers in the same season. After several postponements the Melbourne and University teams finally came together for a challenge match on 18 July 1863. There was a minor commotion when the Melbourne captain suspected that University fielded too many players. He called for a muster and proved that his suspicion was correct. After five surplus University players had been sent from the field, the match went on, adjourning at about sunset after no goal had been scored. The match was resumed in the Richmond Paddock three Saturdays later, and on the wet ground each team scored a goal. The teams agreed to play again the following Saturday but for some reason they did not. At last, one Saturday later, publican Bryant of Wellington Parade kicked the winning goal for Melbourne. After all that effort Melbourne held on to the cup for only three weeks, losing it to Geelong.

To decide at what point in the afternoon the play should finally be halted was often a tantalising question. A team which had attacked for much of the day, and now held the ball in a congested crowd of players only 15 yards from the goalposts, was very reluctant to agree that it was too dark to continue playing. It was never too dark, if the goal was in sight. To set a time for ending the day's play was difficult partly because no player carried a pocket watch on the field: they were too expensive and fragile. Even a central umpire running up and down the field would not have risked his gold pocket watch and chain. In the later years a time-keeper would stand on the boundary and call out 'Time!' Meanwhile it was mainly a game for young gentlemen, and such men were supposed to resolve their disagreements by courteous discussion.

Some matches ended when spectators could barely see the ball. A match in Melbourne between two teams which called themselves North and South ended in a way charmingly described by *The Illustrated Melbourne Post* of 16 August 1862: 'It was not until night had begun to draw her curtain round, that friendly hostilities ceased'.

In this era of low scores, most of the deliberate attempts to kick a goal gained no score. Behinds or near-misses did not count in the final scores until 1897. Australian football was rather like present-day soccer insofar as a team could keep the ball in attack for nearly all the match but gain nothing. Indeed, when the ball went out of bounds on the forward-line, an elaborate rule gave a decided advantage to the defending team. Whereas today the full-back returns the ball to play by kicking from the goal square, in the early decades he could kick from a much larger goal square. The rule stipulated that two kick-off posts, the forerunner of our behind posts, should be erected on each side of the goalpost. These posts were further apart and much lower than the present behind posts, each being 20 yards away from the nearest goalpost.

The kick-off posts marked the extreme edges of what we would now call the goal square, and a player about to kick off could take his kick from any point in front of a straight line joining the kick-off posts and goalposts – as long as he was no more than 20 yards out from the boundary line. In effect the 'goal square' ran 47 yards along the straight boundary line and extended out 20 yards, so that it dwarfed the present goal square.

After the ball had gone out of bounds anywhere on that straight forward-line, the rule decreed that a player on the defensive side must kick the ball with the aid of his 20 yards' advantage and 'kick it as nearly as possible in a line with the opposite Goal'. In short, no matter where he stood on the edge of the goal square, he had to kick it directly towards the goalposts at the opposite end of the ground.* The aim of this rule was to prevent a player about to kick the ball back into play from directing it into the remote corners which on a rectangular ground were far deeper and more of a dead-end than today's forward-pocket. The rule in effect gave the defence a strong chance to clear the ball; but by ordaining that the ball, when kicked back into play, must land near the goal-to-goal line or the central spine of the ground the rule gave the attacking team – especially when favoured by the wind – a chance to return the ball to the goal mouth. By 1866 this rule had been modified and the backman kicking the ball back into play appears to have been allowed to direct the ball more onto the defensive flanks.

During the era of the rectangular ground the kick-in rule applied only when the ball was miskicked over the forward boundary. If the ball went across the side or wing boundary, a player threw the ball back into play, throwing it at right angles to the boundary. This rule possibly came from Eton football. The throw-in by the umpire was invented much later.

*After the early decades of football the big 'goal square' became smaller. By 1885 – and the rule had been operating for some time – the player could bring the ball only 10 yards in from the goalposts or 'goal line' as it was called. But the goal square still embraced the area in front of the kick-off or behind posts as well as the goalposts. A photo of an 1896 match shows the oblong or elongated 'goal square' still in existence.

Most of the early matches did not employ independent umpires. An exception was the well-known match of 1858 between Melbourne Grammar and Scotch College when each school appointed

A plan of a typical football field, with the recommended positions for the 20 players in a team, was published in The Footballer *for 1876.*

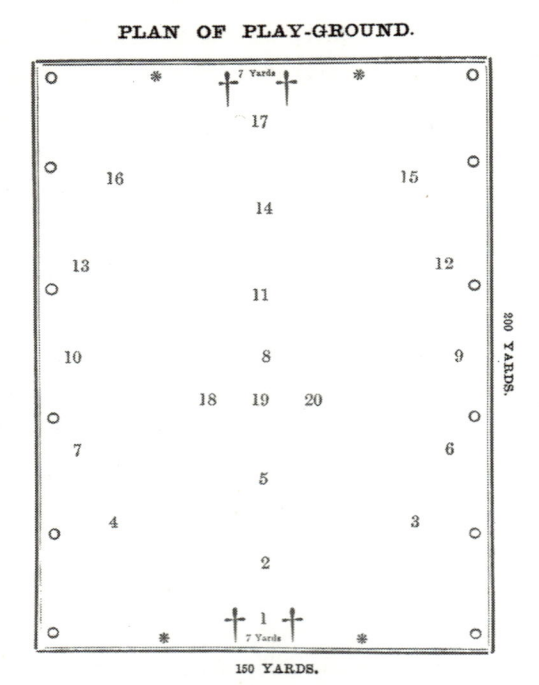

PLAN OF PLAY-GROUND.

†† Goal Posts.　　** 20 yards Posts. Ball has to be kicked off 20 yards in
o Boundary Posts.　　front, if it goes between these and the Goal posts.

1.—Goalkeeper.
2.—Back.
3 and 4.—Backs on the right and left wings.
5.—Half-Back.
6 and 7.—Half-Back on the right and left wings.
8, 9, and 10.—Centre Players.
11.—Centre Forward
12 and 13.—Centre Forwards on the right and left wings.
14.—Centre Forward on Goal.
15 and 16.—Right and left wing Forwards on Goal.
17.—Goal Sneak.
18, 19, and 20.—Followers when the ball is in motion; these also take it from out of bounds.

an umpire, but school matches were probably more in need of central umpires. Generally it was assumed that the two captains would normally be the umpires. While the revised rules of 1860 permitted the appointing of independent umpires, reports of early games suggest that outside umpires were not common. Furthermore, no football association or league existed to appoint the umpires. The football, in its style of umpiring, was more like the cricket, and a player who felt indignant that a rule had been broken appealed loudly just as a cricketer appeals today. A few of the appeals to umpires were less a cry for fair play than for fair comment. When South Yarra's team included gentlemen of dignity, one of its players was incensed to hear a Melbourne player call him 'a lump of blubber'. He promptly appealed for a free kick. The rules then were still tentative and to lose one's dignity was akin to being tripped.

The rival captains were usually the adjudicators. They probably agreed when a blatant breaking of the rules had taken place, but in marginal infringements an agreement must have been difficult. The essence of the game was to play with the minimum of umpiring, and indeed rule 11 in the revised rules of May 1869 suggests that a free kick was awarded to an aggrieved team only if a 'deliberate infringement' was made. What was deliberate? What was accidental? Here was a rule for King Solomon in all his wisdom. At last the rules of 1866 insisted on specialist umpires, and football borrowed the cricket custom whereby each team appointed its own umpire. The umpire who stood nearest the spot where a rule was infringed or a goal was kicked made the final decision on any matter of dispute. The policy of employing two central umpires in the Victorian Football League was revived in the 1970s, by which time the similar practice of a century earlier had been completely forgotten.

The game was often rough. Some of the rules tried to control rough play, and the very wording of the rules showed how rough the playing styles could be. To trip an opposing player was permitted in the early matches if an opponent possessed the ball or was moving rapidly; by mid-1859 it was banned. The art of hacking – the kicking of an opponent's legs, sometimes with the aim of tripping him – was a vital though illegal part of the early game.

Hammersley, an early rule-maker, recalled that many players fitted spikes to their boots, enabling them to draw blood when hacking an opponent's legs: 'My shins now show honourable scars, and often have I had blood trickling down my legs.' Hacking was prohibited in the first written rules but this was not easily enforced when the players were huddled in a pack. Tom Wills, exhorting the manly virtues of football in 1864, left no doubt in readers' minds that the deliberate kicking of an opponent's shins was a noble part of the game. He seemed to believe that a schoolboy footballer would equip himself for the battlefield, should war eventually come to Australia, by his feats on the playing fields; and he admired the boy footballer who 'would kick his hardest at close quarters without showing the white feather, although his shins were streaming with blood'.

Charging was legitimate, and the big players who led the charge against the opposition were fearless. In the 1860s, Tom Gorman of Carlton was celebrated for his powerful shoulders. He was called 'the pocket Hercules'. Of him the verse was written:

That doughty warrior would hold his own,
He had wondrous strength in his collar bone.

Jack Conway, a cricketer with bulging thighs and knotty calves and a chest of 43 inches, was already famous in football circles as the Carlton leader who hurled himself against Harrison the Melbourne captain in the years when those two clubs were supreme. It was said that the 'very ground seemed to tremble' when the two players hit each other. To charge an opponent who held the ball was a normal way of dispossessing him. To hold a man – even if he held onto the ball – was soon prohibited, and instead he was knocked to the ground or given a sly hack or kick in the shins. Pushing was the other popular way of upsetting a player with the ball, and a push in the back was a legitimate method of upsetting an opponent who was running with the ball in hand.

Migrants who first saw Australian football in the mid-1860s were conscious that it differed from every English version of football. For example, one major difference from Rugby was that hacking and tripping were banned in Melbourne. The specific Melbourne rule on rough play leaned towards the more peaceful versions of what became soccer or Association football. Thus the Cambridge rules of 1856 had banned tripping and the Sheffield rules of 1857 had banned hacking and tripping while the Harrow rules seem to have shunned rough play. Of course, these rules cannot simply be taken at their face value. A rule is notable only if it is strictly enforced.

It was not easy to enforce the new Australian rules – so long as the captains served as umpires. If one captain early in the match refused to allow a free kick to be paid against his team, the other captain would retaliate by refusing to concede a free kick for infringements by his own team. So the deadlock continued, rule after rule being broken as the afternoon went on.

While matches could be rough, rarely were they outrageously rough. Broken limbs were few. The first leg said to have been broken was that of Newton Jacomb, possibly in the late 1860s. Shirts were torn far more often than limbs. A former Rugby boy named Morrell who played the Australian game with intense vigour was especially known for the number of shirts he tore during a football season.

A spectator arriving late for a match and surveying the play as he came closer to the boundary was more likely to see a scrummage than fast open play. An early writer observed that the scrummage 'took up a heap of time'. When a player in possession of the ball was tackled and the ball fell to the ground, a scrummage ensued and the rival players formed themselves into two knots and with heads down tried to push their opponents and the ball towards their attacking zone. There is every reason to think that the Australian scrummage was like the scrummage which the secretary of the English Rugby Union described as typical of his code in the 1870s. Each team, he said, 'bent on driving the ball through the ranks of their opponents, set to work to push, struggle and kick, forcing, if possible, a passage through which the ball may emerge'. In the Richmond Paddock and the Royal and Albert parks, a team deficient in physique was crucified in the scrummages.

The scrummage was such an essential part of early Australian football that a goal was scored whenever the slow-moving scrum of players forced the ball through the goalposts. In the late 1860s the scrummage went out of favour, for most spectators and players wanted a faster style of football. In the early 1870s the umpires were to be instructed to throw the ball into the air rather than allow a scrummage to continue. By 1872 a goal could no longer be scored in the course of a scrummage unless it was clearly kicked before passing between the goalposts.

The rough play, the disputes and the occasions when an entire team walked off the field were more likely than good conduct to be reported in the newspapers, thus consigning to silence the numerous acts of goodwill and fairness. While the word 'sportsmanlike' was not yet part of the Saturday afternoon vocabulary, such conduct was frequent. When Geelong played at Ballarat in July 1863 – they played on the public holiday commemorating Victoria's gaining of independence from New South Wales – the slippery grass made for numerous spills and an 'ugly collision' injured a Ballarat player. And yet good humour prevailed. When Geelong kicked a goal and a Ballarat player promptly claimed the ball had touched his hand before passing between the goalposts, Geelong amicably accepted his protest. Eventually Geelong won with two late goals. After the teams cheered each other off the field, the reporter on

Bell's Life noted that the cheering 'proved both teams still had some wind left'. He did not need to observe, for it was normal rather than abnormal, that both teams also retained plenty of fair spirit after a tense match which, with only a single break, lasted from one o'clock until five in the afternoon. The playing time was almost double that of a typical match today.

One puzzling question in the experimental years of this new game is whether an offside rule partly operated. The printed rules are silent on this important matter, but they are silent on many matters. Under an offside rule the permanent forwards as we know them have no place, and players become real forwards only after the ball moves into their attacking zone. When their team is in attack they cannot fan out ahead of the ball but instead must always stay behind or parallel with the ball as it moves towards their scoring zone: otherwise they are offside or, in other words, out of bounds. The extremely low scoring of the early years suggests that perhaps an offside rule was an unwritten custom in certain situations. An offside rule is the strongest of all impediments to scoring.

It is certain that each match began with a minor version of the offside rule by which the player who kicked off did so with all his team mates standing behind him. Moreover, it would have been surprising if, in its infancy, the new code of football used no offside rule whatsoever. That would have been an abrupt break away from Rugby* and Association football, both of which emphasised the offside rule, and such a break would have aroused comment. And yet so far I have come across no early description of Australian football which actually comments on the abandonment of offside.

---

*In the 1850s, six of Rugby's thirty-three written rules elaborated on the offside principle. Of the thirteen written rules of the Football Association (soccer) in 1863, one was devoted to the offside principle but did not use that exact phrase. In soccer the offside rule was to change drastically between the 1860s and 1925.

This suggests that the departure from the offside rule was not an abrupt, emphatic decision of 1858 but came in quick stages.

The scrummage was probably another occasion when an offside rule was applied. The scrummage or scrum was an early solution to the deadlock which is now solved in Australian football by either the ball-up or the free kick 'plucked by the umpire' (as they say) from the pack. Victoria's football rules for many years defined a scrummage as commencing 'when the ball is on the ground, and all who have closed round on their respective sides begin kicking at it'. Oddly, the early Victorian rules, while legislating in favour of scrummages, did not clearly set out the conditions which gave rise to the scrummage, nor the rituals and conduct allowable in a scrummage. It seems almost certain that the footballers formed up in two groups facing each other and abided by a version of the offside rule. In the manner of Rugby players they stood 'shoulder to shoulder, leg to leg, as tight as they can stand' and tried to kick the ball out of the pack.

How far a player could run with the ball remained a topic of argument. By 1860 a player who possessed the ball could not run more than a pace or two: 'The Ball may at any time be taken in hand, but not carried further than is necessary for a kick.' This rule presupposes that unless a player dribbled the ball along the ground his only mode of attack was to kick. To throw – and presumably to punch – the ball to a team mate was forbidden. Another inaugural rule allowed a player to catch or 'mark' the ball and take his time to kick from the place where he caught it. The Harrow and Winchester schools and Cambridge University permitted a mark in their more soccer-orientated version of football, and even Rugby allowed a mark. Commonplace in England, the mark was to decline there but grow in importance in Australian football.

The leather football itself showed the contrasting forces that were shaping the new game. Both the round ball and the oval or

The Day of the Round Ball and the Oblong Ground

By the 1870s big crowds saw the top teams play on the makeshift ground outside the fence of the Melbourne Cricket Ground. **The Australasian Sketcher** *of 12 June 1875 published this lithograph, looking west towards the large houses of Jolimont. The ground had no grandstands or embankment but the terrain was shaped like an amphitheatre and could hold as many as 10,000 spectators.*

Rugby ball were used in Melbourne in the first years. The match between Melbourne Grammar and Scotch College in 1858 may have used a Rugby ball – Scotch is said to have owned such balls – but in most of the early matches between senior footballers a round ball was almost certainly used. Several early rules were probably devised with the round ball in mind. Thus the rule that a ball could only be picked up by a player when it was clearly bouncing or 'on the hop' suggests that a round ball was normal. Indeed, at one stage the rules allowed the ball, in the course of general ground play, to be grasped only on the *first* bounce or hop. As an oval ball bouncing on a rough surface would have been too erratic to give players much chance of grasping it on the first hop, we can reasonably assume that the round ball – what we would now call a 'soccer ball' – was mainly used at that time.

The choice of ball depended not only on whether the soccer or Rugby style of playing was in the ascendancy but also on the availability of footballs. In 1860 George Marshall's sports store in Melbourne was advertising an improved oval or Rugby ball, made in a new way on 'a scientific principle' and capable of flying far. Unfortunately, many of the earlier Rugby balls did not have the symmetry and exact proportions that would enable them to travel a long distance when kicked, nor did they bounce in a reasonably predictable way. *The Argus* on 14 May 1860 criticised the new oval balls for their erratic behaviour.

A football, even when its maker was exceptionally skilled, was not easily manufactured. The first task was to go to a butcher's shop and select the strong, well-proportioned bladder of a pig. The bladder had to be cleaned, and then the bladder was washed in a weak solution of chloride of lime, rinsed with clean water, blown out and rolled under the arm in such a way as to stretch the bladder and make it larger. It was blown as large as possible and, when taut, was allowed to dry. The pig bladder was then enclosed in a leather case made to fit the bladder and hand-stitched by a shoemaker.

Wide variations in the bladder and football were normal. But once the process ceased to be the work of the butcher and cobbler and became the task of a skilled craftsman in a small factory, a more uniform product was possible, though not certain. The more reliable footballs were made by Gilbert of Rugby and Howard of London and shipped to Melbourne just when the Australian code was developing. Everyone in those days knew how a football was made. In sporting prose the nickname of the football was simply 'the pigskin' or 'the polished pigskin', and those names were used long after the pig's bladder ceased to be used.

Once England, the workshop of the world, applied factory methods and careful measurement to the making of footballs – and the growing market for footballs gave a reward for skilled manufacturing – the quality of the average football was certain to improve. The improved quality of the oval-shaped footballs might have been an important factor in shaping the rules of Australian football. Certainly, if the round ball had remained largely in use, the game today would have evolved in somewhat different directions.

Some teams preferred the oval ball and some the round ball. As a football was expensive – some matches were abandoned when the football burst – a match possibly could begin with an oval ball and conclude with a round ball. In 1865 when Carlton played one of its first matches its players were clearly accustomed to a round ball. It so happened that an oval ball, rather small in size, was used that afternoon, and Carlton could not cope with its erratic bounce. That match was long remembered for Carlton's confusion and for an astonishing kick made by one of Carlton's opponents, Henry H Budd, a young solicitor. His kick was inconceivable a decade earlier when footballs were made more roughly. Budd had decided, far from goal, to try a place kick. He sent the ball through the goals with probably the longest kick seen in Australia up to that time. A decade later it was excitedly recalled as '70 yards if it was an inch'.

The round ball was used in some matches as late as 1866. Thus when *The Illustrated Melbourne Post* sent a black-and-white artist to draw a scene from a football match in the Richmond Paddock, all the evidence suggests that he used his eyes and – perhaps exercising a little liberty here and there – drew what he saw. The ball around which the players in long trousers are milling is unmistakeably round. Soon, however, the oval ball was to be supreme. Whereas the official rules of May 1866 did not specify what kind of ball should be used, the rules of the following decade were to specify a Rugby ball.

CHAPTER FIVE

When Harrison Grabbed the Ball and Ran

The champion footballer of the 1860s, if there was one champion over such a wide span of time, was Henry Harrison. He played in every season of the 1860s, one of the few early players to last so long. He was without doubt the game's fastest footballer during those years and he had a strong influence on developing the fast and open play that was to become characteristic of the game when played with high skill. He was the best rather than the fairest footballer, and one old player thought that Harrison was perhaps 'a little vicious in his play'. No doubt the critic had in mind an episode when Harrison jumped on an opponent. A methodical man, Harrison was also one of those who helped to write football's new rules. Such was his role as player and rule-maker that long before he reached old age he was hailed with some exaggeration as the father of Australian football.

Harrison and Tom Wills had much in common, indeed they were step-cousins, and the relationship became closer when

Harrison, approaching the height of his football fame, married Tom Wills' sister, Emily. Both Harrison and Wills had separately come overland as small boys in the early years of the pastoral inflow into Victoria and spent a large part of their childhoods in the 1840s on their parents' sheep stations in central Victoria. Wills called Henry Harrison 'Coldy': his second and more familiar name was Colden.

Henry Colden Antill Harrison, the great footballer of the 1860s. This portrait, sketched by Ruby Harrison long after his sporting career was over, belongs to the T Wills Cook collection.

'Coldy' was the younger by ten months and tended always to look up to Wills, once calling him 'the beau-ideal of an athlete'. The Harrison family settled near the present site of St Arnaud and the sons were brought up amongst horses and sheep, even giving up their educations to serve as shepherds when labour was scarce. Henry was only nine or ten when he and his brother first rode their horses the seventy miles along winding bush tracks to visit the Wills family near Ararat. One horse was injured to such a degree that the brothers returned without it, each boy taking his turn to ride while the other walked. While young Henry was very fit and dexterous, his father was slightly prone to accident, both in work and business. A photograph of the father shows a proud, defiant man with a black sock or covering over his right hand – the result of his gun accidentally discharging.

The Harrisons moved to Melbourne, their pastoral venture not being very successful, just before the gold rushes of 1851. The restless father, excited by the news of gold, bought horse and cart and camping equipment and with two sons set out, first digging at Ballarat and then at Castlemaine and Eaglehawk. Henry, aged only fourteen, worked hard at digging and at washing the gold-bearing soil, but he did not thrive on the rough food and became thin. At night the fleas inside his blankets especially annoyed him. After a year he returned to Melbourne, leaving his father on the gold diggings where he became one of the leading agitators against the government's policy of highly taxing the diggers.

Young Harrison joined the civil service and was posted to Williamstown. As tide-officer he boarded the sailing ships that had just arrived from Britain and numerous other lands and helped to assess the cargoes on which they had to pay import duty. After five years of inspecting the cabins and holds of ships anchored in the bay, he was transferred to the customs house in Melbourne where his hours were more regular and he had leisure for sport. Some sixty years later, in his autobiography, Harrison recalled how he and his friends were advised by his cousin Tom Wills not to play Rugby but to 'work out a game of our own' more suited to grown men. So he and a few friends, he claimed, came together and began to play football, making their rules as they went along. He did not, in any sentence in his own book, call himself the father of the game, but his chapter on football actually carries the title of 'Father of the Australian Game'. In old age in subtle ways he spread the message that he was the father and understandably he accepted the title when it was conferred on him.

So far as is known Harrison did not even play in the first year of football, and certainly he had no part in shaping the first rules. The first match in which his name is recorded is in September 1859 – late in football's second season – when he was captain of one of the ten-player teams for the Melbourne club. In old age he claimed to have captained Richmond in the very first year of football, but Richmond did not play in the first year of football. Soon, however, he was prominent both for Richmond and for Melbourne.

In 1861 – the fourth year of regular football – he was one of the game's most skilled players and Melbourne's regular captain. In May of that year he led Melbourne against Geelong, wearing his team's brilliant new magenta uniform, and was in superb form. After Melbourne had gained an unbeatable lead of four goals to none, it was decided to equalise the sides, and Harrison took off his magenta jersey and donned one of Geelong's coloured caps. In the words of the newspaper, 'the Melbourne captain was given up to the Geelong side'. On his own he was sufficient to bolster Geelong's weak defences and the match was continued without further score until 'the declining sun warned the visitors to retire'. At this time the spectators gained as much pleasure from the falls and tumbles of the players as from sheer skill, but Harrison as much as any other player was to place the premium on skill.

Next year the Customs Department transferred Harrison to Geelong, which by then was declining after a few years of hustle as the main harbour for the Ballarat goldfield. Harrison, elected captain of the Geelong club, seems to have helped to turn it into a powerful team. Next year he returned to Melbourne and again became its captain. In the typical year of the 1860s Melbourne was one of the two best teams, and much of its success came from Harrison. He was a skilled tactician. A bush lawyer, he knew how to gain the most from the existing rules and to suggest changes if they did not favour his team.

Harrison became an official rule-maker. When in 1866 the delegates from the four main metropolitan clubs – Melbourne,

Carlton, Royal Park and South Yarra – met at the Freemason's Hotel, a few paces along Swanston Street from the hotel that became Young & Jackson's, Harrison was voted into the chair. He gained approval for the set of twelve rules he had written out with pen and ink. Though most of the rules were those of 1859,

Royal Park was rough and rural when Carlton originally played there. This may be one of the earliest surviving photographs of a football team. Reportedly taken in 1868, it shows Carlton before coloured socks were worn.

Harrison's central role in the meeting was a reflection of his ability to gain agreement for changes that were both popular and practicable. The footballers themselves still ran the new code of football, and the rules they accepted were essentially those which had been tested again and again on the football field.

As a player Harrison was strong. He was somewhat bigger than the average player of his day, for his height was 5 feet, 10½ inches and his weight in the early 1860s was about 12 stone 5 lbs; later in his footballing career he was probably closer to 13 stone. He found a way past opponents by his cleverly timed use of weight and speed, and he was sure in handling the ball and accurate in his kicking. He was recalled as 'lithe, sinewy, well conditioned, strong and hard as nails'. The unusual paleness of his face and hands gave new opponents the initial idea that he was not fully robust: his vigour and toughness sometimes caught them by surprise. In his heyday, it was speed more than toughness that made him the hero of the Richmond Paddock.

The open style of football demonstrated by Harrison was slow to emerge. Those who favoured the soccer style were still numerous. Disliking the constant handling of the ball, they wanted rules which enforced as much kicking as possible – in short, a game which significantly was usually spelled as two words, 'foot ball'. On the other hand the Rugby players wished to retain as much handling of the ball as was possible. They especially liked to run with the ball, using sheer strength to retain possession. Naturally the young Australian-born players or recent migrants who barely knew the various English codes of football tended to prefer a kind of game that favoured their own personal skills, whether speed, strength or ability to dodge. Harrison belonged to this influential group which was tied to no English code. He was also a captain when the captains possessed the power to experiment with new rules, and the fact that he belonged to none of the English footballing creeds gave him a certain authority and impartiality.

In the 1860 season the players in the soccer mould held a brief ascendancy. The rules seem to have encouraged players to soccer the ball along the ground. It was still permissible for a player, after a ball had been *kicked*, to catch the ball and call 'Mark!' in a loud voice, but if the ball fell to the ground the player's options were more restricted than they are today. The new rule firmly prohibited a player from picking up the ball after it had made more than one bounce. Then he could kick the loose ball by soccering it, but not handle it.

The rule caused many disputes, partly because it was not easily interpreted. Thus if a ball were kicked at a low level some 30 yards into the open, and if a player arrived just when it was hitting the ground, and if his body happened to conceal the low-running ball from the captains and other players, who could tell whether he picked up the ball on the first or second bounce? Presumably such occurrences prompted *Bell's Life*, on 3 August 1861, to inform its readers that the new rule did not increase 'the harmony and pleasure of the game'. Gradually the new rule was discarded and the players picked up the ball even after it had bounced three or four times. That change, favouring an open style of football, was soon followed by another reform which encouraged fast players, when they had picked up the ball, to run with it rather than kick it.

There had been an early agreement that those who gained possession of the ball must kick it as soon as possible. The Rugby-minded players, however, liked to hold the ball tightly and run with it. Likewise, fast players – and the game soon attracted some of the continent's fastest sprinters – also wanted to race away with the ball in their hands. More and more players grabbed the ball and ran. By 1864 the runners were winning the debate on which style of football should prevail. They were winning partly because the game they played was more appealing to the people. The spectators who stood near the boundary flags were therefore to be counted amongst the inventors of the new code of football, for their preferences influenced the rules which, for the most part, were slowly rewritten or reinterpreted to encourage open play.

At Yarra Park and Royal Park in Melbourne and at the Argyle Ground in Geelong, many players were making long dashes of 30 or 40 yards with the ball, but the opponents of this style of play looked for rules which might retard the runners. Those who ran with the ball, the opponents said, must bounce it. As the surface of the ground was uneven, the act of bouncing the ball would increase the risk that the players would lose possession whenever the bouncing ball hit a projecting rock or a mud patch. That risk increased after the oval ball challenged the round ball. The new oval ball at that time was not as pointed as it later became, but compared to the round ball it could still not be bounced with assurance. The oval ball was also difficult to bounce because it lost shape more quickly.

In first-class football today the act of bouncing the ball seems so safe and effortless, except on a muddy day, that we have almost forgotten how severe a penalty was originally imposed by the rule that players must bounce the ball when running. The rule-makers hoped the act of bouncing would severely penalise the runners. The response of the fast players who loved to carry the ball was to bounce it as little as possible. So long as captains served as umpires, they were unlikely to agree on a strict enforcing of this rule. At the beginning of the 1864 season the main sporting paper in Melbourne regretted that 'frequently a player would run 20 yards with ball in hand', not bouncing it once. In the following season, the evidence suggests that a few players were running 40 yards without once bouncing the ball.

Harrison was believed to be the fastest footballer in the first era of Australian football, and under the new confusion of the bouncing rule he had every incentive to grab the ball and sprint. He now ran long distances at full pace without once bouncing the ball. Theodore Marshall, an early captain of Royal Park team, was perturbed at the liberties Harrison took with the rules and decided to challenge him.

In the winter of 1865, on the eve of a game with Melbourne, Marshall privately told one of his fast players, J E Clarke, that if he happened to gain possession of the ball when there was open ground stretching ahead of him he should shun the bouncing rule and run for his life. This might awaken Harrison to the liberties he himself often took, in defiance of the rules. Clarke was said to be the second-fastest footballer in the game and he seized the chance. With the ball in his possession he raced along the wing, dodged several Melbourne defenders and continued to sprint without bouncing the ball. He even ran beyond the 40 yards which Harrison, when the opportunity arose, normally ran without one bounce. In the end

When Carlton played Melbourne in 1881, bare arms were becoming fashionable.

Clarke kicked a goal. Marshall, recalling the episode years later, said that Harrison protested at the long distance his opponent had run, but he must have received the obvious response that what was sauce for the goose was sauce for the gander. As captains and umpires the two men then discussed the matter and, according to Marshall, they agreed 'that the ball should be bounced at least once in every ten yards'. The new experimental rule still favoured the fast, attacking player.

Marshall later argued that this was how an important facet of Australian football came into being, but the bouncing rule in one form or other had a complicated history. And after the marathon dash by Clarke of Royal Park in 1865, the 10-yard rule simply applied to those matches on which Harrison and Marshall and any other captain were able to impose it. In 1866 the formal adoption of a new set of rules – the most important revision so far – virtually settled the bouncing controversy. It stipulated that 'no player shall run with the ball unless he strikes it against the ground every five or six yards'. That marked the end of Harrison's very long Rugby-like sprints with the ball. Thereafter he had to bounce it.

The defenders were quick to retaliate against the swift player who tried to run the field, bouncing the ball as he ran. The defenders increasingly applied vigour. In many matches they grabbed the runner by the neck – an allowable tactic – and threw him to the ground or they pushed him from behind, making him fall headlong. Sometimes they tore the jersey almost from the runner's back while temporarily retarding him, and little 'Billy' Freeman became well known for the jerseys he lost each Saturday afternoon.

With the defenders gaining the initiative through these roughhouse but permissible tactics, the attackers often felt justified in holding onto the ball and continuing to run without bouncing it. As each side appointed its own umpire, and as the nearest umpire made the decision in any matter of dispute, violations of the bouncing rule might have remained frequent. Thus, on 14 August 1869, Albert Park was at home to the Hobson's Bay Railway team and one newspaper report hints that the bouncing rule was not always enforced: 'Some amusement was caused to the on-lookers by Millar taking up the ball, and in spite of some half-dozen of his opponents sticking on to him like leeches, rushing through with it for sixty or seventy yards.' The conclusion is inescapable that Millar was hugging the ball tight and not daring to bounce it.

The fast-running, weaving forwards were often called 'dodgers' in the late 1860s. Some observers of the game objected strongly to the new tendency for the more rugged of the defenders to take their revenge 'on all dodgers who come within their range'. Most spectators – and even then they wrote letters to the newspapers after each new trend or rule – relished the dodgers. Newcomers to Victoria also fell under the spell of this dashing style of football. One Englishman, who for eleven years had played the Eton College's distinctive code of football, first saw Australian football in 1868 and told English friends that the new game was especially exciting because – unlike Association football at home – a player could pick up the ball and dodge to his heart's content until he was shouldered or pushed off balance. He wrote a letter to *The Melbourne Australasian* in 1869 expressing his admiration for six particular players, including 'Wills of Geelong fame' who gracefully ran with the ball, 'bouncing it the whole time, and passing through numbers of their opponents, to the great amusement of the spectators'. The old Etonian even sent to England a copy of the 'Melbourne Football Rules' so that friends could read rule number eight which tried to protect the wonderful dodgers.

While most spectators were pleased that an open and fast-moving game was emerging, there were still numerous passages of play in which sheer physical strength and vigour were at a premium. Harrison was renowned both for his open play and, in his final footballing years, his vigour. On Saturday, 16 July 1870, Albert Park, then the holders of a much-prized Challenge Cup, accepted Melbourne's challenge. Harrison led Melbourne, physically the stronger side, and began to apply what almost everyone except Harrison agreed were strong-arm tactics. In the scrummages he was so vigorous that one newspaper drew attention to his 'rough and savage style'. When an Albert Park star named Gray, one of the finest marks in the colony, was about to mark the ball, he was thrown to the ground by Harrison and then jumped upon. The last action was almost certainly unintended but Gray – a bleeding cut across his eye – had to leave the ground for half an hour; and a few days later he made it known that he would not play football again that season. In the course of the same game his team mate Morris had his nose broken – a mere 'scratch', said Harrison – while another two Albert Park players were hurt in a manner which was also the subject of dispute. Clearly one Albert Park player was injured by his own team mate, but another was hit on the head by an un-named Melbourne player. The extent of that player's concussion was brushed aside by Harrison, who explained that the player was 'knocked silly for a time, but soon regained his usual mental equilibrium'. We glean from Harrison the hint that his opponent, even when in full command of his faculties, paid only nineteen shillings in the pound.

The match gave rise to heated letters in the press. It was generally agreed that Harrison on that day was not the only over-vigorous Melbourne player, but it was also argued that he was the most savage and excitable of them. Harrison replied with a fluent letter in the *Australasian* of 30 July in which he stood his ground: 'Football is essentially a rough game all the world over, and it is not suitable for men-poodles or milksops.' To his credit he himself took hard knocks without complaining.

Harrison was still playing when he was close to his thirty-fifth birthday. He had lost a little of his pace and was receiving more knocks. Now a popular target for the defenders because he was the celebrated old champion and because he could be rough in his own play, he began to feel, for days afterwards, the effects of a vigorous game. In 1871, towards the end of his career, he felt pain after he led fifteen or sixteen Melbourne players against a team of twenty Ballarat players. The odds were too heavy: so were several Ballarat players. Ballarat's Eastern Oval was muddy, play was good-tempered though rough, and after nearly four hours of exhausting football

Harrison's team lost by two goals. For some time he relived the vigour of that game whenever he walked.

At the close of the 1871 season Harrison led Melbourne against Carlton. As the Challenge Cup was at stake, the neutral South Melbourne ground by the Albert Park lake was chosen and a mass of Carlton followers crossed the city on this Saturday afternoon in

South Yarra was for a decade one of the leading teams, and its Presentation Challenge Cup aroused strong competition. The cup was won on a windy afternoon in 1871 by Carlton, who defeated Melbourne in what was Harrison's last game.

October and stood around the unfenced arena. The old champion, having lost the toss, was forced to kick to the least favoured end. A gale was blowing, and when he kicked off the wind lifted the ball and almost carried it back over his head. With tremendous effort he tried to keep the Carlton attackers at bay until it was Melbourne's turn to use the strong wind. Later the wind dropped away, Melbourne gained little aid from it, and Carlton won by two goals. After the match the exhausted Harrison must have been taken to his house in a cab. There he lay in bed, suffering from 'over-exertion'. He did not play again, though half a century later he was still seen at the big matches at the Melbourne Cricket Ground, offering his right hand to those who would be ever so proud, years later, to say that they had once shaken the hand of none other than Mr Harrison.

He belonged to the era when most players were still known as Mister rather than Tom, Dick or Harry. Called Mr Harrison throughout his playing career, he saw football's transition from a game mainly for gentlemen to a game which, by 1871, boys and men of every occupation were playing. He saw it rise from a sport for the few to a sport for the many. That last match in which Harrison played attracted such a crowd of followers that two by two and three by three they encroached onto the arena. The game that had begun with a few spectators in the endless expanse of parklands was about to be reshaped by the crowds it now attracted. It was on the verge of becoming the people's game.

CHAPTER SIX

Rise of the Barrackers and Hissers

Saturday afternoon was normally the time for football, but that afternoon was a holiday for only a few professions and even fewer skilled trades in the 1860s. Even for city clerks in favoured positions, the Saturday afternoon was not always free, and in the period before the overseas telegraph cable reached Australia the impending departure of a mail steamer for England signalled a Saturday of last-minute writing of letters and commercial orders from banks, merchant houses, big shops and factories. We know that on the Saturday of the punishing match in which Harrison was deemed the villain in July 1870, the Albert Park team was seriously weakened by the absence of some to its finest players 'in consequence of the departure of the mail'. Though that phrase means nothing to us today, it meant everything to a city which was still commercially tied to England. Even football had to give way to the mail steamers.

The 1870s were to see a large increase in the number of workers who were free to play football on a Saturday afternoon, but in the preceding decade such workers were few. In Melbourne was one notable exception – the soldiers living in the barracks that still stand on St Kilda Road. Ever since 1788, regiments of soldiers recruited in the British Isles had been stationed in Australia; and during their

Even in wet weather, large crowds went to the football (The Australasian Sketcher, *3 July 1880*).

term of duty they often took part in local social and sporting events. The regiments now stationed in Melbourne had just returned from the wars against the Maoris in New Zealand, and being attracted to competitive sport they began to take intense interest in the football matches played within ten or fifteen minutes' walk of their bluestone barracks. The teams in Melbourne were also eager to play football against the soldiers, for here was the first opportunity to play what could be seen as an international game of football: Victoria versus the British Isles.

Regular contests against the soldiers began in 1867. The difficulty was that the officers and privates did not understand what were called the Victorian rules. Even if they did understand them, they preferred to play according to their own rules which favoured their physical strength. They liked to grab the ball and run, charging and shouldering their way through opponents.

The soldiers were to be long remembered for their liberties with the rules. The 14th 'Buckinghamshire' Regiment team was led by Lieutenant A W Noyes, himself a Rugby player and a clever handler of the ball; and his team's exploits – no doubt exaggerated – were recalled in a verse which appeared in 1877 in *The Footballer* magazine:

> *I've watched the 14th at football play,*
> *In foraging caps and singlets grey;*
> *Lieutenant Noyes,*
> *With his broths of boys,*
> *Charged fierce along with a wild 'Hurrah!'*
> *'Twas 'Go it, Larry: fetch him a lick!'* *
> *Then Larry licked*
> *And Dooley kicked;*

The long verse went on to lament that players in the 14th Regiment thought that fair play embraced hacking and tripping, while their fierce charges could end in a 'nose all smashed, and some teeth knocked out'. But one picture that lingers is of the shouting and barracking by the private soldiers:

> *Pat Kelly cries, with a warlike snort;*
> *'Knock 'em to blazes; bark their shins,*
> *And I'll stake my life the 14th wins.'*

They did not often win against top Victorian clubs but in defeat they were exultant.

Games against a red-coat regiment provided a unique brand of football. On 17 July 1869, Albert Park played the 14th Regiment in a ground at the end of Clarendon Street, obviously the site later of the South Melbourne ground, and about a thousand people arrived

---

*To 'lick' a man in the face was to hit him.

to receive 'an infinity of amusement' from the rough and tumble play of both teams. It seems that several of the soldiers favoured a more soccer-type game and they secured the winning goal by dribbling the ball into the forward-line where at last a strong kick guided the ball through the posts. Curiously, the Albert Park goalkeeper was no more familiar than the soldiers with the rules and tactics, and instead of stopping the ball in front of the goalposts he marked the ball after it had passed through. This match suddenly came to an end in the second half after a field umpire's decision had been fiercely disputed.

Harrison, captaining Melbourne in its first match against the Garrison, wisely allowed the soldiers some latitude. (They probably thought they gave him the same privilege.) In later matches Harrison called for stricter adherence to the rules agreed upon, and the Garrison probably said yes, but what the 'yes' meant was open to doubt. Their mode of play was described as 'hugging and hitting'. With their sturdy physique, a willingness to use heavy soldiers' boots to kick an opponent in the shins, and coloured handkerchiefs tied around their brow in the manner of modern Aboriginal nationalists, they appeared 'pretty awe-inspiring', noted Harrison. He especially relished the soldiers' way of forming a bodyguard to protect their captain when he fell panting to the ground, the ball beneath him.

Matches with the soldiers aroused intense interest. They were considered so important that in 1869 the Melbourne Cricket Ground was allocated for one match in which Melbourne eventually defeated the Garrison by one goal to nil. Such matches heightened the discussion about the emerging rules of Australian football, and the general conclusion was that the local rules were far superior to the soldiers' rules. Impertinently, some observers even said that the soldiers had no rules.

Harrison was especially delighted with one rough incident in June 1868. The soldiers, after they had been defeated by a Victorian team, replied that all would be changed soon: 'Wait till Ensign Crosby arrived!' At last he arrived. Appearing on the football ground in spotless white and wearing a belt which was probably embroidered by an admiring woman, he seemed boyish and lacking in robustness. He was in all likelihood a sprinter with an uncanny

*Women wearing the latest winter fashions would stream into Yarra Park if their favourite team was playing. This sketch of a hurrying crowd in July 1877 shows, on the other side of the river, the grand, new government house (*The Australasian Sketcher, *7 July 1877).*

ability to dodge. He was given no chance to dodge. After about sixteen seconds Ensign Crosby was charged ('collided with' was Harrison's tactful phrase) by a stocky Melbourne footballer named Chubby Forrester. The frail Ensign, all in white, was carried from the field.

Many soldiers went as individual spectators to football matches, particularly those played near the Albert Park lagoon, which was not far from their barracks. When Albert Park played Carlton for the Challenge Cup in August 1870 and the 'great assemblage of spectators' crowded along the boundary of the unfenced arena, the captains of the two teams invited a few soldiers of the 18th Regiment to prevent the crowd from invading the field. The brave soldiers succeeded. That must have been one of their regiment's boldest victories on Australian soil.

All the British regiments in Australia were to leave in 1870, permanently handing over the land defences to the local troops of each colony. In the history of empires it must be rare for the imperial power to withdraw its forces in such a glow of goodwill. In Melbourne their departure was regretted by most followers of football, not only because the two styles of play made matches against the soldiers so unpredictable, but also because these contests were the closest approach that Australian football could make to international matches in its first two decades. For that reason Saturday, 6 August 1870 was especially awaited. Almost on the eve of the 18th Regiment's departure by sea, its officers and privates were to play Carlton, the team with the largest following of all. Rain poured, and the match was called off. Many sports-goers were sad to see the soldiers finally march through the streets on their way to the pier.

They left behind something permanent. They helped to shape a word which has been one of the hallmarks of Australian sport for more than a century, the word 'barracker'. The word became popular about 1880 and was originally an Australian football term, and from football it spread to cricket and then to every kind of sporting contest. For a long time it was a slang word, but it climbed the social and political ladders; and on 5 July 1893 in the Victorian Legislative Assembly, Isaac Isaacs, who was to become the first Australian-born Governor General, could be heard complaining in the face of frequent interjectors that he hoped that their barracking 'would not be continued'.

Apparently the word was still unfamiliar in England, and authors writing for the English market felt a need to explain what it meant. G L James, in his book of 1892, *Shall I Try Australia?*, explained that in Victoria the young men were mad about football, usually wore the colours of their team and were known as barrackers. He explained that 'to barrack' was to 'audibly encourage their own favourites and comment disparagingly upon the performance of their opponents, a proceeding which leads to an interchange of compliments' between the rival barrackers.

The word was said by some to come from the Aboriginal *borak* and by others to come from the Northern Irish word *barrack*, meaning to brag and boast of one's fighting powers. It is unlikely to have stemmed from the Aboriginal, and even an Irish origin is not certain since the little-used Irish word did not mean the same as the new Australian word, though their meanings are similar. More important than the exact origin of the word is the question of why it came to be used enthusiastically in Melbourne's footballing circles – being used infinitely more than in Ireland and used in a different way – and why it then spread throughout the continent. A new word becomes the vogue largely because it sounds right. The word barrack seemed just right amongst football spectators in Melbourne in the 1870s because they recalled the regimental footballers who lived in the Victoria Barracks, knew especially their fighting brand of football, and recalled how Pat Kelly and Tim Dooley and other soldiers, mythical or real, barracked while playing or watching. In a city and a sport where the players from the army barracks made such a stir, the word seemed a neat fit. Where the word actually originated is an important matter for those who trace the ancestry of words, but more significant is why it was virtually reborn in Melbourne, and why it there acquired an energetic life of its own and a distinctive meaning.

At one time many people in Melbourne believed that the word had originated through football's connection with the Victoria Barracks. But the specialists in the Australian language who later emerged – and most came from New Zealand – did not realise the intimate connection between 'barracks' and the rise of Australian

Sydney was much slower than Melbourne to adopt football as a winter game, but by June 1885 its Town and Country Journal *gave a whole page to sketches of the crowd and the game. Presumably the code depicted here was Rugby Union but it could have been the rival Australian code.*

football and therefore had no reason to see merit in the theory. It is now impossible to tell whether the word was invented in Melbourne or imported from Ireland and then resuscitated with a new meaning; but it would not have become so popular but for the fact that in Melbourne it conjured memories of a special group of footballers and their banter on and off the field. Eventually the word in its new meaning was to cross the world, becoming common in English sporting writing from about the 1920s.

The garrison in Melbourne offered a version of international football which was trebly welcomed by spectators because a football match against the other colonies was still out of the question. Even to visit Ballarat was too expensive an outing for most of the metropolitan clubs, and on the few such visits in the 1860s many members of the visiting clubs could not afford the fare or, if they could, failed to gain their employer's permission to be absent from work in order to catch the Friday evening train. To visit Bendigo was even more of an adventure. Harrison probably did not play in Bendigo during his whole football career.

The first city team to visit Bendigo was South Yarra. In 1872, on the verge of its extinction as a football club, it accepted the challenge from Sandhurst Club and sent its available players to Bendigo by train. Only sixteen footballers made the journey and they played Sandhurst's eighteen at the large Kangaroo Flat cricket ground on the outskirts of Bendigo on the public holiday called Separation Day. South Yarra kicked one goal late in the afternoon, before the ball was accidentally burst and the match came to an end. A fortnight later the Melbourne team arrived in Bendigo on the Friday evening train and stayed in the Shamrock Hotel, but the disappointment was keen when the Sandhurst football club heard that only fourteen Melbourne players had made the journey, and so Saturday's game was fixed at fourteen a side. It would be an exhausting day for both teams, for the ground was wet and slippery, the wind was blowing in gusts, and the teams had agreed to play for three hours. Players fell flat on their backs in the mud, those trying to kick against the wind were often lucky to drive the ball 20 yards, and the game seemed likely to end without a goal until Goldsmith of Melbourne took the ball from a scrummage in the centre and ran like a hare. His driving drop kick landed close to the goal and then 'with a good bound, went clean through the posts'.

Further upcountry – far beyond the terminus of the railway system – the football clubs had no opportunity of a visit from footballers living in Melbourne, Geelong or Ballarat. In southwest Victoria, where football was reborn after its quick death in the early

1860s, the inland town of Hamilton and the two ports of Warrnambool and Port Fairy occasionally played each other with teams ranging from 15 to 20 players. Their matches were social events, and when the Port Fairy team came to Warrnambool to play football on the racecourse in May 1868, the play commenced at 1.30, was adjourned in mid-afternoon to enable luncheon to be eaten at the Steam Packet Hotel, and was then resumed with 'the utmost good feeling' until 5 pm. When Hamilton sent its football team by horse coach to Warrnambool one month later, the visit aroused such excitement that the main business at the port closed their doors on the Thursday afternoon of the match. The day was long remembered because Warrnambool was about to score its second goal when a bystander accidentally stopped the ball with his foot.

In these towns the footballers played with a stamina that would have astonished the city footballers. On the great winter holiday of 1868, Separation Day, Port Fairy commenced its home game against Warrnambool in the morning, kicked with the aid of the wind for four hours, and after adjourning for luncheon it proceeded to defend against the wind for one and a half hours until darkness set in, ending the game. Complete exhaustion must also have been setting in by 10 pm because normally the upcountry matches ended with a banquet, songs, speeches and 'loyal and patriotic toasts'.

Ballarat was a special side-window on the way football, in about 1870, was changing. While football was still mainly a game for young men working in stiff-collar professions and possessing ample leisure, it was beginning to attract a few of those who worked long hours at manual tasks. The game thus gained players who often had a formidable strength and a willingness to use it on the football field. The company-owned mines in Ballarat were a particular source of such footballers because their miners, by the standards of the era, worked short hours and thus had some leisure for football.

In a suburb of Ballarat, in the heartland of the big gold mines, the Redan football club was formed about 1870. Possibly Redan's players were the strongest to appear in Australian football up to that time. When they lumbered onto the field, many opposing players, fresh from their office desks, must have shivered with apprehension. Redan's players were mostly tributers – the self-employed miners who leased parts of the famous Band of Hope and other gold mines. Judging by their surnames most were Irish. Upcountry cousins of the soldiers who played briefly in Melbourne, their impact was similar.

The news that Redan would play the Ballarat team on 2 September 1871 – possibly their first encounter – drew a crowd to the wet and rocky surface of Wynn's Paddock, not far from the lake. The game was no sooner started than many of the lighter Ballarat players were skittled. They were bumped, they were charged, they were bear-hugged and they were kicked, though this was more the result of clumsiness than of malice. *The Ballarat Star* even alleged that the Redan bruisers had 'no scruples in tripping, and worse'. The meaning of 'worse' was probably the player's collarbone reportedly broken. The umpire thought Redan was sometimes too rough even for a game which permitted a liberal degree of roughness and had no general rule debarring rough play. When he awarded free kicks against Redan players, they vigorously protested. At times a free fight seemed likely to replace the football game.

The teams played a return match on the same paddock on the very late date of 21 October, and the good spirit of the Redan players was applauded. Their 40 stone of additional weight ceased to be a bonus on a firmer ground and Ballarat kicked the only goal scored during the two encounters. These matches were probably a landmark in the history of Australian football, for they brought together residents of diverse occupations and social classes.

Ballarat was still sufficiently isolated from Melbourne and Geelong to have its own interpretation of the rules, and indeed most Victorian regions during football's first twenty years were inclined to adopt local variations of the rules. So long as a town played no

*A big crowd depicted at the old football ground in the early 1880s with the Melbourne Cricket Club's reversible grandstand to the right. By then the arena was moving from a rectangular to an oval shape (*The Australasian Sketcher, *27 July 1883).*

other team from far away, it could happily follow its own rules. Moreover, so many important facets of football were not yet specifically covered by the formal 'Laws of the Game' that upcountry umpires tended to conjure their own interpretations.

When Ballarat went to Geelong to play at the Corio ground on 19 August 1871, it became entangled in an episode which suggested that its own style of playing was now more rugged than that of the clubs on the shores of Port Phillip and Corio bays. The ball was kicked towards a Geelong forward. He seemed likely to catch it and, as the custom was, call out 'Mark', when at the last moment the Ballarat captain ran from behind. The Geelong forward, to his indignation, 'was pounced upon and brought to earth by the gallant captain'. At once he was awarded a free kick, because the rules prohibited the slinging of a player unless he held the ball. The Ballarat footballers were flabbergasted at the umpire's interpretation. Although the Geelong forward failed to score with his free kick, the Ballarat players were in high indignation as they journeyed home. Their local newspaper shared the indignation. The episode seemed additionally unfair because Geelong specialised in a long-kicking game whereas Ballarat favoured a style that was full of what the *Courier* called 'dodgings and capsizing'. The Ballarat captain was a champion capsizer, it was said, and was simply practising his art when the one-eyed umpire intervened.

For a time the club football in Ballarat possessed a bone-crunching quality seen less often in Melbourne now that the soldiers had sailed away. At Ballarat's first scratch match of the 1872 season the injuries were too numerous for a game of fun. The play was punctuated by pauses in which the sick and injured were helped either to their feet or to the makeshift stretcher. There was apparently no malice, merely mayhem. In the course of a few hours of chasing the ball, or felling opponents who were also chasing it, Killen fractured his collar bone, 'young Fisher' broke a rib or two, and Davidson limped from the field with blood trickling down his leg. Searching for a remedy, Ballarat tried a revolutionary rule which is now a vital part of Australian football – a ban against pushing a running player in the back. The rule was years ahead of its time and before long was dropped.

A footballer's collar-bone was vulnerable so long as the rules specifically allowed a player running rapidly to be pushed in the back. The new practice which Harrison pioneered, of running long distances while holding and bouncing the ball, was still so resented by the backmen that they could not dream of foregoing their legitimate tactic of pushing the running player hard in the back.

Pushing from behind generally remained illegal, but a clear exception was made 'when any player is in rapid motion'.

Most footballers in these years displayed goodwill as well as ruggedness. Goodwill was especially needed to buttress all the unwritten rules, because the unwritten rules must have far exceeded the dozen written rules. One unwritten rule was that players should try to keep the ball in play, but it so happened that a team defending strongly in the face of a gusty wind sometimes saved the match by repeatedly keeping the ball near the boundary flags or deliberately kicking the ball out of bounds. As the rectangular

The Melbourne Cricket Club in the 1870s built an unusual grandstand which could be so altered that it faced the cricket arena in summer and then faced the outside football ground in winter. The grandstand burned down in September 1884.

ground contained deep forward-pockets or corners, and as Australian football did not permit the corner-kick so useful in soccer, and as it did not allow the Rugby method of scoring a try along every point of the goal-line, there was a clear incentive for the back-line players deliberately to place the ball out of bounds near the goalposts. The full-back of their own team was then rewarded with a free kick. He did not have to kick from what is the present goal square but could kick the ball back into play from a position some 20 yards out from the kick-off or behind posts: in an era of weaker kicking that was a big advantage. The defenders were therefore favoured by the early rules, and many backmen gave a foretaste of those famous Melbourne defenders of the late 1950s who drove the ball to the boundary.

When in 1872 the Geelong team visited Ballarat on the great public holiday of the football season, Separation Day, it won first use of the strong wind in the puddles of Wynne's Paddock but failed to score a goal after ninety minutes of attacking. Ballarat then had its turn with the wind but found Geelong defending with ease by playing the ball out of bounds. As Ballarat at the time had a powerful side, the local supporters became angry at the constant thwarting of their heroes' skill. A few spectators actually hissed. Even now, after all these years, we can almost hear the sound of the hisses competing with the rush and rustle of that blustery wind near the shores of Ballarat's lake. We can sympathise with the frustration that gave rise to hiss after hiss from the watching miners. For miners were among the supporters of a Ballarat team which had cunningly strengthened itself by recruiting three heavyweight players from nearby Redan. But to the football officials who wore gold watch and chain and a high black hat, the idea of hissing during a football match was abhorrent. What would respectable citizens say in Melbourne when they heard that loud hissing had swept across a sportsfield in proud Ballarat? Officials of the Ballarat football club, eager to defend the reputation of all sporting clubs on the goldfields, expressed a hope that 'this kind of feeling will never be displayed again in any match or under any circumstances'. *The Ballarat Star* was also shocked, denouncing the hissing as a sign of 'ignorance and bad taste'. What those Ballarat worthies would think of a football grand final or a night cricket match in Melbourne, more than a century later, we can only guess.

It almost seemed as if football had reached a new stage of competitiveness that disowned the old sportsmanship formally praised by the founders of the game. But the founders did not disown the new era; they helped to initiate it. Geelong that day was captained by Tom Wills himself. Now aged thirty-six, he was as shrewd in tactics at football as at cricket. It was he who helped to provoke the gale of hisses. To him football was still to be played like a preparation for war. Once the match was ended, however, he believed in peace, and he made a pithy, friendly speech at the banquet and sang 'Auld Lang Syne' at the railway station when his team was farewelled with handshakes and the waving of hats.

How the footballers behaved on the field was a topic of wider public concern than today. Football was seen not simply as a form of recreation – the blowing away of cobwebs, the recharging of batteries – but as a training ground in character and morality. One reason why the new game received such wide support in Victoria was that it was believed to cultivate courage and self control. 'Muscular Christianity' was the phrase on many schoolteachers' lips as they extolled the virtues of a fair but hard game of football. For their part, many politicians saw the new football code as an ideal training ground for war should an invader threaten Australia. In the aftermath of the revolution in Paris in 1871, football was also seen as a potential soother of civil unrest because it was capable of bringing together on the same strip of grass the rich and the poor, the genteel clerk and the rough foundryman, and men drawn from every economic, social and religious background. In theory, but not always in practice, football broke down social divisions.

The era had not yet arrived when sport was larger than life, and was seen as its own justification. In what was often called the great game of life the footballers of the 1870s still belonged to the little league.

CHAPTER SEVEN

High Marks, Little Marks and Goal Sneaks

The main ground to which the barrackers went each winter Saturday in the early 1870s was still inside the Yarra Park. It was surprisingly accessible to most of Melbourne's 200,000 people. Those living in the main parts of Carlton and South Melbourne, Fitzroy, West Melbourne and North Melbourne, and nearly all those in Collingwood, Richmond, South Yarra and Melbourne city, could easily walk to the ground within three quarters of an hour. In that slower era before the bicycle, cable tram and motor car, even children of ten years of age could walk two or three miles with ease. Those who preferred not to walk could reach the ground either by horse-drawn bus along Flinders Street and Wellington Parade or, if they came from Hawthorn and Prahran, could travel in the train to Richmond station and then follow the crowds walking along the rough paths of the park towards the football arena.

It is difficult now to imagine the wide sweep of parklike country which stretched from the Yarra River – more winding in those years

– northwards to Wellington Parade and the Fitzroy Gardens. Where the Olympic Park and the riverbank now stand was the Friendly Societies' Gardens and arena, a favourite resort for fairs and summer

A player was awarded a mark by the umpire even if the ball travelled only a yard or two from a team mate's boot. The short-distance mark was known as the 'little mark'. This episode was in a Melbourne v Carlton match depicted in **The Australian Pictorial Weekly** *on 12 June 1880.*

sports meetings and easily reached by the small boats which professional watermen rowed along the river. Batman Avenue did not exist nor did the busy Brunton Avenue that now runs between the railway lines and the Melbourne Cricket Ground.

The privately owned railway between Melbourne and Richmond passed through the paddocks, but the whistle of the steam locomotive was not heard very often in the early 1870s because few trains ran during a Saturday afternoon. The vast area now occupied by the railways for marshalling yards was mainly grassland, and indeed a large part of the present yards was occupied by the East Melbourne Cricket Ground which stood opposite the south end of the Fitzroy Gardens. As the building of the railway through Jolimont to Clifton Hill was not commenced until 1899, that side of Yarra Park was peaceful and uncluttered. The short streets of Jolimont already had houses – some of them still stand – and members of the hundred or so families living in Jolimont could walk at the weekend towards the winding Yarra by crossing the single track of the Melbourne–Richmond railway and continuing down Jolimont Road to the river, which they could cross on Brander's ferry.

The northeast corner of this vast parkland – towards the corner of Punt Road and Wellington Parade – did not hold the present suburban houses. Simply known as the Police Paddock, it housed mounted policemen and stabled their horses. In 1881 the police paddock was subdivided into narrow housing lots, and terrace houses were built in Vale Street and Berry Street. The two-storey Yarra Park School already stood on the corner of Punt Road and Wellington Parade, and Arthur Streeton, the painter, attended that school. One of his celebrated paintings – displayed in Sydney, alas – depicts footballers playing in a park at the eastern end of Richmond in 1889.

As early as 1860, three major cricket grounds stood in these parklands, and they were so close to each other that about six or seven minutes of walking was enough to encompass them. The Richmond ground – the present Punt Road Oval – had a pavilion but no grandstand worthy of the word 'grand'. Its atmosphere was rural, with trees standing between the cricket ground and the neat outside fence. Only a few hundred paces away was the Melbourne Cricket Ground, which was also surrounded by large gum trees. This ground was enclosed by an ugly fence to keep out those who refused to pay for the cricket, foot-running and other events held on its arena; while inside a low fence, in part made of pickets and in part of post and rail, prevented spectators from invading the cricket field. The main building at the MCG was a pavilion with a verandah from which members could watch the play; but on public holidays, when an important cricket match was staged, the field was surrounded by marquees and refreshment tents, some of bright canvas striped red and white and nearly all flying their flags.

The cricket ground itself was tucked into a natural amphitheatre with the river-flats on one side and gently sloping hills on the three other sides. On those rare public holidays when an English cricket team was playing, perhaps 10,000 people could be fitted into the area. Spectators who wanted more space stood, the men with their hats and women with coloured parasols, on the northern slope some distance from the edge of the arena. The arena itself was circular in the 1860s and almost large enough to have contained an oblong Australian football field of the regulation size. The Melbourne Cricket Club, however, was rarely willing to permit the footballers to play. It did not fall for Tom Wills' theory that the trampling of the footballers in winter would make for healthy grass in summer. Its committee did not yet realise the recuperative powers of grass in the Australian climate.

So the Melbourne football team continued to play in the Richmond Paddock, now called Yarra Park, just outside the fence of the cricket ground. This football ground on which were played most of the main matches in the first decade of Australian football must have had a decided slope from wing to wing, and moreover a team attacking to the western or Punt Road goal had to kick uphill. In shape it must have been more like a crudely made saucer than a flat plate. Its surface was also uneven, and dusty in dry weather. On parts of the football field the gravel was almost on the surface, and when in the early 1870s many loads of gravel were needed for footpaths and roads within the park, the gravel was dug close to the football arena – perhaps even from it – and the holes were filled with some ten thousand dray-loads of loam. Here, on this patchily grassed field, the early champions of the game dodged and dashed. The only advantage of playing here rather than on the Melbourne Cricket Ground, just across the tall iron fence, was that spectators were admitted without paying. The land was essentially a public park, and the Victorian Government in the early 1870s planted more native and imported trees in small groves surrounded by picket fences, close to the football ground.

A few hundred paces towards the city stood a third cricket ground, East Melbourne. The newest of the three, it was first used by East Melbourne's cricketers in March 1861. Originally belonging to the Abbotsford cricket club, these cricketers had played on various grounds before finally persuading the government to give up a paddock in Jolimont, just below the Fitzroy Gardens. Amongst the citizens of Melbourne who had petitioned the government for that land were Dr John Macadam of Macadamia fame,

Soon after the first electricity was generated in Melbourne a football match was played under the floodlights at the Melbourne Cricket Ground. The match of August 1879 was remembered more for the uneven light than for the fine play (The Illustrated Australian News, *30 August 1879*).

J B Were the stockbroker, Henry Miller who founded the Bank of Victoria, Rev. Dr Cairns the Presbyterian clergyman after whom is named the Cairns Memorial Church, and the ever-present H C A Harrison, who was intimately connected at one time or other with each of the trio of cricket clubs. The East Melbourne cricket ground was planted with rye grass and regularly sprayed with water from the little creek that dawdled through the Fitzroy Gardens. Described by W G Grace as one of the finest cricket pitches in the world, it was the home of the most successful cricket club in Australia for about thirty years. From 1882 the Essendon football team was to use East Melbourne as its home ground, and it was a source of such revenue that before long no other cricket or football ground in Australia could accommodate in comfort a larger crowd.

In retrospect it is hard to believe that three excellent cricket grounds had stood almost side by side and that, over many years, no footballer was allowed to play on them. These three clubs viewed their cricket seriously, and during a long period when Victoria was the premier cricketing colony, one of these clubs was normally the best in Victoria. Between 1861 and 1890, a period forming a total of thirty cricket seasons, these clubs won all but five of the cricket premierships. Their success was one reason why football was kept in exile on the rough ground beyond the cricket fences.

Australian football in its early years was a completely free sport. If a few pence had been charged for admission, football might not so quickly have become a sport for the people. The lack of grandstands and embankments did not much matter, because the contour of the sloping ground at Yarra Park enabled large crowds to view a match. They could not, however, see the play clearly enough during a close finish, and so they began to push forward. Inch by inch the crowd imperceptibly spilled onto the field, sometimes wedging the players into a narrow corridor towards the close of an exciting match.

As most games were played in the public parklands, the footballers usually had no special rights over those who chose to use the park for other pleasures. Footballers wielded little power over the spectators. The line of flagposts that marked the football boundary was easily crossed by spectators, and even law-abiding citizens who watched the football had no hesitation in moving onto the playing field in order to improve their view when the match became exciting. As the game was often static and as the excitement centred on the scrummages and the slow-moving packs of footballers, many spectators thought they were safe in walking closer to the scene of play, forgetting that the game might suddenly break out of the scrummage and burst upon them. One of the sketchers who served as 'photographer' for the illustrated weekly newspapers made a black and white sketch of a football match on the familiar arena just outside the Melbourne Cricket Ground in 1866, and he showed the main line of spectators standing alongside the head-high fence of the cricket ground, but a cluster of some five or six top-hatted spectators can be seen beneath a tall gum some 50 yards inside the playing field, and several other spectators can be glimpsed beneath a smaller gum that also grew on the field. Perhaps these privileged spectators were high officials, friends of the players or – who knows – a justice of the peace and even a member of the judiciary.

Encroaching on the arena was almost a tradition. When Melbourne played St Kilda in 1859 a policeman sent to keep order had to expel from the field the 'knots of small boys'. At a match between Melbourne and Richmond in July 1860, many of the spectators were standing in the middle of the field when suddenly a rush of players pursued the ball in their direction. Escape was impossible, and spectators were knocked over by the stampede of footballers and 'seen sprawling in all directions'. A month earlier a Richmond footballer kicked the ball towards the goal, but almost at the last moment it hit a small boy on the head. Deflected from its course, the ball unfortunately hit a goalpost.

Even when the code of football was ten years old, the gum trees still stood on the main football arena in Melbourne. The spectators wished for their removal because the higher branches obstructed a clear view of the play, while the players were just as eager to chop down the trees. That cricketers could play on public grounds unobstructed by trees while the footballers had to suffer the trees was an injustice that rankled. On 22 June 1868, at his office in the Customs House in Melbourne, H C A Harrison took up a sheet of the office's best notepaper and, adopting his own version of flexitime, wrote an indignant letter to the Mayor of Melbourne who controlled the Richmond Paddock.

> Sir,
>
> I have been requested by the Members of the Metropolitan* Football Club to ask your permission to have five or six trees removed from the play-ground in the Richmond Paddock. The trees have been the cause of great inconveniences & several accidents & their removal will not detract in any way from the appearance of the Park.
>
> Every Saturday during the Winter Season from forty to fifty players are actively engaged upon the football ground & the Club numbers more playing members than the whole of the cricket clubs combined whose grounds are situated in the Paddock and for whose benefit some hundreds of trees have been cut down. I trust that for the encouragement of one of the most manly of British out-door games, you will kindly grant the favor asked for.

Whether Harrison's letter – written with the degree of exaggeration common to exasperated writers of letters – achieved anything is not clear. The answer to his letter has not yet been found in official files. But five or six big trees in a public park were no longer so secure as they were when the game was born. Their

---

*The Melbourne football club and its football ground were often called the Metropolitan club and ground at this period.

protruding, interfering branches sometimes felt a gale of public indignation on Saturday afternoons. Clearly the big redgums were endangered.

We can glimpse what the main football ground of the city must have been like in 1871, the fourteenth season of the code. The ground in the Richmond Paddock was hard and bare with, here and there, an oasis of grass which in mid-July had survived the sliding and pounding of the footballers' boots. In the centre of the ground the surface of a small gully or watercourse was almost certainly bare. A rope tied between the large trees along the boundary of the arena kept the spectators at bay, though if the crowd was large the small boys and even adults could crawl under or jump over the rope. On the day Melbourne played South Yarra in July 1871, a spectator noted the absence of the small boys who normally gathered on the ground itself, sheltering by the big trees with the jutting roots: maybe the police had expelled the boys. Also absent was 'the fringe of hobdehoy larrikins' making loud comments beside the cricket ground fence that formed the southern edge of the football arena. On the northern or uphill boundary, behind the ropes, stood an unbroken line of spectators 'clad in dark and sombre vestments'. On the field itself the trees were so placed that the eastern goal was not easily attacked because large overhanging trees almost blocked the approach to the goalposts, forming a 'tree-encircled space'. And we read how Byrne of Melbourne, approaching the forward-line, actually had to skirt around a tree in order to continue his run towards the goalposts.

The second most popular ground was Carlton's in the Royal Park. Its playing surface, though rather flinty, was almost unique in that it was 'marvellously free from all ruts and rough places'. Unfortunately it had no boundary lines, and visiting players were told that the boundary was an imaginary line linking distant trees. To control the spectators must have required a miracle.

By the early 1870s a few of the matches on these bald patches of earth were attracting as many as 10,000 spectators. As no admission fee was charged we cannot be certain how many people were present, but most of the journalists describing the football probably developed a certain skill in counting the number of spectators. On the normal oblong-shaped football ground one single line of people standing almost shoulder to shoulder along the boundary must have aggregated at least 1,000, and further counts could be made of the people standing further back.

Some football reporters did not bother to estimate the crowd, being content to report that a match was played 'in the presence of a goodly company', but others made an estimate. Thus Geelong – a town of no more than 25,000 people in 1876 – attracted what was described as a normal crowd of 2,000 to a home match against East Melbourne and 3,000 to a match against the local Barwon club. The combined team of Albert Park and North Melbourne was said to have drawn, in successive weeks, 5,000 to a match against Melbourne and 6,000 to a match against Carlton.

The biggest crowds each year went to see Carlton and Melbourne play. These were usually the strongest teams, and when they played on a sunny winter's day their admirers were so numerous that the few policemen who were present had trouble preventing the crowd from straying onto the arena. In 1876 at the Royal Park, the Carlton–Melbourne match was said to have attracted over 10,000 people. As the Carlton ground at the south-eastern corner of Royal Park had no embankment and no grandstand and as the landscape did not slope strongly, those spectators who arrived last must have had trouble seeing the exciting match. Eventually the overflow of spectators prevented the Melbourne players from making full use of the space on the wings. The return match in Yarra Park in July was just as popular. We learn that the 'afternoon was a splendid one, and the admirers of the game (whose name is legion) came pouring on to the ground until they numbered 10,000, every available spot being taken up with the greatest enthusiasm'. As the match did not begin until three o'clock, it was certain to end in the twilight. Late in the afternoon Melbourne gained a lead of two goals to one, but a formal ending was impossible because 'just before call of time the spectators had encroached too far on the ground to continue play'.

These were startlingly large crowds for a football match, by world standards. At the Oval in London in 1872 the first final of the now-famous FA Cup between Wanderers and Royal Engineers attracted 2,000. In 1880 in England the final of the FA Cup drew 6,000 people but as many as 15,000 then attended the important matches of the season in Melbourne. In 1886 the two champions of the decade, South Melbourne and Geelong, are said to have drawn 34,000 to the September match on the shores of the Albert Park Lake. That was probably larger than any English or European football crowd hitherto recorded. It was probably not until 1893 that the game of soccer, anywhere in the world, passed the record crowds of Australian football, and in that year the FA Cup Final between Everton and Wolverhampton at Fallowfield near Manchester drew a crowd of 45,000. In 1895 the FA Cup Final was moved to the Crystal Palace ground in south London, where began the era of huge crowds. A record of 74,000 attended in 1899 and an estimated 111,000 two years later, though large numbers in the crowd glimpsed the ball only when it soared above the heads of the packed spectators. Rugby even in the land of its birth lagged behind Australian football in its capacity to attract crowds, but there was a sensation at Cardiff in Wales in 1899 when 40,000 were said to be present, with spectators spilling onto the edge of the ground and halting the match.

In the city and suburbs of Melbourne as late as the mid-1870s the major matches were still played in the parks and not inside the fenced cricket grounds. Sometimes in the same park two or three matches were under way, each with a big following of spectators. At Albert Park, on the edge of the lagoon, various rectangles of ground were used for football. The park in 1876 was the home ground for the major team, Albert Park, and also for South Melbourne, South Melbourne Imperial, Melbourne City, Rising Sun, South Park, Young Victorians and even the wandering Jolimont team. At the St Kilda end of the park, not far from the railway station, lay the home ground of St Kilda Alma and St Kilda; their playing arena – unlike the present Junction Oval – ran from east to west.

The Yarra Park also accommodated various football teams, including Melbourne (which played in that part called 'Richmond Paddock'), Richmond, Richmond Standard and a team proudly known as Warwick but formerly called Vaucluse, a name associated with Richmond Hill. Not far from Yarra Park was waste ground at Jolimont on which the Victorian Railways team played, while in East Melbourne, along Powlett Street, was a smallish ground where played the promising but short-lived Powlett team in the early 1880s. But the most popular venue for football in the mid-1870s was just north of the city, where the several hundred acres of Royal Park supplied home grounds for the Adelphian club, the Excelsior club, a football team from the big West Melbourne printing factory of Sands & McDougall, as well as the teams known as Victoria United, Victoria Parade, West Melbourne, Brunswick, Hotham United, Hotham Union, Faraday Union and a Collingwood club called Comet. The teams from the vicinity of North Melbourne almost certainly played at the southern end of the park while Brunswick played at the far northern end. Some were minor clubs playing only four or five matches in the season, but a few were big clubs which played nearly every Saturday and attracted several thousands to their main games. As the parklands were also used by people who strolled in fine clothes on Sunday, the football clubs were probably not permitted to leave their paraphernalia and boundary posts in position during the week. Their home ground was not really a home but just a patch of grass. Indeed, the normal name for their football ground was 'playground'.

The big crowds were served by few if any public lavatories, but then people did not drink at the football as a general rule. How the players changed into their football gear is more easily answered: they tended to use the nearest hotel. The Clyde Hotel, still standing in Elgin Street, Carlton, advertised that it kept files of sporting papers including *Bell's Life in London*, served as a rendezvous for Saturday spectators going to Royal Park and nearer football grounds, and provided a dressing room for footballers. Carlton in the late 1870s appears to have used the Clyde Hotel as its dressing room, the players then walking to the nearby football ground at the top of Swanston Street. At a few grounds a dressing shed or room was available for players. At the Geelong ground in July 1872 the South Yarra footballers, returning to the dressing room after the match, found that all their valuables were gone except their railway tickets.

A few miles away from the centre of Melbourne the perimeter of sweeping parklands came to an end, and the football was played on smaller reserves of public land. Collingwood, a junior club, began its short life in 1876 on a ground between Gipps and Vere streets, while the neighbouring Abbotsford Club played at the corner of Hoddle and Reilly streets. The red and black caps of Essendon were to be seen at Flemington Park, the light blue and white caps of Hawthorn could be seen at Grace Park, and Williamstown's dark blue and white colours were worn at the Recreation Reserve in Williamstown. While the Port Melbourne team – known then as Sandridge Alma – played by the Esplanade at Port Melbourne, Fitzroy played at what became their long-time ground in Brunswick Street. Carlton Imperial, a strong team, played in the paddock which presumably was part of the ground now occupied by the University of Melbourne's sports grounds. The university's own team, after blossoming early, seems to have dropped out of senior football, to return again as a member of the Victorian Football League in 1908.

Carlton and Melbourne, the two clubs which regularly attracted large crowds, were perturbed by the lack of amenities for their

On some football grounds the top of a goalpost was clearly marked by small pennants which flapped in the wind. The spectators were kept in order by a rope which stretched along the boundary from post to post (The Illustrated Australian News, *27 July 1881*).

players and spectators. After playing mainly in Royal Park, Carlton negotiated to play on a stretch of wasteland at the top of Swanston Street, only two drop kicks from the Clyde Hotel. The ground, now occupied by Newman College, was controlled by the university which, after several years, withdrew permission for Carlton to play there. Meanwhile, at much expense the Carlton committee levelled the ground, compacted the soil with a horse-drawn roller and erected an ornamental fence around the north-south playing arena. Carlton played there during the later part of the 1876 season and then ploughed the soil and sowed English grass so that the arena came to resemble an English lawn.

The new Carlton ground, popularly known as the Madeline Street Reserve, is perhaps the earliest Victorian football field for which the exact measurements have survived. It was 200 yards long and 120 yards wide, the width having been shortened when the first season's play suggested that the ground was too capacious. By today's standards it was rather a narrow field; and even Hawthorn's old Glenferrie Oval, the narrowest ground for senior football in Melbourne in the half-century from 1925, was wider, being 136 yards wide and 185 yards long. Of course the Hawthorn ground was oval in shape whereas this Carlton ground, as far as we can judge, was rectangular. The new Carlton ground was especially admired because of its unusually tall goalposts which were 32 feet high – enough to reduce the number of arguments which normally arose whenever the ball sailed high above the short posts on the typical arena. Carlton showed the advantage of a smooth playing surface – and a strong team – by defeating the Victorian Railway's team by 10 goals to 1 on the new arena on 2 June 1877.

As an iron fence controlled entry to the ground, Carlton was able to charge sixpence to each spectator until the arena's initial expenses were defrayed. At the first match, a clash with Melbourne on Saturday 19 August 1876, nearly 5,000 paid to enter the ground while hundreds more scaled the fence or found ways of seeing the game by standing on drays and other vehicles and contraptions outside the ground. At first the admission charge virtually halved the crowd attending Carlton's home matches.

Resentment against football clubs charging spectators was deep – unless the money went to charity. The game had arisen, unlike horse-racing and professional athletics, as a completely free entertainment. After nearly twenty years the custom of free entry to football grounds was almost a Melbourne birthright and a strong reason why the remarkably large crowds attended the important matches.

The Melbourne footballers now envied 'The Bulldogs', as Carlton were called. For long, Melbourne had sought permission to play matches on the Melbourne Cricket Ground, and in June 1869 they had played on the sacred grass against a team from the 14th Regiment and in July against a team from the Victorian Police Force. Their experiment was not smiled upon. The Melbourne captain, inspecting the condition of the turf on the Sunday after the police match, was told by several members of the MCC committee: 'Harrison! You have ruined our ground!' No doubt the ground was scarred and pitted here and there. The making of the small mound of turf on which to place the ball for the popular place kick must undoubtedly have pocked the area around the cricket pitch, but such holes were easily repaired after the match by those with an open mind and a spade or strong boot-heel.

Gradually, season after season, more members of the Melbourne Cricket Club liked to watch football matches played in the adjacent open land, and that made it easier to think of allowing the footballers to play on the Melbourne Cricket Ground itself. At last, on Saturday 9 June 1877, Melbourne played Carlton on the very grass which only three months previously had been the scene of the first official cricket test between Australia and England. Eight to ten thousand people were said to be present at the football, the grandstand was crowded, and even the slippery condition of the grass and the frequent tumbles of the players, none of whom wore football stops or leather bars on the soles of their boots, prevented a wonderful display of football. Carlton scored two goals to one, and the kicking of each goal was followed by the throwing of hundreds of caps and hats into the air and a mighty roar of a volume and sound which the football scribe of the *Australasian*, Peter Pindar, had not heard before from a large crowd of any kind. It reminded him of 'the sound of a rushing, mighty wind', a phrase borrowed from the *Acts of the Apostles*.

Football was not yet admitted permanently into the holy of holies. In that same year the Melbourne Cricket Ground completed an elegant grandstand so designed that in summer it was the viewing point for the cricket but in winter was available for members who wished to watch their favourite Melbourne team play football on the Richmond Paddock, on the other side of the iron fence. This grandstand was reversible. Facing the cricket ground in summer, it faced the football field in winter. Whether at the start of the football season it was reversed by a team of heavy horses, by mechanical means, or by employing carpenters and other tradesmen to rearrange the floor and seating is not clear. The grandstand was burned down in 1884. By then Melbourne and other senior football teams were playing many of their matches on a variety of cricket grounds, and indeed the adjacent East Melbourne cricket ground was now the most popular football arena in the city.

In many country towns a cricket ground was already used for football. By 1877 such towns as Avoca, Port Fairy, Coleraine, Kilmore, Stawell, Inglewood and St Arnaud used their cricket grounds for football. It is almost certain that when playing on a cricket ground the footballers initially did not accept the curving cricket boundaries but marked out their own rectangle. The idea of playing football on an oval-shaped arena, however, was now becoming feasible.

Once Melbourne and a few other senior clubs began to play more often on the cricket grounds, one important feature of the game – the rectangular playing field – was quickly challenged. There was little purpose in taking the trouble to erect boundary flags in order to mark out an oblong field of play when the cricket field was fairly similar to the football field both in length and total playing area. Right from the start the rule-makers of Australian football had allowed for variations in the size of the playing field. They had not insisted, like the English codes and the American football, that grounds be uniform in size, and so any proposal to change the shape of Australian football grounds from the rectangular to oval did not represent a revolution nor even require a change of rules. Thus when Melbourne and Carlton played their memorable match before a roaring crowd on the MCG on 9 June 1877 they used the whole circular ground for their game.

Australian football had now moved towards set positions for most players. As a team was normally composed of twenty players, and as the forward-pockets or corners of the rectangular field were shunned by most players (except on windy days when the match was especially defensive in spirit), the field was a little more crowded than today. But already the practice of loosely arranging players in pairs, one from each side, was accepted. Apart from the three followers – the rover was not yet born – each player in theory was allotted a set position for most of the match, with five spaced along each flank and initially standing fairly close to the flag-lined boundary or winds. Whereas today's goal-to-goal line has only five set positions, that of 1877 carried seven set positions:

Goalkeeper
Back
Half-back
Centre
Centre Forward
Centre Forward on Goal
Goal Sneak

In matches between top teams, a goalkeeper and his opponent, the goal sneak, tended to stand very close to the goalposts. The goalkeeper had little alternative but to guard the goals closely, for a score of one more goal was often enough to win a match. If he could simply touch or deflect a ball about to pass through the goalposts, he was the saviour of his team.

The short distance separating each team's key player along the goal-to-goal line or spine of the ground was possibly a result of the thinking of the late 1860s when most players did not yet kick the ball very far and preferred to run with the ball. But by the 1870s the ball was kicked long distances by many of the players. The football itself was now more kickable, being a product of a modern factory rather than of a workshop at the end of a farmyard. The bladder from a pig was being replaced by one made of the new rubber, and air pumps or 'inflators' were available for filling the bladder with air. The outside of the football was still made of leather, but the football was regular in shape, and that shape was more likely to be maintained throughout the game. A match was less likely to be abandoned because the football burst, and any club worthy of the name now possessed in its changing shed or pavilion a spare football.

By the early 1880s, or perhaps earlier, Boyle and Scott of Melbourne were making their own footballs which they sold at one shilling less than those imported from Gilbert of England, and both balls were made to a precise weight and measurement. The governing body of Victorian football could actually stipulate for the first time that the football used in matches should be the Number 2 size of Rugby ball, with a circumference of 26 inches. A football remained expensive, however, and a man on the wages of a carpenter or skilled tradesman worked for two full days in order to earn enough to buy a football.

With the aid of the precision-made football and the more open style of the running and bouncing game, players were realising the advantage of the long drop kick. Many players now practised their kicking. As the primary schools turned to football in their crowded school yards, young players began to practise kicking from an early age. School teachers must have realised the advantage of kick to kick at playtime in the school yard, for it prevented a live football match with boys rushing around the yard, skinning their knees, tearing their clothes, and knocking aside small or dreamy children wandering along. Kicking was becoming an art form in the 1870s, and at the end of each season many of the football clubs ran an athletics meeting at which the long kick was one of the spectacles. The competitors were usually permitted to kick with the wind, and so on windy days the distance they covered could be impressively long.

In 1872 the longest kick in the annual Carlton sports meeting had been a mere 50 yards. The typical player was probably lucky to kick more than 35 yards, and it is significant that on a beautiful day at the Gardens' Reserve at Williamstown in 1877 the best kick by a footballer of the reserve team or 'Second Twenty' was 44 yards. But already there were champions whose kicking boot deserved to be placed in a folk museum or raffled for charity. At the series of athletic meetings held on the football grounds at the close of the 1877 season, several long kicks were seen. At the Williamstown club's 'playground', J Ulbrick, not at his best that afternoon, booted the ball 54 yards, while at Warrnambool W G Kelland kicked 58 yards to win the local jeweller's trophy. At St Kilda Park a distance of $61\frac{1}{2}$ yards was achieved by Terry, at windy Essendon a kick of 62 yards by Angus was considered a fine effort on a blustery day, and at the north end of Royal Park, to the popular music of the band of the Northern Rifles, Pigott of the Brunswick club dropkicked the ball 68 yards. At this period all the kicks which measured more than 60 yards appear to have been aided by the wind.

At least 2,500 people went to the new Carlton ground at the cemetery end of Swanston Street in October 1877 to see the sports.

A strong northerly was blowing, the air was heavy with dust, and the Carlton followers hoped to see a kick of record length. St Kilda, Melbourne, Hotham, Albert Park (which amalgamated with South Melbourne a few years later), Ballarat, Barwon and Geelong as well as Carlton each sent one of their best kickers. With the Carlton brass band playing favourite airs, and every now and then a ball travelling far when it was 'caught in the nick of time' by the dust-laden northerly, it was a day to remember. Eventually the Carlton champion, H Nudd, carried home the exotic trophy, a vase with a silver-mounted emu egg, after kicking the ball 71 yards. Earlier that day, competing against Carlton team mates, he had actually kicked 74 yards. The new emphasis on long kicking was a sign of how much the game had changed since the days when most of the stronger players carried the ball forward by sheer strength.

The little kick was also coming into favour. The rules allowed a player who marked the ball to take his time and, unimpeded, kick with deliberation. The rule, however, did not stipulate how far the ball had to travel before it could be marked. Ingenious forwards soon realised that if their team had possession of the ball near the goal but on an impossible angle, they could work it around to the front of the goal by a succession of short kicks, each of which was marked. This stratagem was known as the 'little mark' but was really a little kick. Rewarding to an attacking team and its loyal barrackers, it was boring to many neutral spectators.

Carlton perfected the little mark. By 1877 even the bush teams were trying the little mark, and when Sale played the neighbouring Gippsland town of Stratford, a Sale player who marked 20 yards from goal on an impossible angle initiated a chain of little marks or 'little uns'. After the fifth little mark, the ball was so centred that a goal was kicked with ease. The little mark was originally the ingenious attempt to deliver the ball out of those deep forward-pockets which, in an oblong ground, make it impossible to kick a goal from

George Coulthard (right) was the star footballer of the late 1870s and in the opinion of some he was the most skilled footballer so far seen in the Australian game. He was always depicted with the football in his possession. The ball, it was said, rarely eluded this Carlton champion.

The Australian Pictorial Weekly of 24 July 1880 gave his weight as 12 stone and his height as 5 feet 10 inches, making him bigger in physique than the average player of that time.

the nearer boundary lines. Later the oval arena eliminated those impossible kicking angles near the behind posts.

While the little mark captured the limelight, the high mark was about to become a highlight of Australian football. By the mid-1870s a few players were beginning to leap into the air in the hope of catching or marking the football. At first the gallant leaps were noticed more on the forward-line where, in a game in which goals were scarce, one high mark in the goal mouth could virtually win the day. Thus, on 22 September 1877, when the senior club, Barwon, played Carlton at the riverside ground at Geelong, an excited crowd of 4,000 saw W Bracken of Carlton make 'a splendid mark high about his opponents' heads, fifteen yards in front'. Unfortunately he was not allowed to kick and thereby level the score because the Barwon backman complained of an infringement. The crowd echoed the complaint. The umpire, who was said to favour Barwon more than a two-eyed umpire should, bowed to the clamour.

Bracken, described as 'a neat and active little forward, and a pretty drop', became brilliant in judging and marking the ball. But high marking was still considered dangerous, especially as the surface of the main arenas was not level and was often too hard for a player who, trying to mark high above the ground, fell awkwardly from a height. The hints to players printed in *The Footballer* at the end of the 1876 season condemned the high mark as a menace. Its glory was exceeded by the risks: *Jumping for marks is dangerous. 'I pray you avoid it.'*

The high mark could be hazardous, though much of the hazard came from the tendency for a cluster of players to treat the high mark as a kind of aerial scrummage in which pushing and even kneeing and elbowing were common. One high mark was to end tragically at Ballarat. That city, one of the five biggest cities in the continent, was now engrossed in football, and undoubtedly a larger proportion of the population attended football there than in Melbourne.

John Mills, 'a steady and industrious workman', was captain of a leading team, the Ballarat Imperials, and at the age of twenty-seven he was one of the finest footballers in Ballarat. On 15 September 1883, his team played the top team, Albion Imperial, at the Western Oval. After half-time he 'jumped to obtain a mark' and fell, and in his fall he seems to have collided with other players. He felt groggy but did not immediately leave the field. When questioned he said on the Saturday evening that he had fallen on another player's knee, but later he said he had been kicked.

He went home to bed in his parents' house at the suburb of Soldier's Hill and did not improve. Early on the Monday morning, feeling that the water of the public baths would ease his pain, he set out in a horse-drawn cab but died during the short journey. The post-mortem revealed that Mills had ruptured a small intestine.

His funeral drew a crowd said to number 4,000 or 5,000 and a Baptist minister gave a fine sermon over his grave, while *The Ballarat Courier* delivered its own sermon on the evils of aggressive barracking and the hazards of players hunting in packs. The attempt at high marking, significantly, was not blamed for the tragedy. In a flurry of finger-wagging the *Courier* urged footballers to keep to their set positions, like cricketers in the field, rather than hunt like hounds.

High marking was sometimes frowned upon, but jumping for the ball after the umpire threw it into the air was forbidden. When the ball went out of bounds the umpire threw it back into play, but the revised rules of 1874 stipulated that the ball – after leaving the umpire's hands – must touch the ground before any player could again kick or touch the ball. Possibly this same practice had been followed almost from the birth of Australian football, but it was a custom rather than a strict and formal rule until the 1870s.

Under the out-of-bounds rule there was no scope whatever for a tall or springy player to leap and catch or palm away the ball. Likewise, when in about 1870 it became the agreed procedure that teams change ends not after each goal was kicked but simply at half-time, a new rule – confirmed in 1874 – decreed that the second half of the match should begin with the umpire throwing the ball into the air. Again the practice was to wait for the ball to hit the ground before any player grabbed it. This code of conduct was not in the rule book but was clearly the accepted practice. Presumably if the rule were broken by a tall follower leaping up and grabbing the ball, the umpire simply rebuked him and, calling for the ball, again threw it into the air to inaugurate the second half of the match. There was thus little call for leaping prowess in those roaming players who as early as the mid-1870s were called 'followers'. The three followers then playing in a senior team were more usually the bullocking type of player, strong in the crushes, rather than the present type of taller follower whose special skill includes an ability to leap high at the throw-in or the centre bounce. All in all, ground play remained the chief skill, though the overhead mark and the long kick were becoming more frequent in the best teams.

The high mark and the little mark, the running with the ball, the new rules against very rough and unduly defensive play, the abolition of scrummages and the preference for an open style of football in which players kicked to team mates who had made position on their own, were all changing the appearance of football.

Certainly goals were becoming easier to score. The low scoring of the early years had come partly from the frequent scrummages which clogged the game. A typical match was then deadlocked for long periods, and players did not find it easy to break out of the packs partly because the act of throwing the ball – and presumably punching the ball – was strictly prohibited. The ball did not easily move quickly from one end of the arena to the other, partly because the typical kick did not travel a long distance. Moreover, in the era of the rectangular arena the defenders, when under severe pressure, could push the ball into the deep pockets or corners, from which it was not easily bullocked back towards the goal front. But the main obstacle to the kicking of numerous goals in a match was probably the defensive spirit. Australian football, like the rugby and soccer of those days, was seen as a defensive game. It was a version of chess. The main aim was to protect the route to your own vulnerable fortress, namely the goal, and so men were placed on the defensive rather than on the attack.

Each sporting game, in each era, has a particular spirit, and football by and large remained defensive in spirit in all parts of the world in the late nineteenth century. Indeed, the prevalence of the offside rule in nearly all codes of football reflected the desire to make the scoring of a goal as difficult as possible. Victorian footballers in 1870 still clung to the defensive way of thinking that characterised the rival codes. Today we have gone almost to the other extreme, viewing high scores as innately superior and forgetting that a match with no score can at times be far more interesting than a match in which forty goals are amassed.

Victorian footballers inherited from England that defensive attitude. In the early era 'our goal' was the one which our team was defending. This makes reports of old football matches hard to understand when first read. Thus when we read of a Carlton player marking the ball in front of the Essendon goal in 1875, we think that he was a defender when in fact he was, by definition, a forward. As Australian football became more an attacking game, a team's goal was to become the one which it was kicking towards. This change in terminology illuminates a vital change in the spirit of Australian football.

The high-scoring forward was virtually unknown in any code of football in the late nineteenth century, but he was beginning to emerge in Australian football. His early name was 'goal sneak'. What a miserable title for a hero! In Australian football nowadays the centre forward is far too glamorous and conspicuous to be given such a snivelling pickpocket of a name; but the habit of calling a forward a 'goal sneak' came from England where any footballer who in a season kicked a dozen goals was almost by definition a sneak. A high goal-scorer just could not exist in such a defensive sport unless he cut a few corners and made carefully timed but almost illicit dashes. In the English codes of schoolboy football a 'goal sneak' was actually the description given to a player who technically was offside: the Eton College rules of 1846 so designated the practice of 'sneaking'. But in Victoria where nearly all vestiges of the offside rule had been discarded, the goal 'sneak' by 1880 had emerged as a specialist in the legitimate scoring of goals. To *sneak* was to act like a stylish highwayman rather than a cat-burglar. The word *sneak* was to persist as a noun of praise well into this century; and Dick Lee of Collingwood, who was often to kick a tally of goals such as English football had never seen, was widely called the 'champion goal sneak' just before the First World War.

Meanwhile, in the 1877 season, the top goal sneak for Melbourne, C Baker, kicked the huge tally of fourteen goals, while Carlton's goal sneak kicked nine. Ten years previously an entire team might not have reached such a tally in a season. The kicking of goals was ceasing to be a rarity, and inflation of the final scores was to be rapid in the next two decades.

While more and more goals were scored, the drawn game was still common. In the 1880 season, Melbourne actually drew 8 of its 22 matches. South Melbourne drew 5 out of 20 and Hotham 5 out of 19, while Carlton and Essendon each drew four matches. As would be expected, the very top and bottom teams, with their clear margins of superiority or inferiority, were less likely to draw. In 1880 the two bottom teams, West and East Melbourne, drew only one match each while the top of the eight senior teams, Geelong, drew two matches.

A behind was now recorded but did not yet count in the final scores. A behind was scored when the ball went between the goalpost and the kick-off post, which later was to be called the behind post. Behinds gave a little glory but they did not alter the result even when two teams were level on goals.

Tantrums were common in the early era when one goal in a whole afternoon had often been enough to win a match. As each team provided its own goal umpire, and as certain umpires were highly partisan, disputes about goals were frequent. Perhaps one in every four major matches in the 1876 season was marred by scoring disputes. Thus Geelong, playing against Geelong Imperial, kicked a goal from a place kick and nearly everybody but the umpire vowed it was a goal. Barwon, playing against Geelong, kicked what was agreed to be a goal, but the goal umpire decreed, to everybody's astonishment, that it had gone outside the goalpost. At Royal Park, Carlton defeated East Melbourne by two goals to none and the goal umpire negated the third because he said the goalpost was leaning at such an angle that it allowed the ball through. L Bracken of Carlton suffered a similar disappointment at Albert Park when the umpire said the goalpost had been tampered with, presumably by a Carlton player. Melbourne, playing at home against the weak East Melbourne, actually walked off after the third dispute about goals in the course of an afternoon. Twice the East Melbourne goal umpire, who was now notorious for his strange eyesight, was blamed. He was eventually replaced, but his successor was no fairer. Most fair-minded spectators in the big crowd were so outraged that they thought Melbourne's conduct in abandoning the match was excusable. Melbourne was in another contentious episode at the new Carlton ground where the central umpire allowed a dubious goal. Melbourne won by two goals to one, but later the loquacious umpire apparently told all he met that he had made a mistake.

The game of football was changing more quickly than the rules were changing, but the changes in the formal rules between 1866 and 1874 were also decisive. On 12 May 1874, at Nissen's Café in Melbourne, new rules were agreed upon by a dozen delegates drawn from six of the main clubs – Albert Park, Carlton, Geelong, Melbourne, North Melbourne and St Kilda. If during that winter an old player, after spending seven years on remote goldfields, had returned to see his old club play, he would have been bewildered by the new rules. The main change was the increasing speed and flow of the game, and the decline of those congested episodes in which sheer physical strength was vital.

Under the new rules a player could no longer cling to the ball even when held by an opponent. It had been the practice for a player holding the ball to try to force or dodge his way past opponents; and if they grabbed him he tried to cling to the ball as long as possible, even when slung to the ground. These wrestles were usually resolved by the scrummage in which players assembled on their respective sides in a tight Rugby-like situation. Under the 1874 rule, however, the player running with the ball and trying to pass his adversary could no longer hold onto the ball when grabbed. He immediately had to drop the ball. The subsequent wrestling was thus forbidden, and so too was the subsequent scrummage. Instead the ball which the player had let fall from his hands was now a target for every available boot because it had to be kicked in soccer fashion – it could not be touched or handled again until a kick of the ball had taken place. The player who, when forcefully grabbed, dropped the ball often managed to kick it just after it had bounced up again. Sometimes his opponent kicked it. Once kicked, it could again be handled by all players.

The rough practices of tripping and hacking had long been forbidden. The 1874 rules also specifically banned 'rabbiting', which was defined as the act of a player who caused 'another to fall by placing his body below the other's hips'. A further tightening of the rules in 1877 prohibited a player from catching an opponent by the neck and 'slinging' him to the ground. We gain some idea of the roughness of the early game when we realise that for nearly two decades 'around the neck' was quite legal and that slinging was one of the soundest methods of stopping a player who was trying to run with the ball. What the heavyweights from Redan thought of these effeminate changes to the rules can easily be guessed. At least they still possessed the privilege of pushing or shouldering or chesting a running player in the back and riding him to the ground. They could use the full weight of their bodies against either the front or back of a player running with the ball – if they could intercept him. To charge or to shirt-front an opponent was still legal after the reforms of the 1870s, so long as the opponent was actually running and was within five or six yards of the ball.

It was now unusual to witness the old Rugby-like method of a pack of players pushing the ball through the goalposts by sheer momentum. Until 1874 it had been permissible to score a goal

South Australia played Victoria on the East Melbourne ground at Jolimont on 1 July 1879, and every forward seemed to be tagged by a defender. The New Treasury Building in Spring Street, can be seen in the top left corner and the Fitzroy Gardens near the top right (The Australasian Sketcher, *2 August 1879).*

through a slowly moving scrummage, so long as it was not a hand or arm which finally propelled the goal between the posts. The chest, knee, stomach, head or shoulder or foot of a player could push the ball between the goalposts, and the goal was allowed. By 1874, however, the goal could be scored only by a kick, and no goal resulted when the ball was touched by either friend or foe on its way from the boot to the goalposts.

We can virtually reconstruct what had slowly changed in the first two decades of the new game. A contest ruled by the pack of players had been converted to an open, fast-moving game in which congestion was discouraged, though still visible on wet or muddy days. In the early years, when the pack was dominant, the scoring of goals had been so difficult that allowances had to be made for a goal that simply emerged from the combined actions and reactions of a heaving pack of players just in front of the goalposts. There can be little doubt – though the rules do not specifically mention the situation – that the episode known in soccer as an 'own goal' was permissible in the first years of Australian football. In essence, if a backman was defending fiercely within a few feet of the goalposts and mistakenly kicked the ball through, he thereby scored a goal for his opponents. The 1874 rules, for the very first time, stipulated that the attacking player must score the goal from his own boot.

What if the ball hit a tree or a spectator before going through the goalposts? The rules remained silent on these matters, though we know that a ball which hit the branch of a tree before passing through the goalposts was usually considered a goal. But the increasing practice of spectators encroaching onto the playing arena was addressed in the 1877 rules. A spectator who stopped or interfered with 'the progress of the ball going through' was now wasting his time. The goal umpire was entitled to call it a goal.

In the twentieth season of football in Melbourne, there was still no official premiership ladder or points table. The football reporters, the players and the public could usually agree on which team was the best throughout the season, but if two teams were about equal in performance there was no accepted way of judging which was the premier team. The main teams did not all play the same number of matches in a year, and sometimes they gained victories at the expense of weak rural teams, and sometimes they conceded a handicap by deliberately fielding three fewer players than their opponents. Comparison of performances was difficult. Thus in the 1876 season, Carlton played in 20 matches, Melbourne 17, St Kilda 15, East Melbourne 13, Geelong 12, Ballarat 11, Carlton Imperial 11, the combined team of Albert Park-cum-North Melbourne 10, Barwon 8, Geelong Imperial 5 – to name most of the teams which were classified as senior clubs. Such clubs as Collingwood, Hawthorn, Essendon, South Melbourne, Williamstown, Hotham United and West Melbourne were unofficially classified as junior clubs and normally played about 10 to 15 games in a season. Occasionally, near the close of the season, the best teams might meet, and the game would carry some of the excitement of a grand final, even though no flag or cup was awarded to the winner.

Victoria did not possess a formal football league or association until 1877. The fixtures listing forthcoming games were the result of negotiations by individual football clubs. Without a formal association of clubs, discipline was not easily imposed. No club could be suspended or debarred from playing, and no player guilty of misconduct could be suspended from future games except by individual agreements between two clubs. When the football rules required revision, the delegates from the main clubs would meet, but their decisions affected only their own clubs. Significantly, these occasional meetings of the delegates of half a dozen clubs managed to secure agreement on the complex matter of trafficking in players; and the final sentence in the 'Victorian Rules of Football' for 1874 decreed that no footballer could play with more than one club during the season. A few years later a rule allowed a country player to join a city club and a city player to join a country club during the playing season, so long as the player permanently changed his residence. Transfers between city clubs during the football season were still forbidden.

In May 1877 the main clubs came together to form the Victorian Football Association to promote and control the game in Victoria. Only senior metropolitan clubs were permitted to join, and in the first year five senior clubs of the city were members: Albert Park (whose scarlet and white banded jersey was to survive when the club merged to become South Melbourne), Carlton,

Hotham (soon to change its name to North Melbourne), Melbourne and St Kilda. In addition two Geelong clubs, the Geelong and the Barwon, joined as senior members. The rules also permitted country or provincial clubs of some ability – clubs which did not seek a handicap when they played senior clubs – to send one delegate. In the Association's first year, the four goldfields clubs of Ballarat, Beechworth, Castlemaine and Inglewood and the rural town of Rochester paid to send delegates. Indeed, three of the upcountry delegates won seats on the seven-man committee which was set up to watch the form of the best players and select a team for any intercolonial match that might take place. The big city clubs, however, held the most influence in the new Association; and Melbourne and Carlton between them supplied the secretary, the treasurer and the two vice presidents, one of whom was the retired champion, H C A Harrison. The president of the VFA was William Clarke, later Sir William, possibly Australia's richest squatter whose grand townhouse, Cliveden, was to be built a decade later right opposite the Yarra Park on the site now occupied by the Hilton Hotel. Under the rules the president and two vice-presidents were figureheads and forbidden from taking part in management.

The main task of the Association was the setting of the rules of the game, the settling of disputes between member clubs, and above all the financing and conducting of matches against teams from other colonies. Indeed, the formal constitution specified only one task: to control and manage all intercolonial matches. The first Association therefore was not an all-powerful body such as leagues and associations later became but a tentative step away from the irregular alliance of club officials which had loosely managed the game in the past. A club could still give one month's notice and leave the Association. Upcountry clubs could become voting members even though they intended to play no senior Melbourne club during the year. And no rule debarred clubs who were not members from playing many of the season's matches against clubs belonging to the Victorian Football Association. For years to come the VFA clubs continued to play matches against a variety of non-member teams and these matches were recorded on the informal premiership ladder.

The hope of conducting intercolonial matches was the special aim of the new Association, for nothing in Victorian football seemed more exciting than the prospect of at last playing against the neighbouring colonies of New South Wales and South Australia. Football's era of isolation seemed about to end.

CHAPTER EIGHT

'Victorian – perish the thought!'

Melbourne, as late as 1870, was the only capital city in Australia where football of any variety was widely played. Other capital cities showed more enthusiasm for cricket. New South Wales played very little football, and it was easier to find a football match in Adelaide on a winter Saturday than in Sydney. Most Australian boys living outside Victoria had not seen a match played under Victorian rules and most had not even played one of the English versions of football.

In Victoria, the new football flourished to a degree that surprised visitors from overseas. Whereas soccer was not yet played in Europe and South America and Asia, football was becoming a spectator sport in Melbourne. It is little known that in the infancy of football as a major sport, Melbourne was probably more enthusiastic than any other city of the world towards the game, though playing it according to its own distinctive rules.

Victoria remained virtually an oasis for the Australian version of football. Meanwhile, many Victorians who played football in the 1860s were moving to other colonies where they thought of

'Victorian – perish the thought!'

forming new football clubs. But there also arrived, in Brisbane and Sydney and Adelaide, even larger numbers of young immigrants who had already played versions of soccer or Rugby in England

James Pearce, like many footballers, wore his white cricket trousers. He played for Kapunda, S.A., in 1879 (South Australian Archives).

and were eager – if football was to be played – to adopt the familiar rules of home. The conflict between various football codes actually impaired the spread of football as a winter sport within Australia. In contrast, the game of cricket faced no such obstacle, for its uniform rules were accepted both by native Australians and new immigrants from the British Isles. Moreover, in Melbourne cricket was usually played on fenced grounds, and so revenue could be collected from the public in order to finance the visit of cricket teams from the nearer colonies. Victoria played cricket against New South Wales, Tasmania and South Australia long before an intercolonial match of any kind could be organised for a Victorian football team.

Outside Victoria the South Australians were the first to play football regularly, though not too regularly. There, the game probably took root two years later than in Melbourne. Those who read the public advertisements in *The South Australian Register* on Wednesday, 25 April 1860, would have seen, below notices of insolvency at Echunga and debt at Gawler, an invitation for young men to meet at the Globe Inn in Rundle Street, Adelaide on the following evening at seven o'clock and form a football club. About sixteen men attended, rules were adopted and the Adelaide Football Club began its life. Wasting no time it summoned footballers to the North Adelaide Park Lands on the following Saturday for a match that was to last three hours, only darkness preventing the play from continuing. 'The weather was fine', said the *Register*, 'and there was a large muster both of members and spectators'. On the results of the match the newspaper was astonishingly vague, merely reporting that one team 'obtained one or two goals more than their opponents'. Vagueness still surrounds these early matches on the parklands of Adelaide, and it is not clear what code of football they were playing.

Football matches in Adelaide attracted to the sidelines a procession of dignitaries such as no football match in Melbourne could yet hope to attract. Indeed, Adelaide newspapers listed the names of distinguished spectators rather than the leading players. The governor attended, sometimes with his wife. Often present too was the Anglican Bishop of Adelaide as well as an occasional dean and archdeacon, judge and police inspector, and various members of parliament of whom a few sometimes ran onto the field to play. On the sidelines the *Register* reporter observed many of 'the elite of the colony', including Duttons, Stows, Fishers, Spences, Morphetts, Torrens's and Lindsays. One man almost invariably named amongst the Saturday spectators on the south or north parklands was a leading politician, Henry Ayers, who a decade later was to lend his name to the famous rock in central Australia. And of course the ladies came, 'gracing the scene' as the journalists wrote, while Herr Schrader's band was usually hired to play music in the open air during pauses in the match. A social sport, football seems to have been confined to the one club, Adelaide, whose favourite fixture was to divide its members into those living south and those living north of the river. One team wore pink caps and the other wore blue.

The printed accounts of the first matches give little guide to the rules. As in Melbourne the number of players seems to have had no clear limit; as few as ten and as many as thirty-five players were on each side. A goal was not common and some matches were scoreless. No time limit was assigned to a close match except that it was usually halted just before the players became blurred in the creeping darkness. If heavy rain fell in mid-afternoon, the match was abandoned. When rain on the Saturday morning was prolonged, most players did not bother to go to the parklands. Football, however, was sometimes played on slippery turf, and the falls and tumbles of the players gave endless amusement, especially to the women standing along the boundary. Fun was very much part of the day, as hinted in a report of a match between pink-caps and blue-caps near the present Adelaide Oval in May 1862: 'Considerable amusement was created by the antics of a number of aboriginal natives who came from a camp close by and were permitted towards evening to take part in the sport.'

Unlike in Melbourne, the early practice in Adelaide was not to single out those who scored goals. Only the captains were mentioned in the newspaper reports and, as in Melbourne, they were elected by the players before the start of each match. The only other player mentioned in an early match was George Barclay. Colliding with an opposing player – not named – Barclay hit the ground with the back of his head and was unconscious. A spectator rushed onto the arena with a container of that trusted medical remedy, Cold Water, which apparently revived him, and to the relief of the players standing around he was lifted to his feet before

Adelaide Football Club, photographed in front of the grandstand in 1886. The footballer's cap was no longer part of his uniform.

the doctor could arrive. The game was resumed while Barclay went home 'with only a few slight bruises on his face'. The common bruise in those days was on the shin, for indiscriminate kicking was part of every code of football.

The football played in Adelaide in 1860 is now sometimes described as Australian football. Such a conclusion seems risky. As far as is known, the early sponsors of the game in Adelaide were South Australians, not Victorians, and the teams in the first recorded match in 1860 were captained by J B Spence, who was the brother of Australia's first famous feminist (Catherine Spence), and by John Acraman, a young merchant who is said to have been interested in football as early as 1854 when he reportedly paid for the first goalposts to be erected on the sportsfield of St Peter's College in Adelaide. South Australia was in spirit the most independent of all the Australian colonies in 1860 and the least likely to imitate quickly a social or commercial custom originating in Melbourne or Sydney; and there is no visible reason why it should have suddenly decided to adopt the new Victorian rules rather than one of the English codes.

In support of the argument that Adelaide quickly copied the

'Victorian – perish the thought!'

Melbourne game, it is sometimes said that Henry 'Coldy' Harrison himself made a promotional visit to Adelaide early in 1860, just before the Adelaide Football Club was formed, and that his visit was influential. Harrison, writing his own life story, mentions no such visit. Moreover, at the start of 1860 he was not yet a major figure in Melbourne football and so it is unlikely that he should embark on the rough voyage to Adelaide mainly to propagate a code of football in which he had no more proprietorial interest than twenty other Victorian players. Evidence could some day emerge to link the first football matches in the two cities, but at the moment the evidence is thin. If by chance Adelaide did at first adopt Victorian rules, then we have to explain why it soon abandoned them. A decade later, the football being played by most clubs around Adelaide was certainly not like Victoria's.

In its attitude to football, Adelaide in 1860 probably resembled Melbourne, being knowledgeable about the various English codes of football but unwilling to adopt any code in its entirety and therefore inclined to experiment. That the first club, Adelaide, had a fashionable following and perhaps an exclusive membership, suggested that it would not have been too eager to modify its rules merely in order to play other local clubs; and it seems likely that in the city and suburbs at least two and perhaps three versions of football were played throughout the 1860s.

Football did not flourish in Adelaide, it existed. How could it flourish when clubs could not agree on the rules? The level of disagreement rose and fell and sometimes a brave mediator presided over meetings in the hope that common rules of football could be drafted. Charles Cameron Kingston, soon to become a politician and a father of the Australian method of industrial arbitration, presided over such a meeting in March 1873. The young arbitrator seemed to succeed. The delegates from three of the stronger clubs – Adelaide, Port Adelaide and Kensington – agreed upon rules that were said to be closest to soccer or Association football, except that about nineteen rather than eleven men were allowed in each team. But once the playing season began, the new rules were not fully accepted by the clubs.

Umpiring disputes imperilled the game. In 1875, Adelaide and Port Adelaide met twice at the Adelaide Oval and gave nearly as much mental effort into disputing the rules as to playing the game. Next year Adelaide seems to have reverted to a kind of Rugby with its charges and scrummages rather than stick to the so-called Kensington rules. According to Bernard Whimpress, in his *South Australian Football Story*, football 'almost died out in the city itself' in the mid-1870s. There was little indication that within a year one code would be dominant in Adelaide and that the code would be Australian.

Meanwhile in Tasmania, football made slow headway. On Saturday afternoons the thud of the football and the shouts of spectators were not widely heard. As in Adelaide, football was at first a game for Tasmanians of money and leisure and nobody else could play the game except on the rare public holiday that fell during winter. In Tasmania most boys over the age of twelve and most men worked throughout Saturday, and many were still working long after poor light ended play at the nearest football ground.

Football was played in Hobart in May 1866, and perhaps earlier. We cannot be sure whether the code initially played was Australian football, for the few descriptions of the matches played are meagre; but Hobart had strong commercial links with Melbourne, and each month many tiny passenger steamships linked the two colonies. Few immigrants from the British Isles were coming to Tasmania, so a British source for the football rules adopted in Hobart is unlikely.

New Town was probably the island's first football club. It was followed by the Hobart Town Football Club whose playing president was Dobson – almost certainly the Henry Dobson who later became the Chief Justice. Hobart Town prepared to play New Town for perhaps the first time at the main cricket ground in Hobart on Saturday, 26 May 1866, and E Swan and H Grubb were elected to lead the teams. The Hobart *Mercury* gave this pithy commentary:

> There was a good attendance of spectators, and some capital play. The first goal was won after about an hour's tussle, the lucky ball being kicked by G Wright of the New Town Club. The sides then changed bases, but at about half past four o'clock the rain came down sharply as to prevent a continuance of the game.

The match was resumed on the following Saturday, and *The Mercury*'s report was even shorter:

> The match lasted a considerable time, and finally the goal was kicked by Mr J O'Dodd of the Hobart Town Club, so that the match is now a tie.

Football slowly attracted supporters in Hobart, gaining from its opportunity to use the ground of the southern Tasmanian Cricket Association, from the eagerness of the boys of the High School and Hutchins School, and the arrival of soldiers of a British regiment which had already played football on the other side of the strait.

New clubs were formed. Stowell team, playing in a paddock near Battery Point, took the field about 1866, and a club with the magnificent name of Break O'Day appeared. Meanwhile the game spread to rural areas, and in July 1871 *The Mercury* noted that 'the football reigns supreme in the various academical playgrounds throughout the colony'. Even then the newspaper, in reporting the recent sporting meetings, gave precedence to the hunt at Melton

Mowbray where about 80 riders and their hounds pursued a stag for nine miles over rough country.

The football was as unpredictable as the hunt. In the winter of 1868, two matches in Hobart were abandoned because the football

This team from southern Tasmania played in 1890 in Sydney when that city still had several strong Australian Rules clubs (The Illustrated Sydney News, *19 July 1890*).

burst, and several matches were postponed because of wet weather or abandoned when rain poured down. Furthermore, a match could be abandoned for reasons which twenty years later would not have been accepted. On Saturday, 12 August 1871, at the New Town ground, Myles Coverdale kicked at the ball at the same time as a Break O'Day player. Their legs collided, and Coverdale fractured the tibia of his right leg. The match was abandoned after Coverdale was placed on a door and carried to his home at the Queen's Asylum.

Launceston, the other large Tasmanian town, is said to have played football as early as 1867, but the game possibly died, and a new football club was formed at a meeting at the Criterion Hotel in July 1875. An Anglican clergyman, Rev. W H Savigny, was elected president – usually players held the main offices and so presumably he was a player. It was an era when players, rather than receiving pay, themselves paid an annual subscription; at Launceston they paid half a crown a year. Other clubs also played on the Windmill

Hill, and one memorable match was between a team called Bankers and Lawyers versus virtually everyone else. Everyone else called their team the All Comers. Unfortunately, only eleven Bankers and Lawyers appeared while double that number appeared for All Comers, who were augmented by another three or four players as the game went on. The Bankers and Lawyers, being so outnumbered, were allowed to kick with the wind for most of the afternoon. This particular match was closer to Rugby than to the football normally played in Melbourne, for the players on various occasions obtained 'a touch down' and with it the right to kick for goal. Four years later football in Launceston, unmistakeably, was played according to the Australian rules.

The small town of Perth – now in its final phase as a convict settlement – had its first taste of football when the Barrackers arrived on a tour of duty. Two battalions of the 14th Regiment – a few officers, eight sergeants, four drummers and 157 rank and file – had left Melbourne for Hobart where they played vigorous football before sailing away in May 1868. They were followed to Perth by their wives and children, including the dozen women who had married soldiers during their brief stay in Hobart.

Three months after reaching Perth the regiment played football against a team of Western Australians in the grounds of the Bishop's Collegiate School, close to the Perth barracks. In the opening match, on Friday 19 September, Perth scored a goal. Halted by darkness, the play was resumed on Saturday week when the soldiers scored two goals to win the match. Next month a scratch match involving both the soldiers and the civilians was played in Fremantle. As in the early days of football in Geelong, the temperance movement in Fremantle fostered football in the hope that the game would offer more excitement than rum and brandy.

Whatever were the exact rules of this brief Western Australian season of football, they were presumably influenced if not moulded by the Australian code which the 14th Regiment had already played in Melbourne. This regiment sailed from Australia in the following summer. Thereafter football in the small towns of Perth and Fremantle was played intermittently. It began to flourish in the 1880s when at first Rugby and then Australian football became the dominant codes.

The game spread to New Zealand. It would be surprising if it had not made headway there because many Victorian footballers went to New Zealand in the 1860s in search of gold or as clerks, bank tellers and merchants. The South Island of New Zealand was in commerce almost a province of Melbourne, and any journalist who chanced to tour its goldfields would have found Victorian shopkeepers, publicans, teachers, mine managers and labourers in every town worthy of the name. Early football games in most towns on the South Island – except perhaps Christchurch – were as likely to have been played accordingly to 'Victorian Rules' as English rules. Indeed, the port of Nelson, in the warmer part of the South Island, is said by *The Oxford Companion to Sports and Games* to have been the birthplace of Rugby in New Zealand, but the first football there in 1869 was played partly or fully according to Victorian rules. In 1870 the Rugby game was adopted through the persuasion of Charles J Munro who had just returned from college in North London. On the North Island the Rugby game spread quickly and Wellington formed a Rugby club in 1871 and Wanganui in 1872.

In Dunedin, then the largest city in New Zealand, the Victorian and the Rugby codes lived uneasily side by side. In 1876 the city had two clubs – the Dunedin club which was favoured by the Scots and played Rugby and the Union club which played according to the Australian rules. The Union's best player was Cleverdon who came from St Kilda while his team mate Barrass had been well known in Victoria as a sprinter. When the two Dunedin clubs agreed to play each other, the choice of rules was not easy. In the initial match the Dunedin players in their red jerseys and knickerbockers selected Rugby rules for the first half while the Union, in the white, chose the Victorian rules for the second half. The hybrid match was won by Dunedin. To play another team which specialised in Victorian football, the Union club and its 'capital goal-sneak named Israel' had to travel all the way by horse-drawn coach to the gold town of Balclutha.

The Victorian supporters in New Zealand were confident missionaries, believing they could convert all footballers to their code. They hoped that within a year all the football matches on the South Island would be played under 'Victoria's Popular Banner'. They were too optimistic. The Australian game would continue to gain followers in New Zealand but by 1880 it was clearly the minor code.

Whatever the reasons were for the ultimate failure of the Australian code after such a promising beginning in New Zealand, the population movements were important. Victorian gold seekers had mainly emigrated to the South Island, and their Victorian code had gained its footing, but the South Island lost its dominance as the gold era faded; and the city of Dunedin was steadily challenged as the main city of New Zealand by Auckland and then by Christchurch and Wellington. The population mainly expanded in the North Island whose Australian links were strongest with Sydney, and that increased the likelihood that Rugby would become dominant there. Moreover, the major source of immigrants to New Zealand in the period 1870–90 was the British Isles, and they came in such numbers that their footballing tastes and preferences prevailed, thus pushing the Australian game to the outer paddocks.

While New Zealand in the early 1870s was seen as the promising arena for Australian football, it was South Australia which experienced the sudden conversion. It was then playing a brand of football unknown in Melbourne and probably unknown in England. It used a round ball at a time when the oval ball was supreme in Melbourne. It employed no offside rule and in that sense was closer to Melbourne football, but it was like soccer in that it allowed neither pushing nor holding the man. Adelaide's version of football also stipulated that a ball could be picked up only when it was on the hop – otherwise it had to be kicked, presumably as in soccer. The distinctive facet of the Adelaide arena was the goalposts which at first sight resembled those of Rugby. They were 18 feet apart (compared to $18\frac{1}{2}$ feet in Rugby Union and 21 feet in Australian football), but 8 feet from the ground was a wooden crossbar as in Rugby, and 16 feet from the ground was another crossbar made of rope. The ball had to pass above the wooden crossbar but below the rope. That cramped opening made the kicking of goals very difficult.

At the start of the 1876 season, South Australia's leading clubs moved towards Australian football, even abandoning their own distinctive goalposts. The main difference was that South Australia did not yet insist that a player with the ball must, on being held, drop the ball at once; instead he could be 'held and thrown until he has dropped the ball'. Under the new Adelaide rules a player with the ball could also run as far as he wished, whereas a running player in Melbourne had to bounce the ball every five or six yards. In the first season of the new rules, low scoring was the vogue, and in only one of Port Adelaide's matches did both sides manage to score.

There was a sharp increase in the enthusiasm of players and spectators for the new code of football, and Woodville played fourteen matches in the 1876 season, and Port Adelaide and South Adelaide each played nine. The leading team, called 'Victorian', played less frequently. Staging its home matches at the foot of Montefiore Hill and wearing orange and black colours, it won six of its eight matches. In contrast Adelaide was the weakling and its best performance was to draw twice against South Adelaide which was then led by a former Carlton champion, George D Kennedy.

Curiously it was a new English migrant who made the final step that ensured that Adelaide and Melbourne codes of football should become almost identical. Richard E N Twopeny had studied at Marlborough College in England where he was a skilled player of a Rugby-type of game before emigrating at about the age of nineteen to South Australia where his father had once served as an Anglican clergyman on the wheatfields. In his first year in Adelaide, Richard Twopeny took to the strange local code of football and put on the red and white striped jersey and red and white cap and white knickerbockers of the recently revived team of Adelaide. He was noticed at once for his fearless charging and his Rugby instinct of holding onto the ball at all costs. He held the ball even when felled, and his tenacity caused 'much merriment' amongst supporters of other clubs. A poor mark but accurate kick, he was noteworthy for kicking his team's only goal for the season.

In the next year Twopeny was elected captain of Adelaide, by now a stronger team, and he enterprisingly called together the captains of Woodville and South Adelaide, much older men, and suggested that the time had come for the main clubs to form themselves into the South Australian Football Association. Under the presidency of the Chief Justice, Samuel Way, the new association based on the Victorian rules came into existence in May 1877, and its foundation clubs were Adelaide, Bankers, Kensington, Port Adelaide, South Adelaide, South Park, Victorian, Woodville and a ninth, Prince Alfred College, which was not a playing member.

South Australia hoped to send a combined team to play Victoria in 1877 but negotiations on the choice of a ground were slow; the South Australians felt they had been snubbed. Two Adelaide clubs then responded by inviting two Melbourne clubs to visit them.

Though loyal supporters of South Australia knew only too well that their colony did not possess so large a population as Victoria and that their players were still new to Victorian rules, they hoped that their teams would prove to be strong on their home ground. Perhaps the Victorian players would be not quite themselves after spending several days on a rough sea. Perhaps they would miss the cheers of the thousands of faithful followers, of whom only a dozen or so could hope to travel to Adelaide.

On Saturday, 11 August 1877, more than 2,000 people – a large crowd for Adelaide – went to the Exhibition Ground to see their own club, the Victorian, play Melbourne. In the presence of Sir Henry Ayers the local team played valiantly until ten minutes before the end when Melbourne, which had an advantage in weight as well as in 'long telling kicks', succeeded in scoring the only goal. Two days later combined players drawn from four Adelaide clubs – Woodville, Port Adelaide, Victorian and South Park – proved to be so lacking in teamwork that only once did they succeed in advancing the ball as far as the flags on their forward-line. Melbourne in contrast kicked five goals and once hit the post in the powerful cross wind.

The following Saturday – the day of the match between Adelaide and visiting St Kilda – was awaited with excitement. St Kilda were stylish but, not being as strong as Melbourne, could perhaps be defeated. All other football matches in the city were postponed for the chosen day, and the governor and the lord bishop of Adelaide – he was patron of the Adelaide team – and 3,500 people went to the Adelaide Oval. After Twopeny won the toss for Adelaide and chose to kick with the help of the stiff breeze, everything seemed to favour his team, and in the first half it kicked two goals to one. Bishop Short at half-time might well have dared to hope for a dash of divine intervention and a change of wind, but as the match progressed he saw only the black and scarlet stripes of the St Kilda

At the Adelaide Oval in 1888, on a slippery and windy day, Norwood scored 2 goals 7 behinds to Port Adelaide's 2 goals 5 behinds. 'Our artist has made merry sketches' of the match, announced The Pictorial Australian *in May 1888.*

players as they raced away to kick four goals. On the following Monday, the visitors played a team of locally born players drawn from all clubs. Sandilands of St Kilda amazed the crowd by taking off his boots, running in bare feet and kicking a goal at lightning pace. The final score – St Kilda 7 versus South Australian Natives 2 – seemed to pinpoint the contrast between football in the two cities.

Twopeny's career as Adelaide captain and as the reorganiser of South Australian football was brief, for in 1878 he went with the South Australian delegation to proclaim the colony's virtues at the

Paris Exhibition. Already he was evangelical toward the new code of football, and five years later his book *Town Life in Australia* gave a verdict that delighted all except the sports followers in Sydney and Brisbane. Pointing out that cricket was the popular sport in Sydney and football in Melbourne, Twopeny enlarged on the merits of Melbourne's football; how people will actually pay to see the football there, how ten times as many will watch it in Melbourne as in Sydney on a typical Saturday afternoon, and how nine of the ten thousand attending a big match in Melbourne 'watch its every turn with the same intentness which characterises the boys at Lord's during the Eton and Harrow match'. As he himself had played at least 200 matches of Rugby and maybe a few dozen of soccer as well as about forty of Victorian rules, he felt sure that he could speak with authority to the English reading public: 'I feel bound to say that the Victorian game is by far the most scientific, the most amusing to both players and onlookers, and altogether the best.' To Twopeny, a fine football match in Melbourne was one of 'the sights of the world'. He insisted that the best half-dozen clubs in Victoria played football of a style and quality superior to that of the two best clubs he had seen in England, the homeland of football. He named Blackheath and Old Etonians as his two yardsticks. He did not have to add supporting details because in Melbourne in 1883 the well-informed followers of the sport knew that Blackheath was a famous Rugby club in London, and that Old Etonians, in this fading era of the amateur, had defeated the Lancashire mill-town's Blackburn Rovers in the FA Cup Final of the previous year.

Sydney remained the citadel which the new Victorian code of football had to capture if it was to become the popular game of the whole continent. If by chance Sydney and most of New South Wales were to adopt the Australian code, then Queensland was likely to follow. Even in 1870 the first major schoolboys' match in

Queensland, between the Ipswich and Brisbane grammar schools, was played according to Victorian rules. Similarly, if eastern Australia were to play primarily Victorian rules, then New Zealand might follow too. So in the 1870s it seemed that events in Sydney could largely determine the pattern of Australian football for a century to come.

Football was still a minor sport in Sydney. A successful invasion by the Victorian game was therefore feasible. Even after the forming in Sydney in 1874 of the Southern Rugby Football Union,

In depicting an episode of open play from Rugby football, Sydney's Town and Country Journal *of 20 May 1882 regretted that Rugby was too often a game of 'beef and weight' whereas the Melbourne game was more 'a game of science'.*

with a book of nearly fifty rules that made Victorian football seem bereft of rules, the way was still open for Melbourne football to move in. Patently the Victorian code was capable of attracting the larger crowds. While several of the best Victorian footballers, moving north to work in Sydney, played Rugby as the only game available, they persisted in arguing the superiority of the Victorian code.

Those who governed the Rugby Union in Sydney were effective tacticians and knew how to defend the game they liked; and eventually they were to meet the Melbourne challenge by changing several of their rules – regulating the scrummages and opening up the game – to counter strong points of Victorian football.

For Sydney people the Rugby game had other sources of appeal. It was played on a smaller field, and that was an advantage in an older, more cramped city which did not have inner Melbourne's vast domains of parklands. Likewise Sydney's earth was damper and softer in the normal winter – the footballers fell on softer ground.

While Australian folklore assumes that Sydney is a city of dryness and warmth and Melbourne of cold and rain, the comparable facts are not so neat. Melbourne's annual rainfall is much lower. Moreover, July and August, both of which are footballing months, are normally two of Melbourne's four driest months, whereas Sydney's peak rainfall comes in March, April, May and June – in short in the first half of the football season. Thus, contrary to accepted opinion, Sydney's parklands – unlike Melbourne's – helped players to cope with the more physical Rugby game.

The Victorian Football Association had been formed early in 1877 largely with the hope of arranging for the first time a football match with neighbouring colonies. The desire to play Sydney teams was intense but they all played Rugby. This was considered only a minor obstacle by the Victorian Football Association, which decided to write to Sydney suggesting that one match be played according to Victorian Rules and the other according to Rugby Union. On 7 May 1877, in Sydney, the representative of Rugby clubs in New South Wales met and replied 'no'. One reason for their 'no' was shrewdness. There were already divisions within Rugby. About one-third of the clubs, led by University, believed that the Rugby game was being ruined by the incessant scrummages and they pleaded for a faster, more Victorian kind of game in which the drop kick in all its glory and the swift ebb and flow of play could prevail. It was feared that to play a Victorian team now would perhaps widen the dispute among footballers in New South Wales. The official reason for rejecting Victoria's invitation was rather more guarded:

After mature deliberation, it was decided not to entertain the proposal at present, the Union being of the opinion that the intricacies of the 'Off and On Side' Rules of the Rugby game were far too difficult to be readily understood in such a brief space of time to ensure perfect harmony, and prevent any possible unfriendliness from arising through imperfect knowledge generally of the game's fundamental principles, and that the contest had better bide the time when the rules in the respective colonies had become more assimilated.

Sydney, however, did give permission for an individual club to play a Victorian club, which rather undermined the 'perfect harmony' argument set out above.

Waratah, a Sydney club ranking about third in strength, organised the intercolonial match. Founded a mere four years previously, it normally played in the Inner Domain and on Moore Park. It had a strong following of inner Sydney people and had the added advantage of a former Carlton champion, W Newing, amongst its best players, and perhaps for that reason it boldly invited the champion Carlton team to come to Sydney. As no railway linked Melbourne and Sydney, the Carlton players had to arrange a long absence from work in order to make the round voyage as saloon passengers in the small coastal steamship *Barrabool* (588 tons). They arrived in Sydney – a few were white-faced after the rough voyage – and prepared to play their first match according to Rugby rules. On Saturday, 23 June 1877, at the Albert Cricket Ground, more than 3,000 spectators gathered – the biggest crowd so far seen at a football match in Sydney. The ball had not long been in play when the governor, Sir Hercules Robinson, arrived; and to honour such an important visitor the teams halted play and, assembling in front of the grandstand, gave him three rousing cheers.

The match aroused intense interest and was discussed for weeks afterwards. Waratah wore white knickerbockers and caps with jerseys and socks striped red and blue, while Carlton appeared in caps, jerseys and knickerbockers of dark blue, along with spectacular socks in blue and white stripes. The physique of the teams was almost as different as the uniforms, for the Waratah players tended to be tall and wiry and the Carlton players tended to be short and thickset. Much of the game was taken up with scrummages, and at one time 23 of the 30 players 'lay piled one on top of the other on the ground', but at times the ball was carried long distances with lightning speed, the Carlton players usually puffing in the rear. The Carlton champion George Coulthard made several brilliant dashes, but in the end Carlton was no match for Waratah and lost by two goals to nil. In the oblique and charming words of one reporter, Carlton 'struggled in the most valiant manner to cope with difficulties an imperfect knowledge of how to master rendered doubly embarrassing'. It was Waratah's turn to be embarrassed on the following Monday when the Victorian game with 20 men a-side replaced the 15 a-side Rugby game. Towards the end Waratah began to grasp the new game. It was too late: they lost by what for those days was the big margin of six goals to none.

More and more matches were played between combined or individual teams from Victoria, New South Wales and South Australia, which then were the three most populous colonies in Australia. In 1878, after the feast of travelling during the previous year, the 'Victorian' club from Adelaide visited Geelong and Ballarat and Melbourne. A year later, in the first formal intercolonial match between combined sides, South Australia was defeated by Victoria in Melbourne. In that same year the Geelong team, which was entering a triumphant decade when South Melbourne would be its only real rival, travelled by steamship to Adelaide where its style of football aroused excitement.

The following year, 1880, was almost a carnival of intercolonial football, and some players who had not travelled more than sixty miles from the city of their birth boarded the steamships and endured the bucketing of the ocean in order to play on 'foreign' football fields. Norwood, which was the strongest club in Adelaide and a haven of former Victorian players, set out on a tour to end all tours, and at first found nothing but rain. On the capacious East Melbourne ground, now a chain of puddles, Norwood played like mudlarks against Carlton. Buoyed up by their drawn game against such a celebrated team, they moved over to the Melbourne Cricket Ground where on another day of rain they played Melbourne. While Melbourne tried to pick up the greasy ball, Norwood dribbled it, splashing their way to victory by two goals to none. At last a Victorian senior side had been defeated by a team from across the borders.

Norwood, in a mood of some elation, went by train to Geelong, where on the Corio Oval they were crushed. The score, when first sent across the telegraph wires to South Adelaide, sounded respectable: Geelong 1 v Norwood 0. Geelong, however, had also kicked 29 behinds to Norwood's none – a clear sign of superiority though the behind did not yet count formally in the final score. Back at the East Melbourne ground, Norwood recovered confidence and lost narrowly to Hotham and then drew with South Melbourne, before going upcountry to Ballarat for their sixth game which they won with ease. Such a successful tour by such a disciplined club gave all of Adelaide the hope that when the Victorians, a month later, arrived to play a combined South Australian team, they would be defeated. The 4,000 people who had gathered at the Adelaide Oval were disappointed. Even without players from Geelong and Carlton and Melbourne, the Victorians were too strong, winning their three matches against South Australian combined teams.

In 1881 it was the turn of New South Wales' footballers to try their luck by sending a combined team to play Victoria. At the Melbourne Cricket Ground they swallowed their pride. Their defeat, by nine goals to none, was slightly redeemed in Sydney later that season when a visiting Victorian team managed to win by only

Queensland sent this team to play in intercolonial contests in 1888. By then Australian football was losing ground to Rugby in Queensland, but in the 1870s the native game had perhaps been more popular. The big secondary schools played only Australian football, and as late as 1886 few boys at Brisbane Grammar School even knew the rules of Rugby. The first club in Toowoomba (1883) and several other important towns played according to 'Melbourne' or Victorian rules, but by 1888 the Rugby code was ascendant (John Oxley Library).

nine goals to one. The goal Sydney kicked – a 60 yards' place kick – was long remembered, at least in Sydney. In the same year, the Melbourne club voyaged in the coastal steamer to Sydney and won all games, twice fielding a team of twenty against a Sydney team of twenty-three. It was sad for the future of Australian football that

Sydney teams were so humiliated. Defeat gave some critics the opportunity to say that Rugby Union, already popular on the parks of Sydney, was really the superior game.

In fairness to Sydney it should be explained that it was still the less populous city and possessed only a small number of footballers, and moreover their loyalties were divided between Rugby and Australian football and, from the early 1880s, the newly imported soccer. Defeat by Victoria in a match of Australian football was therefore to be expected. But the effect of heavy defeats was to deepen Sydney's suspicions of anything that came from Melbourne. In the words of a football reporter who wrote under the name of 'Orange and Blue':

> The great objection to the rules in New South Wales was that they were styled 'The Victorian Rules of Football'. Had they been dubbed the Scandinavian rules, well and good; but *Victorian* – perish the thought!

'Orange and Blue' saw merit in calling the game 'The Australian Rules of Football', but his call was premature.

In that era of slow sea-voyages, Queensland was too far away and its population too scattered to be able to think of fielding a team against Victoria, though the Victorian game was relatively stronger in Queensland's ports and goldfields than it would be some twenty years later. Tasmania was much closer to Melbourne, and in 1881 the rather low-ranking Hotham team – the present North Melbourne – made the first tour of Tasmania, defeating Launceston but delighting 1,500 spectators by failing narrowly against a combined southern Tasmanian team drawn from Hobart, Richmond and Oatland clubs. In that match, each team fielded seventeen men rather than the customary twenty. There was still flexibility in the rules as well as in the public's attitude to the game.

In Hobart, more than in the British Isles, women gladly attended the football; and they were so numerous on that sunny July afternoon that their enthusiasm, we learn, was 'most gratifying and cheering to the players'.

In Victoria, the new code of football gained support from women as well as men, rich as well as poor, Catholics as well as Protestants, gaining it so completely that all rival codes of football were virtually excluded. Players and officials confident that it was a special game and soon would charm and even conquer Sydney. Deep was the disappointment when Sydney refused to be charmed.

CHAPTER NINE

The Hidden Money

In the 1880s, football was a magnet for increasing crowds. Melbourne, still the biggest city in Australia, extended its suburbs, each of which created new football grounds: cramped or normal, long and narrow, or short and wide. New teams joined the Victorian Football Association, the premier body. Their entry was made easier because the older clubs, East and West Melbourne, were being squeezed out. In the three seasons 1884 to 1886, nine new teams joined: Fitzroy, Williamstown, Richmond, University, Footscray, St Kilda (after a time of absence), Prahran, Port Melbourne and South Williamstown. All were serious about winning.

Cable trams, laid along the streets of inner suburbs, enabled people, when their Saturday work was over, to travel quickly and cheaply to the football in time for the 3 pm start. Suburban steam trains carried supporters to St Kilda, Port Melbourne, Williamstown, Footscray and other grounds. Teenagers with no pocket money but plenty of time could walk from Clifton Hill or Moonee Ponds to the South Melbourne or East Melbourne grounds, see the match and walk back home again in the failing light. In those days, people readily walked long distances to work and to play. Even with the new web of transport, however, most spectators

*As people flocked to the Melbourne Cricket Ground to see the football as well as cricket, grand buildings arose: the new pavilion of 1881 (*The Australasian Sketcher, *30 July 1881).*

saw only their team's home matches and those at nearby grounds. At lunchtime on Saturday they hurried home from work, scrubbed up, put on their better clothes and went to the football in style. There was little time to spare for those who did not finish work until 2 pm. Of course, a host of people, including shop assistants, worked throughout Saturday.

The main Saturday fixtures were becoming more suburban. More working people followed football, and they could not afford the fare or the time to follow their team to such distant cities as Geelong and Ballarat. Even to visit Geelong for the day was an adventure. Occasionally, a special Saturday train was arranged to encourage metropolitan supporters. The train left Spencer Street at 1.15 pm – when most supporters were still at work – and usually did not arrive back until close to midnight. Ballarat was even further away. Teams travelling there had to take the train to Geelong and then go inland, a journey of over 100 miles. The direct line from Melbourne through Sunshine to Ballarat was not open until the end of the 1880s, and steam trains were slow in climbing the steep hill beyond Bacchus Marsh. Slowly Ballarat – then a much larger city than Geelong – dropped out of senior football. There was a prospect in 1894 that both Ballarat and Bendigo would be drafted into a powerful breakaway Victorian league centred in Melbourne, but it is not clear whether a league with such scattered teams would have survived.

Meanwhile the annual competition worked in a do-it-yourself way. Clubs organised most of their own fixtures. A weak club naturally had trouble in arranging a match with a top club. In the course of a season the clubs rarely played the same number of games. Sometimes Association clubs played country teams and junior suburban teams, and all these results were included in their season's final tally.

Newspapers and sports magazines printed annually a ladder of wins and losses. It was not always reliable because, given the way fixtures were organised, some teams faced a series of hard opponents while others played more of the struggling teams and even junior teams. There was no official premiership, but several sporting journalists tried to decide which team had performed the best. The published list of premierships for the 1880s has to be consumed, on occasions, with a grain of salt.

Thus 'Peter Pindar', in reviewing the 1881 season, had to decide which was the best team in a rough-and-ready way. Geelong and South Melbourne had each won fifteen games but Geelong had played one fewer game. That was in itself a problem. South Melbourne had played in more draws than Geelong, though one contest – recalled Pindar, weighing his imaginary scales – had been drawn in wet weather. Geelong had kicked 94 goals and South had only kicked 63 but Pindar decided not to take this difference into account.

Significantly, South Melbourne had beaten Geelong once, though in their respective games against the other top teams South Melbourne had not played quite as well. And should matches against weaker teams be eliminated from the calculation? He decided to delete East Melbourne's results, and yet that club had won more matches than Essendon which he proceeded to place fourth. During the 1880s no finals matches were played – otherwise his calculations would not have been needed. After much verbal shuffling, he awarded the premiership to South Melbourne. It is slightly surprising that such an arbitrary and unofficial way of selecting the top four teams is treated today as gospel.

While such lists are not quite fit for *The Guinness Book of Records*, they are a rough guide to which teams were the stronger. From 1877 to 1888, the best-known list shows Geelong with seven unofficial premierships, South Melbourne with three, and Carlton with two. That period was far and away the heyday of the team that was then called the Pivotonians. In one span of nine years, ending in 1886, Geelong won seven of the unofficial premierships and was runner-up once. It did not win again for thirty-nine years.

For the 1889 season the Association, in a bold step, organised the fixtures on a rough principle of equality. An official premiership now existed. It is tidier for the historian but was not ideal for the game. Previously the weak clubs could sometimes be ignored: now they had to be played against regularly. The match was likely to be one-sided and the gate receipts poor. Ironically, the innovation of the fair and equitable fixture was to be one of the main causes of a dramatic breakaway in 1897, when the stronger clubs seceded and formed the Victorian Football League.

Money crept into football. The jingle of sixpences could be heard behind the grandstand. Those attending Association matches on Saturday afternoon had to pay a silver coin at the entrance gate. Crowds were often so large that money accumulated in the bank accounts of the stronger clubs: they quietly paid many of their players. Payment was banned under the rules, but who knew when a direct or indirect payment was made? Sometimes the payment was to the woman who ran the boarding house where the player lived.

A champion player's weekly rent, in the football season, might be paid to his estate agent. Money was lawfully given to a player in the form of a silver watch, a valuable trophy or a diamond ring for his girlfriend. Rich local supporters gave money to the best players or employed them – in a hotel or factory – when they were not very employable. The football club in its annual balance sheet might list some of these payments under the heading of 'training expenses'. It would now be called the 'gravy train'.

The Victorian Football Association threatened suspension for the remainder of the season to any player receiving hidden or open payments. But who could enforce the rule? It is difficult enough to enforce a parallel rule today, when specialist investigators can be hired and the taxation department can be expected to swoop on offenders. At that time, income tax in Victoria did not exist.

The avalanche of silver coins was used to help charities, to pay existing players and to poach others from rival clubs. A few banknotes easily persuaded a young player – especially one who was newly married with a rented house and inadequate furniture – to join a wealthier club. In most teams, however, were players who remained amateur in spirit. They believed that a love of the game, not love of money, should be the goal. Some genuinely combined the acceptance of a little money – they needed it – with the belief that football transcends money. From a lofty height a waterfall of morality splashed down on players of that era, and many viewed sport both as an enjoyable contest and a way of displaying practical Christianity. The more devout believed that good footballers should turn the other cheek when they were hit unfairly by an opposing ruckman. In some senior teams in the 1880s and long after, nearly all the players attended church where they sometimes heard sermons – occasionally from their own team mate – on the virtues of what was called 'muscular Christianity'. The first VFL player to be killed at Gallipoli has an eloquent memorial in the Anglican church

Cigarette cards of players from the 1880s, presented as part of the series 'Past and Present Champions', issued by Capstan Cigarettes between 1905 and 1910.

closest to the Melbourne Cricket Ground – his home ground – and it recites all the Christian organisations for which he was a worker. How he found the weekend hours to be also a backman for Melbourne, right until the eve of his enlistment, is a mystery.

Even the poorer clubs spent money on their players. They could at least promise an end-of-season trip, not to Bali but to Bendigo. In an era when travel was expensive and a holiday trip was reserved only for the honeymoon, a players' excursion was a delight. In 1893, the Port Melbourne players went on strike on the eve of their match against St Kilda. It transpired that they had been promised a free weekend trip to Bendigo at the end of the previous season, but the club's officials at the last moment could not afford it.

Most delegates who attended meetings of the Victorian Football Association knew sooner or later of the existence of certain silent financial ideals. They did not denounce their colleagues, maybe fearing that their own club would be denounced in turn. Every few years a player spilt the beans. In 1895, Webb of Essendon, wanting a transfer to Richmond and being refused it, made allegations. He said that Essendon had paid him. Certainly he was a storeman employed by an Essendon official. When he refused to be cross-examined and instead sailed to South Africa, he was not necessarily making a hasty escape – many Victorians were emigrating to Johannesburg. That gold-mining city even ran its own Australian Rules league.

Bookmakers slipped through the football gates. There was public gambling on the outcome of important matches – more gambling, probably, than half a century later. Bookmakers attended certain grounds, paraded at a prominent spot and made bets. Sporting newspapers encouraged their readers to gamble. Those who read *The Sporting Standard* in 1891 found a printed football coupon which they could cut with scissors, inscribe with their tips for three designated matches and deliver to the newspaper office no later than 6 pm on the Friday. To forecast the exact number of goals – not behinds – scored by each of the six teams was to win the handsome sum of ten guineas. The prize must have been rarely paid.

The danger, then as now, was that footballers would gamble on games and, just occasionally, under persuasion from bookmakers try to influence the result. The sporting leaders of that era were not very skilled in investigating allegations of bribery. In any case, evidence is not easily gathered from an all-cash transaction. Nonetheless, Collingwood, as a club, had no hesitation in its first years in expelling several players who accepted or probably accepted bribes to play dead. The religious and political pressures against match-fixing were to become stronger between 1902 and 1910 when Prahran, Richmond and Carlton players were amongst those suspended by the League for long terms or even disqualified for life.

The placement of Australia's population had originally favoured the native game but that favour was being withdrawn. Victoria was the most populous colony but by 1890 it was virtually overtaken by New South Wales, which was a Rugby land. South Australia, in love with Australian football, lost third place in population to Queensland, which was rapidly becoming a Rugby land. Tasmania, a home of the native game, ranked fifth in population but was soon to be surpassed by Western Australia.

A palmy era for Victorian football was coming to an end. Even before most of Victoria's banks temporarily closed their heavy doors in the autumn of 1893, unemployment was high. Football clubs felt the pinch. Attendances fell. The roar of the crowd, on windy Saturdays, did not travel so far. Many players went to the country or other colonies to find work. The severe depression temporarily helped Australian football as a nationwide game. Tens of thousands of Melbourne and Adelaide players and fans crossed the Great Australian Bight in little steamships and settled in Perth or the new goldfields of Western Australia. By the winter of 1896, the tall goalposts – sometimes not so tall – could be seen on booming goldfields where many of the Victorian and South Australian stars of two or three years ago now scrummaged in the red-brown dust.

The champion Victorian – some said the finest footballer so far produced – was one who went west. He was not only the best footballer but he was the heart of the best team: Essendon. Albert Thurgood, the son of a builder, went to Brighton Grammar School, then small and little-known. As a teenager he began his career with Essendon, the team often favoured by private schools. The East Melbourne Ground was its home, and on that turf he carried out prodigious feats. He was tall – maybe six feet – and a fine high mark; he was fast and could pick up the ball on the run; and he was strong enough to withstand most bumps. He could roam the back-line or patrol close to goal. Most of the time he spent at centre half-forward where some of his drop kicks were majestic. They went high above the goal umpire and far out of the ground. In 1892, he kicked 56 goals, and in the following years he kicked 64 and 63. Those annual tallies of 60 and more goals stood as a record in senior football in Victoria until Dick Lee of Collingwood passed them after years of trying. Thurgood's record lasted for twenty-two years.

The dashing play of Thurgood had prolonged Essendon's winning run. Essendon won four premierships in a row, beginning with the 1891 season. Between July 1892 and September 1894 – two and a half seasons in the old playing year – Essendon competed in forty-seven games without one loss. In the same period it won another nine games against country and other clubs. It was so

Satirical illustration from The Australasian Sketcher, *July 3 1880, comparing football to a gladiatorial contest.*

indomitable that it made officials and captains think of the forming of a new league of fewer teams. It was pointless for Essendon, except on a freakishly windy or muddy day, to play half of the other

Association clubs. It was just so far above them – until Albert Thurgood left.

Thurgood must have caused dismay when he announced at the end of the 1894 season that he was about to try his luck in the west. He was only twenty years of age – his glory days must surely lie ahead of him. He refused to budge in his decision. Whether money was initially offered to him from afar is not clear. There was money in his family but whether it was still with them, in these lean years, is not certain. He stayed away for four playing seasons, mostly in Fremantle where those Essendon followers living in exile loved to see his driving kicks as well as the play of the clusters of other Victorians in the side. Thurgood carried success in his pocket. His new team Fremantle (later called South Fremantle) were premiers, and he was their star goalkicker.

In the first year of his absence, Essendon slumped alarmingly. It was not alarming, however, for its rivals. Fitzroy and the new team of Collingwood, founded in 1892, began to usurp the place of Essendon near the top of the ladder. The centre of gravity of Victorian football was moving away from the teams playing near the Yarra River and Albert Park Lake, and the Port Phillip and Corio bays. Essendon, incidentally, was also one of these waterfrontage teams, its home ground at Jolimont being only three drop kicks from the Yarra River. From the mid-1890s these waterfrontage teams were overtaken by a trio of clubs in the near-northern suburbs: Collingwood, Fitzroy and Carlton. The three clubs and their grounds were within easy walking distance of one another. Carlton, old and temporarily senescent, was the lesser of the three, but it would rise again. The three were to dominate football in many years between the 1890s depression and the 1930s depression.

Meanwhile, when would Thurgood return? The telegraph line across the Nullarbor sometimes wired reports that the wonder-man was on the move. For the 1899 season, at last, he was back with

Essendon. His moustache denoted a new laid back look. A few onlookers, however, suspected that a touch of the dingo, a touch of the eagle, had departed from him. There was a little less audacity, slightly less determination and less inspiration in his play. But the way he kicked the ball was still an eye-opener. In a match against Carlton in 1893, using the place kick, he had booted the ball the dazzling distance of 104 yards. Now, home again, he thought he could kick further. On Thursday, 22 June 1899, at his team's East Melbourne Ground, within hearing distance of the passing trains, he set out to perform one of the memorable feats in the history of the game. He placed the ball in the carefully scooped hole in the turf and walked back to take his kick. With a little help from the wind, he place-kicked a football well over 100 yards. Spectators ran out a tape measure or measuring cord. The kick was 107 yards, 2 feet and 1 inch – or 98 and a half metres. It is probably the longest of all measured kicks in the history of the game. Two years later, at practice, another of his kicks went 101 yards. Meanwhile, in Saturday matches he sent punts, drops and place kicks to the far end of the ground. A gasp went up as the trajectory of his awesome kicks was observed by the spectators.

The game was perhaps not as fluent, not as stylish, as in the previous decade. For much of a match the play might have been congested. The reformers wondered whether drastic changes to the rules were again needed to lure back the spectators. Some said the drawn matches were too numerous. Actually the draws were fewer than two decades previously. In 1896, during the home and away matches, about one match a fortnight was drawn. That year Port Melbourne, Footscray, Williamstown and Geelong each played in three draws. They were then middle-ranking teams but, in contrast, the teams at the top were less likely to be in a draw – they were too strong. One reason why the drawn match was common was that goals alone were counted in the final score, and not many goals were kicked each day. There was a simple solution. If the behinds, already recorded as a matter of course, were actually counted in the final score, the drawn matches would become few. Other reforms of the rules – even a crossbar above the goal – were discussed with the same eagerness.

Near the end of the 1896 season the top clubs, or rather the ones most financially secure, finalised their plot to break away. For months, on and off, various clubs had met behind closed doors. The time had come. Collingwood and South Melbourne, the two grand finalists, joined in the new League, Collingwood's being a late-hour decision. The next three clubs on that year's ladder – Essendon, Melbourne and Fitzroy – had long agreed that they would join. On the next rungs of the ladder stood North Melbourne, Port Melbourne and Williamstown, but they were not invited. In the loyalty of their supporters they were formidable, but financially they were brittle. Footscray and Richmond, also poor in money and sometimes in crowd support, sat on or near the bottom of the ladder. Only a miracle could admit them to the new League. No miracle occurred.

There were still vacant places in the new Victorian Football League. Geelong, though finishing eleventh of the thirteen teams, was sure to be a member. It had such a long tradition; its teams were usually successful; and it was financially sound. Indeed, Geelong had been one of the original plotters working away for an exclusive League. Carlton was not chosen so easily. It had finished twelfth that year – twelfth out of thirteen – and it did not even possess a secure home ground. Finally it acquired Princes Park. When the first game was played there in June 1897, Princes Park was a primitive arena, far below the League's expectations, with no grandstand and not even a press box.

The selection of the inaugural eight clubs was not completely logical. Friendships perhaps played a part. Past grievances may have played a part. North Melbourne and Port Melbourne would have had a stronger chance of being selected if their home crowds had been less inflammatory. Wishful thinking also played a part in selecting the final club, St Kilda. It had one distinct weakness: it proved incapable of winning even one match in its first three years. Many critics thought that Port Melbourne, which had played such impressive football on Charity Saturday at the MCG in 1896, should have been chosen.

The opening of the 1897 season was eagerly awaited. Football was somewhat in the doldrums – Melbourne as a city was also in the doldrums – but perhaps the novel League would draw the spectators back to the native game. Anticipation was quickened by a set of new rules, perhaps the most innovative for the last two decades.

The League, slowly, was to prove a success. Becoming the dominant body in all Australia, irrespective of code, it supervised many facets of the game and its growth. Most historians now view the new League as the bold introducer of the rules that in 1897 helped to galvanise the game. It was not so. The old Victorian Football Association still operated with the five leftover teams and a new team, Brunswick. Stranded but not dispirited, it was even more the innovator.

The season opened on Saturday, 1 May – the season was starting earlier and earlier. The country was in drought, the grounds were hard, but the weather was lovely for football on the day when the shrunken Association launched its season. Here were the real experiments. Its teams each played with eighteen men – the League still allowed twenty in a team. Its teams that day were the first to put into practice the new rule outlawing the 'little mark'. Hitherto a ball kicked – or surreptitiously thrown – as little as 2 yards constituted a mark. Now the ball had to be kicked 10 yards before the privilege of a mark was allowed. The Association teams also adopted the new rule that behinds now counted in the final score, 1 behind equalling

1 point. So for the first time in the history of the game a team could win by kicking fewer goals – but far more behinds – than its opponent.

On the following Monday, the barrackers opening their newspapers thought how strange the new scoreboard seemed:

> Port Melbourne 8–19–67 defeated North Melbourne 2–6–18
> Richmond 5–8–38 defeated Brunswick 2–3–15
> Footscray 4–5–29 defeated Williamstown 3–4–22

Many of the country clubs adopted what were simply called 'the new rules' – even before the League itself formally was able to apply its version. On the same Saturday, near the banks of the Murray River, Albury defeated Wodonga under 'the new rules'. Whereas the opinion of the Association teams in Melbourne was that the abolition of the little mark – and the elimination of two players on each side – had opened up the game, *The Age* received a telegram from the Murray revealing that the footballers longed for the return of the little mark. They decided that the innovations 'detract much from the attractiveness of the game'. A Saturday later, a nearby league tried the new rules and the Beechworth Wanderers – perhaps because it won – did not seem to disapprove of them.

While the rule book was in mid-air, the League developed its own ideas of the most sensible set of rules. On the evening of Friday, 7 May, one of its committees met at the Port Phillip Club Hotel in Flinders Street to clarify the rules that would be applied on the following day. The League, unlike the Association, was introducing a new 'charging' and 'pushing' rule, and it had to be explained carefully, the umpires presumably being present. The question then arose: how should the new 10-yard mark be defined? An official explained that if the ball went 5 yards horizontally and 5 yards vertically before being caught, it was not legally a mark. So the puzzlement was dissolved. Curiously, the meeting was especially concerned that the matches of the new League should end before the light failed. The final message for the umpires was clear: they must allow each team no more than ten minutes' rest at half-time.

The next day was still and hazy. It promised exciting contests in the breakaway League. For the spectators, however, perhaps the most gripping moments came from the new method of scoring

The Melbourne First Twenty playing '... one of the stronger suburban clubs'. (The Illustrated Australian News, *circa 1877*).

rather than the rules governing the play itself. For example Fitzroy – it won three premierships in the second half of the 1890s – dominated a scrambling game in the first half but kicked only 11 behinds. Carlton in turn kicked 1 goal 3 behinds. While the players rested for ten minutes at half-time, there were the most animated discussions within the crowd. Under last year's scoring rules, Carlton would be winning, whereas under the brand-new rules Fitzroy was 2 points in front. As the game went on, and Fitzroy raced away, the new way of scoring temporarily ceased to matter.

At Collingwood's much-improved oval, the early excitement seemed to stem from the mistakes and mishaps. The visiting St Kilda team arrived fifteen minutes late, and the previous year's premiership pennant was unfurled by the mayor's wife with difficulty because of the faulty ropes and knots. As for the game itself, Collingwood finally won by 5–11–41 to 2–4–16. It was one of St Kilda's more dashing performances for the season.

On that opening day, one of the League's own experiments led to embarrassment. It had introduced a rule that made it legal, in certain conditions, for one player to push another in the back. If the players were stationary, the hard push in the back was legitimate. This new rule – not adopted by the Association – was favoured by those who wished to see strength and vigour still rewarded. After all, another new rule – the banning of the little mark – was certain to open up the game, encouraging longer kicking and discouraging the scrummage and thus reducing the impact of the strong ruckman on the flow of play. It was as if the two new rules were the result of a bargain. On the field, the bargain suddenly broke down. The pushing rule was too rough, and those with long memories recalled that at least two Tasmanian footballers had been fatally injured by rough pushes. The new liberty to push a player hard in the back was widely condemned. Next Friday night the League hastily altered the rule.

Football probably gained from the two rival competitions in Victoria. The League was seen as dominant but not unbeatable. In June, at the Fitzroy ground, a combined League team played a combined Ballarat team in a high-scoring game, and Ballarat won decisively with 13–11–89 to 8–6–54. While the League drew the larger crowds, the Association continued to experiment. It persisted in playing eighteen men in a team, and eventually – in order to open up the game – reduced each team to sixteen. Even in its first year its umpires enforced a backline rule which at first was deemed odd but eventually, in modified form, became part of the game. The first time that this new kicking-out rule came under public scrutiny was in June 1897. At Port Melbourne the full-back kicked off and the kick went out-of-bounds. The umpire promptly awarded a free kick to the Williamstown player and, applying the new rule to the letter, allowed him to take it from the exact place where the Port player had taken his kick. The result was an easy goal to Williamstown.

Why not stage morning matches? Why not play twice in the one weekend? The Association's leaders were tempted. In 1897, on a long weekend, they decided to stage a full round of fixtures on the Saturday and another on the Monday. All six teams played on the Saturday afternoon and all six teams played again on Monday, the games beginning at 10.30 am. In this way they did not clash with the two League matches staged at 3 pm that day.

Amidst these experiments the game remained casual. Football was part of life but did not dominate it. Useful players of one season would not turn up at the start of the next season: it was assumed that they had perhaps gone to Kalgoorlie in search of work or had returned to their home town or farm. At Collingwood's opening match it was simply noted that three of its old players had 'left Melbourne'. At North Melbourne one Saturday in mid-season it was learned that the team's two stars had just gone west to the goldfields. The opening of the football season was casual in another way. The end of the cricket overlapped the start of the football, and star players would desert their football club if their cricket team was in a final. When Fitzroy met St Kilda in the second VFL round in 1897, key players were missing because they were wanted at the cricket, while at Port Melbourne a player donned his football gear, disappeared to play cricket, then returned to the oval to resume his place. Likewise, in the uniforms worn on the field there was not uniformity. While all players wore trousers which they tucked into their long socks, they did not fully agree on the wearing of guernseys and caps. At the grand final on a hot day in 1896, some Collingwood and South Melbourne players wore a felt hat with wide brim, some wore a peaked cap and others were bareheaded. In 1900, at the grand final, the Melbourne captain Dick Wardill wore a long-sleeved woollen jumper but some of his team mates wore lace-up jackets with short sleeves.

Spectators picked up much of the football news by word-of-mouth – the daily newspaper rarely reported football news midweek. Even the final scores from the other Saturday matches were usually passed on by word-of-mouth sometime that evening. And who would take the field for your team? You discovered the answer when you saw the players emerge from the dressing room. There was of course no players' race: the spectators stood aside and made a corridor through which the players passed. As for the umpire, he was sometimes jostled as, quite unguarded, he left the ground. He might even be jabbed by a woman's umbrella. Women still attended in large numbers, and at Collingwood they were attracted by a special ladies' grandstand.

A love of the game was spreading far and wide. Admittedly, hundreds of thousands of Australians merely enjoyed it and hundreds of thousands of others simply liked it or half liked it – their enthusiasm went no further. Perhaps their children went to the football and they shared their children's interest, though not their zeal for the game. Maybe they felt a loose loyalty to their own suburban team but would attend a match only if it seemed likely to win a premiership. Some went regularly to the games: it was a Saturday habit but not an obsession. Some women stood and watched the football because their boyfriend liked the game or even played it. Some people went to a match on sunny days but would not dream of standing in the slippery mud, an umbrella above their head, in the depth of winter. But amidst all these followers, whether in Kalgoorlie or Collingwood, whether in Port Adelaide or Port Melbourne, was a growing band of ardent and vocal lovers of the game.

These fans longed for the coming of winter because it brought football back to them. When they heard in the parks and vacant allotments, for the first time in autumn, the smack of a football being kicked, their pulse-rates increased. These people, as much as the players and club officials, owned the game. By their enthusiasm they had made it part of the nation, or well over half of the nation.

At the football grounds, these intense barrackers were at the centre of the roars and sudden silences which the football journalists tried to evoke in Monday morning's paper. Listen to the journalist 'Observer' describing a match between Melbourne and Essendon in July 1893: 'I doubt whether a football crowd has ever been worked up to such a pitch of excitement'. In May of the following year, sitting in the little press seat at another football ground, 'Observer' again marvels at the electrical excitement when Footscray caught up to South Melbourne. He tells his *Argus* readers that the cheers of the crowd could be heard far away, that a small boy fell from a tree in his elation when a goal was kicked, and at another stage 'the excitement was so great' that a fence collapsed and a boy broke his leg under the weight of the spectators pressing forward. 'Observer' was not prone to exaggeration. Quiet and thoughtful, he liked the calm and the serene. He was a Green before that name was coined; and those supporters who read his nature observations in the same newspaper knew that he liked nothing more than watching a blackfish or platypus in the river, or hearing the warble of the magpies nesting in the Fitzroy Gardens.

CHAPTER TEN

The Tribulations of the Man in White

The umpire held a special place in Australian football. Nobody quite realised that. Not even the umpires quite knew the dilemma unwittingly imposed on them: otherwise they might have tried to ease it.

Australian football by the 1880s was distinctive and most who saw it regularly had no desire to attend another code of football. The Australian game was so successful that in winter in Victoria, South Australia and Tasmania, it had no competition, even from soccer which was now booming in England and Scotland. Most British soccer fans who had migrated to Melbourne or Adelaide were, to their surprise, soon converted to Australian football. The difficulty with a code of football that was so triumphant and pervasive was that it was seen only in its own light. As a result the umpire suffered.

The herculean task imposed on the umpire, compared to the umpires or referees in other games, was simply not appreciated. It is probably not adequately appreciated, even in the early 2000s. Right from the start the playing arena was much larger than that of other football codes. The players were also more numerous. Even when, after nearly half a century, the teams were reduced to eighteen players, that was still a large number by the standards of other codes. An Australian football umpire had to run further in the afternoon, partly because each match was longer than a soccer or Rugby game. The large playing arena also meant that many spectators, at any one time, were a long distance from the site of play. In their enthusiasm, they sometimes glimpsed from afar clashes, mistakes and incidents that hadn't happened.

The difficult task of the umpire in Australian football was accentuated by the absence of an offside rule. In other codes that rule served as a giant magnet: it virtually grasped the players by the feet and compelled them to spend much of the game in a confined part of the field. That helped the umpire to watch and control the players. In contrast, in Australian football the players and the ball could race up and down the whole field without impediment. As the umpire's task was formidable, he was more often criticised. Too much was expected of umpires. Even when they excelled they might be hooted and jeered by the home crowd. Their reputation was roasted: for many spectators it was almost part of the experience of attending the football. Even the benign football writers in the daily press were capable of judging an umpire by too strict a standard. At other times they correctly assumed that the umpire was almost powerless, in the last resort. When Collingwood and Melbourne met in June 1896 it was observed that the numerous 'instances of spiteful play took pretty well all the pleasure' out of the spectacle. The umpire was not blamed for the persistence of the spiteful incidents: what could he do?

The role of the umpires had evolved. Originally, most were older players who, when their footballing days were over, decided to take on a new role. Often the club appointed them to act for the day. They usually had close links to the teams over whose matches they presided. In a valiant move in 1883 the Association decided to appoint its own umpires, paying them one pound a week. It was high pay for a sport that was ostensibly amateur. A young clerk or a senior carpenter who umpired on a Saturday afternoon added about one-third to his winter salary or wages. But to pay the umpire increased, at times to an exorbitant level, the public's demands on his eyesight, common sense and impartiality.

There was still only one official – the central umpire – to control that vast arena. It was surely possible to ease his workload. He was helped by goal umpires, one at each end, but usually they

'Goal in danger', Geelong v. Melbourne in The Australian Pictorial Weekly, *26 June 1880.*

were selected by the rival teams. Most were citizens of goodwill but their goodwill flowed more to their own club. They gave no help, certainly no impartial help, in pointing out players' offences: they could not 'report' rough play.

The central umpire in 1880 did almost everything. Spurred on by a helpful or pained shout from spectators, he decided when the ball crossed the boundary line and went out-of-bounds. He himself had to fetch the ball and throw it back into play. For an instant he had to turn his back on the players before throwing the ball. In that way his throw could not be said to favour waiting members of one team rather than the other. After 1888, the umpire at last was permitted to face the players when he threw the ball into play. Now he could more easily detect infringements of the rules.

A boundary umpire running along each wing would have lightened his load. In the late 1890s, at special occasions, the boundary umpires were tried as an experiment. Their presence was mostly praised for speeding up the game, bringing the wingmen into play, dispersing the scrummages and taking a burden off the field umpire. But the two boundary umpires did not begin to appear regularly in Victorian matches until the first years of the new century. They were given seven shillings a day, whereupon the umpire's salary or honorarium was promptly increased from twenty to thirty shillings a match. Players, officially, were still unpaid – everyone knew otherwise.

The umpire also had to keep the time, just as soccer referees still keep the time in great international matches. In a fast-moving game, however, it was easy to overlook that the quarter had come to an end. In 1887, official timekeepers, equipped with large bells, took over the duty of calling the end of each quarter. That offered a slight relief to the central umpire. Moreover, he had been given a whistle to blow – that saved some strain on his voice when it was husky.

Meanwhile another duty descended on the umpire. At one time, after each goal was scored, the teams had assembled in the centre of the field, and one player kicked the ball into play. Now the umpire bounced the ball in the centre of the ground after each goal was kicked. More and more goals were kicked in a typical match, and therefore he had to become more skilled in the difficult task of bouncing the ball so that it favoured neither team.

Even to find, in the exact centre of the ground, a vacant space on which to bounce the ball was not always easy. Footballers jostled and crowded around him. At last, in 1908, in time for the grand Australasian football carnival, a circle five feet in diameter was painted in the centre of the ground, and no player could intrude into the circle. That small circle was the only official marking line, the only white line, in the sea of grass between the white-painted lines of the respective goal squares.

The umpire had less authority than an umpire in Rugby, soccer, Gaelic football or other kinds of football played in the English-speaking world. And yet he needed authority in order to handle the violence that was increasing on the field. From the late 1880s, the games in Melbourne – perhaps less so in Adelaide – tended to become more violent. There were probably more incidents on the fields, and more were initiated by knuckles and elbows and boots,

'Let go the ball': In 1880 the holding-the-ball rule was already as contentious as it is today (The Australian Pictorial Weekly, *26 June 1880*).

and certainly more were reported in the newspapers. A typical match was played fairly, but in some matches players used the elbow to flatten an opponent, or hit him in the jaw, or blacken his eye. Just occasionally a player was kicked deliberately by an opponent. Every now and then a brawl broke out and the umpire had trouble in halting it. A player could be suspended by a tribunal that met in the week after the match but not many players were suspended. Fortunately, around 1900 the suspensions were becoming more frequent.

Footballers who disliked the umpire's decisions gave him a sharp piece of their tongue: sometimes the tongue was vituperative.

H 'Ivo' Crapp, a fine umpire, was subject to taunts. Crapp was the only VFL umpire in history for whom the spectators did not have to invent a nickname. In 1900, the Collingwood captain Condon was suspended for three weeks after swearing at an umpire, and in the final match of the year he was warned by umpire Crapp. He then tripped a Melbourne player and was penalised. Suddenly, without provocation, he told the umpire what he thought of him and his girlfriend: 'Your girlfriend's a bloody whore.' At the tribunal, Condon was suspended for life – an incredibly stern penalty. The Collingwood club did not defend its captain's behaviour. Eventually it relented, gave evidence in his favour and the life suspension imposed was virtually overturned. Condon was allowed to play again for Collingwood.

On occasions the antics of the spectators were as wild as events on the field. There was a disturbing incident at North Melbourne in July 1896. Roberts the umpire did not please the rowdy home-ground supporters, though the neutral opinion was that he had umpired capably. At the end of the match, narrowly won by Collingwood, he would have been badly injured by North supporters but for the efforts of footballers including McDougall of North Melbourne and Proudfoot of Collingwood, who was also a constable. Those trying to defend the battered umpire were themselves hit many times.

'Rover', the football writer whose articles in *The Weekly Times* were devoured in rural kitchens and on township verandahs throughout Victoria, opened his weekly column with a growl of indignation at this episode: 'Savagery again, and of the most brutal kind. Football is fairly in the mire this time. Respectable supporters of the game may well hang their heads.' It was the opinion of 'Rover', after describing the men and women concerned as 'veritable fiends', that a club should perhaps be disqualified for the rest of the season if it failed to maintain law and order.

In 1897 the new rules were introduced in the hope of lessening the crushes, scrambles and scrummages that often gave rise to congested and rough play. When Melbourne played South Melbourne on the opening day of that season, 'Follower' of *The Age* reported sternly: 'It was, on the whole, a disappointing game, the players too frequently going for each other, and often without the excuse of an attempt for the ball.' His opinion, it should be said, was not shared by 'Observer' of *The Argus*. At the start of the same season at Broken Hill, which was becoming the bastion of the game in New South Wales, the South Broken Hill team, led by their captain and his black eye, walked off the ground. They said the umpire had failed to defend them from their ruffianly opponents, a team significantly known as the Victorians. The umpire, while 'jeered and hooted', was in one piece when he left the field. Whether he was adjudicating under the new or old rules is not clear.

About that time, Collingwood was visiting South Australia where it played against the fine South Adelaide team. The umpire complained that the Collingwood players questioned his decisions and even obstructed him. At least for the questioning there was perhaps some basis, because the two colonies did not always follow the same rules.

It would be unfair to emphasise unduly the episodes of violence, but they were common enough to worry admirers of the game. Conspicuous violence enacted in front of a big crowd was dangerous: it could gallop out of control. After some matches, the umpires had to be escorted past angry crowds or bundled secretly out of dressing sheds or grandstands so that they could catch their tram or train. Some were lucky to be able to walk, a stone or brick having been thrown at them while they were umpiring. In 1908, at the Fitzroy ground in Brunswick Street, a stone hit the umpire. No wonder the Victorian government began to think of sending plainclothes police to some of the grounds where the crowd's behaviour was inflammable.

Another fiery episode took place in May 1910 when, just before the final bell, a Carlton player, seriously provoked, felled a South Melbourne opponent. That in itself was not abnormal, but on this afternoon it incited spectators to run onto the field. As a result of these events George Topping, a lightweight and impetuous forward, a member of two Carlton premiership teams, was suspended for several seasons. He tried to make amends, of a kind, by becoming an umpire for a year.

Australian football belatedly acquired the dubious idea that the player was always more important than the umpire. If the player was selected in a team he was entitled to remain on the arena for the remainder of the match. His captain could remove him – no replacement was allowed – but the umpire could not. But what if the player ran wild and began striking players, right and left? What if he so provoked other players that the ground became as much a battlefield as a football field? The rulers of the game said an offensive player was entitled to continue playing, and even to kick the winning goals for his side.

The enthroning of the footballer had occurred slowly. At first Australian football was a gentleman's game in spirit, though sometimes rough. Players were honour-bound to obey the rules and accept every decision made by the umpire. It was the captain's task to discipline his own team. If he utterly failed to control his players, and allowed a member of his team to disobey an umpire's decision, the umpire was entitled then and there to award victory to the other team. As late as the 1880s that was the Association's rule. But if the umpire was presiding at a ground where the mass of supporters was hostile, how could he formally terminate the match to which people had paid for admission, and gather the ball under his arm and walk defiantly from the oval? He would have been confronted at the boundary by an angry crowd – unless it was the visiting team he was penalising. A sensible umpire, once the game was drawing large crowds, was conscious of his limitations.

Stringent rules in a democratic, confident colony needed the certain support of the players and the regular support of the spectators. If the umpires were to exercise the supreme power entrusted to them, they had to do it early in the history of the game. They had to establish the precedent for decisive intervention. That opportunity was not seized. By 1890, in Melbourne at least, it was probably too late for the umpire to call off a senior game in the presence of an over-excited crowd.

Sending off was an easy option – much easier than disqualifying the whole team. The game could still continue but the team thereafter was short of a player. Other codes applied this rule. In Australian football, with teams of twenty players, the dismissal of a player would be less severe than a dismissal in soccer where he was one in eleven.

At times a sending-off rule was discussed in Australian football, but it did not become part of the fabric of the game. Supporters mostly opposed the introduction of the rule. They had come to watch their team's champions. They had paid their money: they wanted to see them play, come what may. The majority of players also supported their right to stay on the field. Certain umpires must have had a contrary view, but they were never influential as a group, at least not in the years when a sending-off rule was feasible. And yet probably by 1890, and certainly by 1900, and emphatically by 1910, there was a clear need for a sending-off rule as an extreme penalty for dirty play.

It is revealing to consider the rules of Gaelic football. They moved swiftly towards empowering the umpire rather than the player. From the start they imposed a sending-off rule. In the mid-1880s the twin Gaelic games of football and hurling permitted the

When the ball crossed the boundary line an umpire threw the ball back into play. The big men then had to wait until the thrown ball hit the turf before they touched it. South Melbourne players predominate in this ruck duel of 1882 (The Leader, 27 May 1882).

umpire to 'stand aside' – in other words to send from the ground – players in disgrace. The discipline in these games became severe in the early 1900s. A rule severely punished players who, losing their temper, abused the umpire. The rule was the same for both games: 'Any player threatening or insulting the referee shall be suspended for not less than twelve months, and his team too shall be liable to disqualification.' On the other hand, in Australian football many senior players could abuse the umpire and escape any punishment. The culture of the game, inch by inch and year by year, came to condone unsportsmanlike conduct at the highest level of excellence; and the whole game and its reputation suffered.

At that time a sending-off rule should probably have been introduced and enforced, especially in the Victorian Football League. Of course, each new rule imposes losses as well as gains, and sometimes the losses are rightly judged to be dominant both by spectators and players. Such a rule would have been a confession of failure. Opponents of it would not budge. Moreover, they were probably influenced in part by the relationship between cricket and Australian football: cricket has no sending-off rule. The very concept was quite alien to the spirit, the self-disciplining spirit, of traditional cricket. It emphasised fair play, and the fairness had to come from the players.

For a long period the relationship between Australian cricket and Australian football had been tight – far tighter than between English cricket on the one hand and English soccer and football on the other. Since the time of Tom Wills, scores of famous players had excelled both in Australian football and in top cricket, and many played in both senior football and Test cricket. For decades the spirit and culture of the two games had much in common.

The opposition to the creation of a sending-off rule came not only from cricket but from Australian popular culture. As the power of the one declined, the power of the other increased. In Australia, in everyday life, there had long been a suspicion of authority; and the white-dressed umpire, especially in football, was one such symbol and an easy target for the barracker. There was also an intense Australian desire to enthrone the champion player – why should he suddenly be made powerless and dismissed from the arena by an officious umpire? There was also a belief that in Australian football the umpires as a breed were not competent enough and therefore should not be awarded large and almost arbitrary powers. If the belief was valid that the umpires were inadequate, that belief was a reflection of the formidable and unique task unfairly imposed on umpires by a huge ground, many players and the absence of an offside rule.

In football played at the highest level, a novel solution was to be sought much later, in the 1990s. It was the appointment of three field umpires, aided for punitive purposes by a television camera, permanently roving. In years to come, the three umpires may well be seen as a strange solution, but it recognised the persisting dilemma.

CHAPTER ELEVEN

Myths: Gaelic and Aboriginal

Australian football is widely said to be an offspring of Gaelic football. One hundred years ago such an idea was unknown, but now it is probably the dominant view amongst those who view football seriously. The tourist books assume it, advertisers affirm it. The story is not specific, and sometimes the game is said to have been brought here from Ireland and first played on the goldfields by Irish gold diggers or garrison troops, and sometimes its growth is vaguely said to have been strongly influenced by Irish migrants. That massive work of reference, *The Oxford Companion to Sports and Games*, explains that Australian football is 'manifestly based on the old-time Kerry pastime of Caid'. Professor John Molony, in his excellent *Penguin Bicentennial History of Australia*, offers a parallel conclusion: 'The Victorian goldfields in the 1850s gave rise to a unique code of football based on the Irish game.' Some footballers and officials who visit Ireland have little hesitation in accepting such theories, for the two games do seem to have more similarities than any other two codes of football.

The case for a strong Irish influence on Australian sports and institutions is persuasive at first sight. In 1860 Victoria possessed one of the largest concentrations of Irish people outside Ireland itself, and so it would not be surprising if Gaelic football influenced the Australian game in infancy. Perhaps one in five of the population of Victoria was Irish or of all-Irish parentage, and most had derived from rural Catholic Ireland, where the Gaelic game

Whenever children played in the open air in winter, the boys were certain to produce a real or imitation football. This was a game at the Melbourne suburb of Mt Erica in 1879 (The Illustrated Australian News, *2 August 1879*).

was mostly played. Furthermore, in early accounts of kick-about football in Australia, Irishmen were often conspicuous. The first recorded football match, in Sydney in 1829, was between two Irish regiments. Several of the early matches of football in Melbourne were held during Irish celebrations. In the last fifty years many players of Irish name and Catholic religion have been stars in Victorian football, and two schools which in the public eye show an obsession for Australian football are the Catholic country schools, Assumption College in Kilmore and St Patrick's College in Ballarat.

Above all, those Australians who have watched matches of Gaelic football in Ireland have an uncanny feeling that this must be the game from which their own has descended; and indeed the new tradition of Test matches between Australian and Irish football teams, playing composite rules, could not have arisen if the two codes of football were far apart in rules and spirit and skills. On the surface, the case for a common inheritance between Australian and Gaelic football is appealing.

The difficulty of the Gaelic theory is that it is backed by scant evidence. It is eminently plausible until the search for hard evidence takes place. If the early players and rule-makers of Australian football believed that they were playing or modifying Gaelic football they would probably have said so; in fact they gladly mention other English codes from which they borrowed or thought of borrowing but give not even a whisper of Irish influences. The early sporting journalists with knowledge of how football was played overseas sometimes discussed influences on the Australian code and often mentioned Rugby but not Gaelic. No visitor or newcomer to Melbourne in the 1860s, when the new game of football was taking shape, seemed to sense that here was a colonial version of Gaelic football. Most historians of sport who in recent years have begun to dig into the history of Australian football – Bill Mandle, Ian Turner, Leonie Sandercock, Anne Mancini and Gillian Hibbins, Garrie Hutchinson and Rob Hess – have concluded that the Gaelic influence cannot have been strong. Mandle, the first professional historian to write about the early decades of Australian football, is also an authority on the history of the Gaelic Athletic Association which fathered Gaelic football in its present form. He does not view Australian football as an offspring of Gaelic. Rob Hess, commissioned by the National Football League of Australia to assess the Gaelic influence, could discover no strong Irish influences in the early years.

Not even one piece of positive evidence for a Gaelic origin of Australian football has so far been found, and I can see strong circumstantial evidence against such an origin. The seven men who formed a committee to draw up the first rules of Australian football included only one Irishman, redheaded Thomas Henry Smith, and as a student he had gone from the County of Monaghan to Trinity College, Dublin, a Protestant university which in football probably was more in the Rugby than in the Gaelic style. The four men who wielded most influence on the first rules of Australian football came from the universities and private schools of the British Isles, and not from the rural Ireland where Gaelic football was played. In the first ten years of Australian football the number of Irish surnames is actually fewer than one would expect in a city where two in every ten of the people were Catholics and the wearing of the green was common on St Patrick's Day. Furthermore, the whites and reds and blues, not greens, were the favourite colours of the early football teams. In 1880 not one of the dozens of senior and suburban football teams in Melbourne and Geelong wore the green of Ireland in their colours; and yet a green dye was available – in the Irish-inhabited potato lands near Port Fairy the Tower Hill team wore a cap of green and white, while earlier one club in Melbourne with an Irish component had worn a green cap with a scarlet band and red button on top.

The schools which were prominent in the beginnings of the new code were Protestant schools with headmasters from England or Scotland. If Australian football had stemmed from Ireland we would perhaps expect the Catholic schools to be early spearheads of the game and to excel in it. The first Catholic school in Melbourne to figure noticeably in the football season was St Patrick's College which stood at the side of the rising bluestone cathedral on Eastern Hill: it became prominent because in the season 1877 it scored not one goal while its opponents – the Protestant schools – scored 33.

Myths: Gaelic and Aboriginal

Significantly, the first challenge cup presented for competition amongst the senior teams playing Australian football in Victoria was not an Irish cup: rather it was the Caledonian Cup, presented by Scots. The first president of the first football body, the Victorian Football Association, was not a Catholic but one of the most influential Freemasons in Melbourne. It may also be significant that the first major re-writing of football's rules took place in the Freemason's Hotel, not a hotel frequented by the Irish.

It would be surprising if the Catholic Irish had been numerous amongst the game's founders. Football in Victoria was initially a game for young men with money and leisure, and the Irish were to

A scratch match of football being played at the Orphan Asylum in South Melbourne. In the background the boys are playing games of cricket and hoops (The Illustrated Australian News, *7 September 1874*).

be found far more frequently amongst the poorer workers for whom a free Saturday afternoon was a rarity. Later, as the popularity of the new code spread, and as more factories gave their employees a free afternoon on Saturday, the workingmen's suburbs – and the Irish too – provided many brilliant footballers. By 1880 the Carlton team did not lack Irish names, while the strongest of the

191

Irish suburbs, North Melbourne, fielded various teams. The existing evidence suggests that the Irish players came into the game and made their mark more in the years of expansion than in the founding years. A careful piecing together of the names of players would probably reveal that by 1880 several teams had a powerful core of Irish players and supporters and that they were conscious of their Catholic loyalties, especially when playing against teams seen as overwhelmingly Protestant. But in the first years, British and Anglo-Australian players dominated the game.

Another simple test can be applied to the theory that Australian football was an offshoot of the Gaelic game. If the numerous Irish settlements in Victoria really rejoiced that their native game was conquering the parklands of Melbourne, many of the English immigrants, wary of the Irish and their customs, would have deliberately shunned the new game and retreated to what they saw as English versions of football. There was no such retreat by English purists. Likewise in the strongest Irish towns in Victoria, the Irish people would have revelled in Australian football in the winter time if they had been convinced it was a Gaelic offshoot. Instead, in the vicinity of the south-west Victorian towns of Warrnambool and Koroit and Port Fairy, as late as 1881, many young men of Irish descent actually shunned football and instead played the Irish game of 'hurley' or hurling. Many Irishmen around Kyneton also played hurley rather than join in Australian football.

If Ireland by chance did influence the first matches of Australian football, it affected only a few minor facets. Indeed, when the committees of young men met in Melbourne to write down the first rules they could have learned little from Irish football because its rules were not in writing. Whereas the rules of the various English versions of football were in print and were actually consulted at these key meetings in Melbourne, Gaelic football did not yet follow clear and accepted rules that were precisely set down in print.

Not until 1884, when a young Irish civil servant named Michael Cusack founded the Gaelic Athletic Association in Dublin, was a successful attempt commenced to formulate and write down the rules of Gaelic football. By then the game was little played in Ireland. The famine of the 1840s, the massive outflow of people to the United States and then the arrival of the rising English sports had dislocated the old sporting customs in rural Ireland.

Cusack's aim was to revive the decaying sports and make them distinctively Irish, and his friends in the Irish Republican Brotherhood were eager that Irish football and hurling should have little resemblance to the English games now making headway in Ireland. In one sense, Cusack and his friends re-invented Gaelic football. They sought a distinctive game that would attract young Irishmen and make them proud to be Irish. Picking and choosing from what they believed were the unwritten rules of the game once played on Irish farmlands, and then infusing new rules and rituals, they wrote out the first rules of Gaelic football in December 1884. They were experimenting and – like the founders of Australian football – were later to change the rules according to the experience of the players and umpires.

The traditional Gaelic game was apparently a free-for-all played over many hours. It was rather like Rugby without the rules. The new version played by the Gaelic Athletic Association in 1885 copied part of the roughness of the old game but tamed other parts. At first wrestling was allowed, but it was soon banned along with tackling. Gaelic football moved, as had Australian football, from a contest of fierce bodily contact and congested play to an open and fast-moving game. In the first ten years the rules were altered so often that the game became startlingly different.

The Gaelic and Australian games had curious parallels and differences in the arranging of the goalposts and the means of scoring. Gaelic football had a crossbar 8 feet above the ground, and the ball had to pass underneath the bar to count as a goal. The Gaelic goalposts at first were 15 feet apart, but they were soon moved to the exact Australian distance of 21 feet apart. The Australian game had long used behind posts, and soon the Gaelic game used behind posts. By 1889 in Ireland the behinds counted in the final score – if both sides had scored the same number of goals or no goals. The Australian game already counted behinds – merely as a guide to lost opportunities – but did not count them in the final score until 1897. Indeed, Australia went slightly further. A team could win even though its opponent had kicked more goals, a result unthinkable in the early Gaelic football.

Originally a Gaelic team could field twenty-one players, but the number of players was reduced in stages: there were only fifteen to a team by the start of the First World War. The first Gaelic rules specified a small playing arena by Australian standards. Perhaps that was the ideal arena when the Gaelic game was to be played by teams of only fourteen men rather than the maximum of twenty-one. Quickly the arena was enlarged. When twenty-one players were picked for each team, the optimum arena was specified as 196 yards long and 140 yards wide. An even larger arena – perhaps larger than the largest Australian football grounds in 1890 – was soon authorised. As the Gaelic game was played on an oblong ground, its playing surface at this stage was potentially larger than a large Australian football ground. By the start of the First World War the Gaelic teams were reduced to fifteen players, and so the very large grounds were no longer justified.

Each game of Gaelic football began with what seemed both a ceremony of brotherhood and a ban on stealing an unfair advantage. In the centre of the field the two teams stood side by side in parallel ranks, with each player 'holding the hand of one of the other side'. Under the 1889 rules the actual play began with the referee throwing the ball into the air – at that time the Australian game began with a kick off. The referee was accompanied by two central umpires, each presumably representing a team, with a goal umpire at each end. The umpires appear to have acted rather as the two umpires acted in the first years of Australian football, each advocating his own team's cause; but whereas Australian football in the 1870s moved from two partisan central umpires to one independent umpire, the Irish game relied on the two partisan umpires who, if they could not agree, appealed to the referee whose word was final.

The Irish rules – unlike the Australian – allowed the referee to send a player from the field. The referee could also permit a team, when one of its players was injured by a clear breach of the rules, to bring on a substitute. The Irish rules regulating play were distinctive. They did not allow a player to mark the ball – using 'mark' in the orthodox sense of permitting a player not only to catch the ball – but to take his time and kick without fear of interference from an opponent. They did not allow a man with the ball to run more than four steps. They awarded free kicks, on condition that the ball was placed on the ground and then kicked.

The Irish game was of short duration compared to Australian football, occupying a mere one hour of play. The kicks too were rather short, for initially the round Irish football itself was heavy, though today it is lighter than an Australian ball. The ball did not have to be kicked through the goal but could be punched or driven; and one hallmark of the Irish game was the ability of players to propel the ball a long distance with a swipe of the hand. The Irish code was nationalistic and exclusive, and banned players who persisted in also playing the English sports.

An Irishman who regularly went to the football in Melbourne and then in 1890 returned home to County Kerry where he saw the matches of the reborn Gaelic football was unlikely to say: 'These two kinds of football are uncannily alike.' In the two codes the shape of the field and the ball was different, the penalties – not the least the power of the Irish umpire to expel a player from the field – were different, the method of scoring goals was different and most of the rules were different.

The Australian and Irish footballers did share several major similarities. They could handle the ball – using handle in the orthodox sense of using the hands – and were not permitted to throw the ball. Unlike Rugby, both codes had a tendency to restrict the frequency of bodily contact and to encourage an open brand of football. Certainly they were alike in that they did not enforce an offside rule, and in both codes a team could break away with the ball and make a swift approach to the forward line. In essence the absence of an offside rule remains the chief similarity between Gaelic and Australian football, but in each code it arose independently and not through imitation.

If an historian of football wishes to press the argument that one code must have copied the other, then this conclusion would be difficult to escape: the style of play which Gaelic and Australian football share today was visible in Australia long before it was visible in Ireland. By that line of reasoning the Gaelic football must have been the imitator. The present evidence, however, suggests that Gaelic football made its own way in its own direction which happened to be – in the style rather than the formalities of play – more the Australian direction.

Today's similarities tell us little about the complicated history of each game. Just as two games can grow apart over time, so they can become more alike over time. At one period Australian football and Gaelic football grew apart; in another period they converged in spirit more than in rules. Australian football in the first years had virtually no likeness to Gaelic football as played today. It is the modern versions of Gaelic and Australian football which gives rise to the dubious belief that the two codes are first cousins or even father and son.

The history of American football offers a similar lesson. It warns us of the hazard of assuming that a code of football alters so little in the course of a century that we can deduce its parentage and its manner of birth simply by examining its present rules. Today no two codes of football are further apart than Australian and American football, and yet both were the offspring more of Rugby than of any other code.

A younger game than Australian football, American football quickly shed its British origins. Beginning in the universities of the east coast, its original base was soccer. The first intercollegiate game, between Princeton and Rutgers in 1869, was primarily a kicking rather than a handling game. In the mid-1870s Harvard and Yale turned more to Rugby, and their version of Rugby soon became the dominant code. American footballers, like Australia's, found their own solutions to many of the dilemmas and conflicts that arose in the course of a football game. Whereas the Australian game became more flowing in the first twenty years, the new American game became more congested. In America every inch of territory was painfully won by the attackers, and in 1882 the slow progress of an attack could be pinpointed for all to see by the experiment of painting the football field with the white lines on the gridiron pattern. A slow-moving and fiercely fought code of football no longer required such a large playing arena, and the length of the American football field was successively reduced from 140 to 100 yards, or a mere half of the length of an Australian football field.

Physical strength became crucial in American football. In the 1880s, in defiance of the spirit but not necessarily the letter of the offside rule, an American footballer carrying the ball forward was escorted by a protector who, running a step or two ahead, fended off those trying to tackle the ball-carrier. The opponents, losing the initiative for several years, eventually recaptured it by tackling the protector and the ball-carrier at the knees.

Rough play was now accepted. The attackers, in order to weaken the new tackling power of the defenders, resolved to move forward with the ball in one pack. Every player in the team was part of that slow-moving attack which, shaped like a V, forced its way forward, with the man carrying the ball bringing up the rear. This 'V trick' formation was the vogue from about 1885 to about 1894, enabling the massed players to retain possession of the ball while slowly advancing. No padding was worn at the time, and bodily clashes between attackers and defenders led to injury and death.

In the 1880s, the American fervour for keeping the ball within a team's possession by employing a military formation was paralleled in Australia in a less physical way. Here the attacking team retained possession of the ball with a series of 'little marks'. A forward would kick the ball a few feet to another forward who would 'mark' the ball. The little mark favoured nimble position play and quick movements by individual forwards. This was very different to the 'V trick' but the principle of retaining possession of the ball at all costs, and of making small but slow advances towards the goal, was pursued simultaneously by Americans and by Australians each in their own way. All the time their styles of playing were drifting apart. The American game was becoming fearfully rugged. In 1905, it became almost too dangerous to be tolerated. The United States' President, outraged by the eighteen deaths in the same football season, called together representatives from Yale, Harvard and Princeton and demanded less warlike play. Next year the forward pass was made legal. The strict offside rule was in retreat. The original Rugby-type rules fell further apart and American football became less congested. It is relevant to observe that so much has been written on the history of American football compared to the history of Australian football that Americans are far more conscious than Australians of the way in which a game steadily changes. They do not ask, as we ask, 'Where did the game come from?' They know that their code of football was essentially a game that grew. Like Australian football, American football was home grown.

Australian football in its infant years borrowed heavily from England, especially from Rugby football, when the differences between Rugby and soccer were not as stark as they are today. On the other hand, American football borrowed heavily from Rugby when that code was becoming more distinctive. Neither the Australians nor the Americans borrowed blindly, and much of what they borrowed was soon discarded or was modified almost beyond recognition. The Australians and Americans slowly invented their own way of playing, their own rules and tactics and skills.

Since their beginnings both Australian and American football have invented more, adapted more and changed more than have the main codes of Rugby Union, Rugby League and soccer, all of which were English codes which eventually became international. Australian and American football, being confined each to the one nation, were able to change rules, tactics and skills more rapidly: no international conference had to be summoned in the hope of amending the rules. Nationalist or one-nation games, whether Australian or American or Gaelic football, are more likely than international games to travel far from their original rules.

Cricket, more popular than football in Britain in 1850, also helped to shape the conduct of the early footballers in Melbourne. Tom Wills and other Melbourne cricketers were prominent in shaping the Australian game of football, and they adopted some of the habits and rituals of cricket. Thus their football match began, as did a cricket game, with a toss of the coin, and the winner of the toss had the choice of the goal favoured by the wind. Just as a cricket team could bat all day on a favourable wicket with no time limit, so a football team could kick with the wind all day until at last it scored a goal. In early Australian football, as in cricket, a match was continued over several Saturdays. The clock was not yet the dictator, and an afternoon of football or cricket continued until poor light halted play. The weather was more the dictator of each game, and if rain fell heavily the footballers, like the cricketers, hastily left the field. Likewise, in early Australian football, as in cricket, each team appointed a central umpire. After a few years, Australian football broke loose from these specific cricketing influences, except in one important matter: its attitude to the umpire. The early footballers

St Kilda sent a team by sea to play matches in Adelaide in 1877.

adopted the cricketing custom of appealing loudly to the umpire to redress an infringement of the rules, for the umpire did not adjudicate unless he was formally called upon. Even in its twenty-fifth year as a separate game, Australian football still assumed that the field umpire should not adjudicate unless formally appealed to. Ultimately football, with its emphasis on the clock, was to influence modern cricket. The one-day cricket test of the 1970s, with equal batting time for each team, was simply the application to cricket of one of football's innovations of a century earlier.

Australian football was shaped not only by English cricket and football but by the new environment in Victoria. Its style of play was shaped by the large playing fields. A game born of cheap land, it clung to the big arena long after the overseas codes of football allowed their arena to become smaller. Amongst all the football codes the playing field in Australian football is the largest.

Australian football in its opening year was also influenced by a very dry winter. The hard playing surface of 1858 probably helped to accelerate a trend away from the severe physical contact of Rugby. Likewise the winter climate of Australia, by English and North American standards, was mild, and that encouraged spectators to stand in the open air in big numbers and watch the matches. In Victoria the new game quickly won an astonishing unanimity of support, allowing no other code of football more than the tiniest of footholds. The game attracted remarkably large crowds by the standards of English cities. The crowds and their preferences helped to shape the game. They longed for the spectacular: they wanted to see the long run with the ball, the high mark, the clever dodging and the sudden physical clash. They shunned the slow-moving play and especially the scrummage.

Quickly it became a game of the people, and indeed the experts holding forth in the newspapers began to lament that the crowd's applause was affecting the way the game developed. In 1877 one critic complained that too many footballers were playing to the gallery and running with the ball instead of kicking it. Albury, the first New South Wales town to adopt Australian football as its main game, was singled out because so many of its young players were like show ponies in the presence of an admiring crowd. In Melbourne, the prince of football writers, Peter Pindar, reviewing the football season of 1881, criticised those footballers who 'play exclusively for the crowd'.

So the spectators, players and the shape and texture of the playing surface quickly helped to shape the game, and the game itself gave rise to the new rules, tactics and skills. And in time these innovations could only be thwarted by even newer rules, tactics and skills. Of the names of innovators, the hundreds of innovators, we often know nothing. Many of the important changes in skills and tactics came quietly in the space of a few years. Who began them was usually not known, for they began imperceptibly and at first they did not always succeed.

In trying to understand the origins of the present game of Australian football, we forget that it was moulded by many people and influences, decade after decade. Instead we imagine that it was

Marcus Clarke, author of His Natural Life, *was perhaps the best-known novelist in Australia, and after his death in Melbourne in 1881 a fancy-dress football match was staged at the East Melbourne ground to raise money for his widow and large family.*

largely shaped in its first years, and we hope that if only we can uncover those years we will find its birth and the single most formative influence. So we look for a dramatic person or event in the first years. The game, it is variously said, was founded by the gold diggers of the 1850s, by Gaelic footballers, by the match between Melbourne Grammar and Scotch College in 1858, by Rugby or Aboriginal players, or by the pioneer footballers and rule-makers, Tom Wills and Henry C A Harrison. We all seem to prefer a simple theory. We still hope to find an original landmark or founder in the belief that the game was a once-only invention or derivation rather than a long chain of inventions and adaptations that still continue.

In many regions of Australia, the Aboriginals played football, and in recent years it has occasionally been suggested that they provided the special ingredients of Australian football. We know that in southwest Victoria they traditionally made their own football from an opossum skin filled with crushed charcoal and tied up with kangaroo sinews. They kicked the ball with the instep of the bare foot, and they made strong leaps – sometimes reaching 5 feet above the ground – in an attempt to catch the ball. On the basis of the sparse existing evidence, however, it is unlikely that this Aboriginal game influenced Australian football. In Melbourne, the early teams seem to have included few if any Aboriginals. Generally, the new settlers from the British Isles learned almost nothing from Aboriginal rituals and customs, even when learning could have been to their advantage. One possible exception is the high mark of Australian football. It seems to be primarily an extension of the 'mark' of English football, but it is just conceivable that several of the early exponents of what became a distinctively Australian form of marking had seen Aboriginals at play in rural areas, gained confidence from watching them and even imitated their style of leaping.

At the Aboriginal colony at Coranderrk, near Healesville, a few Aboriginals were still skilfully playing their native football in the 1860s, using a football made not from the heavy opossum skin but from strong, light twine made of opossum hair. Except for the high leaps, it is very doubtful whether their game resembled the football played at the time in Melbourne parks.

The Australian Football League in 1999 issued under its logo a handsome Aboriginal-sponsored booklet and calendar which rightly praised the stunning skills of the new breed of Aboriginal footballer entering the game. The booklet also went a surprising distance in arguing that Australian football in its infancy was strongly influenced by a traditional Aboriginal game.

Three major obstacles seem to face this interpretation of history. Firstly, in the mass of evidence on the early game, especially in the period from 1858 to 1868, there is no evidence to support this theory and a wide array of evidence opposing it. Secondly, the idea that the game in its essential form was invented around 1858 and that the high mark – borrowed from Aborigines – was an integral part of that original game has no present evidence to support it. The high mark was not part of the early game played on the Melbourne parklands: it came later. In essence, the modern game is the result of a chain of inventions, nearly all made since 1858 and nearly all documented by records at the time. Even if by chance the game had been invented by the Aborigines and generously loaned, ready made, to white footballers in 1858, that game would bear virtually no resemblance to the present game. And yet the whole Aboriginal case rests on the naïve idea that the game played now is akin to the old Aboriginal game: 'Today's game still retains the essential character of the original.'

The Aboriginal theory has recently come to depend more on Tom Wills. He spent part of his childhood with or near Aborigines; he felt goodwill towards them even after his father was murdered by Queensland Aborigines; and he was an initial coach of the remarkable Aboriginal cricket team which went to the British Isles. But if Wills had really learned to play or observe a football game while with the Aborigines he would have given them credit: instead he wrote not a word. If he had known Aborigines who were skilled at football he would have encouraged them, just as he encouraged the cricketers. On the present evidence the behaviour and testimony of Wills, rather than supporting the Aboriginal theory, is a blow to it. In the 1860s Aborigines played senior cricket in Victoria and in the British Isles. None, so far as is known, appeared in senior Australian football matches at that time. Their brilliance as football players belonged to the twentieth century.

Ball games have been played, presumably, for thousands of years in many parts of the world. To link those games with modern games requires careful argument and new evidence; but the theory stressing an Aboriginal origin has so far skimped the task of accumulating evidence.

H C A Harrison did much to spread the mistaken idea that Australian football as we know it was shaped in the space of a few years. At the age of eighty-seven he completed the story of his own

H C A Harrison lived to see what he once called 'a game of our own' develop into a national pastime. His portrait by Sir John Longstaff is in the Melbourne Cricket Club.

life, entitled *The Story of an Athlete*, and his version of history had wide influence. He loved the game, played it superbly, worked for its continued success and did not cease to express his pleasure in the early matches of Australian football as 'happy, glorious days'. But the title he accepted as 'father of the game' was more a title of courtesy, and his memory was at fault when he claimed to have been a player in the very first season. Likewise, the rules he was prominent in drafting in 1866 were not, as he implied, the first rules of Australian football. Nor did those rules really form the basis of those played in Melbourne sixty years later when the game was becoming recognisably like our game.

It seems impossible to accept this widely held idea that the basis of the present code of football was laid in the space of a few years. Even after the writing of the new rules in 1866, football had few likenesses to the present Australian game. It was played not on an oval but on an oblong ground with trees in mid-field. Each match began in Rugby or soccer style with a kick-off, most players hunted in packs and the slow-moving game was interrupted again and again by the scrummage. A goal was a rarity and a behind did not exist. A player could be charged by his opponent or pushed in the back while running or slung by the neck or up-ended by 'rabbiting'. The game had no regular quarters and halves, and no time limit. There was no limit on the number of players in a team, nor any rule compelling opposing teams to field the same number of players. So far as we know an offside rule probably operated in several minor facets of the game, and likewise, as in today's soccer, an 'own goal' could be scored by a player of the opposing side. Back in 1866 the high mark had not been born and the little mark – famous in its day – was probably still unknown. Even the stock-in-trade of today's footballer, the drop-punt kick and the quick punching of the ball to a player on the move, was probably unknown. In 1866 the difference far exceeded the resemblance to contemporary football.

Tom Wills, who did much to arouse interest in football in Melbourne in 1858, and who did more perhaps than anyone to adapt English football to Australia's climate and social conditions, has probably the strongest claim to be the originator of the first phase of Australian football. It is far too much to say that he founded the game, but it would be too little to say that he was simply one amongst many founders. His knowledge of the Rugby game, his reputation as a dashing cricketer, his position for one crucial year as secretary of the Melbourne Cricket Club, his zeal as a publicist of both the pleasures and morality of sport and his ability as a footballer all helped to set football in orbit. If Australian football's distinctive qualities can be seen by 1880 as the outcome of a long chain of inventions and ideas and tactics, Tom Wills himself should be seen as the most active proponent of the first in the chain of ideas: that football should be regularly played in Melbourne and that the English codes of football should be reshaped to meet new conditions. Even in this idea he was not alone. The headmasters of St Kilda and Melbourne Grammar Schools and Scotch College were also sympathetic to football, fostering it in their schools in 1858, sometimes in collaboration with Wills, for we know that he was one of the two umpires in the famous schools' match in the Richmond paddock. Wills, however, went further than any headmaster. He captained many of the early matches and, by his ingenuity and advocacy, helped steer football in new directions. Wills made this main contribution to football between 1858 and 1860.

In those experimental years we cannot be sure of the sequence of innovations and compromises which quickly made the game different to English football, but there can be little doubt that Tom Wills' fertile mind was devising new ways of defeating his opponents and that some of those ways were eventually to become part of the game. In July 1860, in the third year of football, he captained Richmond on a cramped pitch actually marked out by flags on the turf of the Richmond cricket ground. After his unbeaten Melbourne opponents had gained the initiative, Wills devised what is probably the first recorded example of position play in the modern manner. According to the sporting magazine *Bell's Life*, he prepared to trick his white-capped opponents by temporarily abandoning the congested play and the constant scrummages: 'Mr. Wills, their indefatigable and untiring captain, then tried a *coup de main*, and placing his men right down to the goal, by this means succeeded in getting the ball safely landed between the posts.' How many of the tricks and stratagems of the first years came from this clever tactician we will never know.

Suddenly Tom Wills' link with football was broken and, when later renewed, would never again be as strong. Early in 1861 he left Victoria, and with his father, Horatio Wills, went by sea to Brisbane. In February they began a long, slow overland trek with

Alfred Tappy the Melbourne tailor advertised himself as a football outfitter in 1876. More and more tradesmen catered for the booming sport of football.

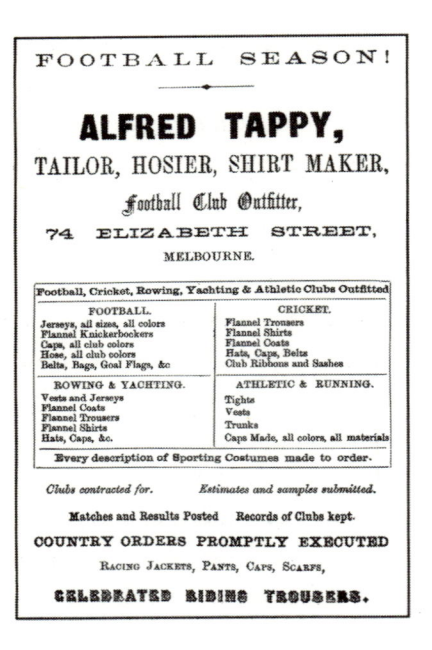

> **FOOTBALL SEASON!**
>
> **ALFRED TAPPY,**
> TAILOR, HOSIER, SHIRT MAKER,
> Football Club Outfitter,
> 74 ELIZABETH STREET,
> MELBOURNE.
>
> Football, Cricket, Rowing, Yachting & Athletic Clubs Outfitted
>
> | FOOTBALL. | CRICKET. |
> |---|---|
> | Jerseys, all sizes, all colors | Flannel Trousers |
> | Flannel Knickerbockers | Flannel Shirts |
> | Caps, all club colors | Flannel Coats |
> | Hose, all club colors | Hats, Caps, Belts |
> | Belts, Bags, Goal Flags, &c | Club Ribbons and Sashes |
>
> | ROWING & YACHTING. | ATHLETIC & RUNNING. |
> |---|---|
> | Vests and Jerseys | Tights |
> | Flannel Coats | Vests |
> | Flannel Trousers | Trunks |
> | Flannel Shirts | Caps Made, all colors, all materials |
> | Hats, Caps, &c. | |
>
> Every description of Sporting Costumes made to order.
>
> Clubs contracted for. Estimates and samples submitted.
> Matches and Results Posted Records of Clubs kept.
> **COUNTRY ORDERS PROMPTLY EXECUTED**
> Racing Jackets, Pants, Caps, Scarfs,
> **CELEBRATED RIDING TROUSERS.**

thousands of sheep to a new pastoral run – about 250 miles west of Rockhampton – that his father had bought. Tom Wills spent the whole of the 1861 football season travelling with flocks. At the new station called Cullinlaringo, the Wills family and their employees began to build huts and stockyards as well as stores for the supplies coming by bullock drays and wagons. On 17 October 1861, Aboriginals attacked the camp killing nineteen men, women and children. Horatio Wills was one of those killed. Tom Wills had the good fortune to be away from the camp on the day of the slaughter, for he had just set out for Brisbane with bullock teams to buy more supplies.

Tom Wills remained in the district managing the sheep station, and eventually returned to Victoria where he resumed his sporting career in the summer of 1863–64, playing cricket for Richmond and Victoria and football mostly for Geelong. His influence on football was now intermittent and he was not a member of the committee which substantially revised football's rules in 1866. Certainly he had been a vehement supporter in May 1865 of the idea that Australian football should adopt the crossbar of the Rugby goalposts, but his proposal for a crossbar 8 feet above the ground was narrowly defeated. In the early 1870s he was still captain of Geelong, but when he played his last game of football is not certain. Two of his younger brothers, Horace and Egbert, who were schoolboys at Bonn in Germany at the time of the Queensland massacre, also became well known in the Geelong football team, and in the sparse descriptions of several later Geelong matches it is not always clear whether Tom or his younger brothers were playing. In 1876, living near Geelong, Tom Wills was the donor of a fine challenge cup for the best football team in Geelong and Ballarat and districts. Curiously, the shilling magazine *The Footballer*, reporting his generous gift, referred to him simply as 'the veteran cricketer'. His fame as a footballer had ebbed.

In cricket his fame did not diminish. He had spent part of the spring and summer of 1866–67 in Edenhope in western Victoria, coaching a team of Aboriginal cricketers. He escorted them to the Melbourne Cricket Ground on Boxing Day of 1866, where a crowd of some 10,000 people watched them play, and then he led them on a cricket tour of New South Wales. He did not accompany them on their cricket tour of England in 1868, but their victory in fourteen of their games partly reflected his skill as a coach of bowling and batting. When they finally returned from England in 1869 and played a three-day match at the Melbourne Cricket Ground, Wills was in the Victorian team against which they played. A portrait painted of him by William Handcock in 1870 shows him in his cricketing creams, a red cap shading his bearded poker face, and a slight air of weariness about him. When Adam Lindsay Gordon in 1865 wrote his long poem 'Ye Wearie Wayfarer', he wrote of Wills the cricketer:

> *If you hold the willow, a shooter from Wills*
> *May transform you into a hopper,*
> *And the football meadow is rife with spills,*
> *If you feel disposed for a cropper.*

Gordon, at one time Australia's most popular poet, did not have to explain who Wills was. Every Victorian reader interested in cricket knew that a fast low ball from Tommy Wills would rattle their ankles. In all the land perhaps no cricketer was held in more affection by the crowd, and he was almost thirty-eight when his name was widely discussed as a possible player against W G Grace's visiting English team. By then, alas, a certain unreliability on and off the field virtually debarred him. Hundreds of cricket followers in Melbourne had hoped that he would be selected, and *The Australasian Sketcher* movingly wrote in November 1873 of the loyalty he still commanded. In that era when the title of Mister was courteously extended to most men who batted or rowed, he was one of the few Victorian sportsmen to be known widely not by his surname but his Christian name. He was 'Tommy'. Everyone knew who Tommy was.

Wills in his last years was in debt. He had no job. He was drinking heavily. Many of his old friends had retreated. In 1878, in his early forties, he was still fit enough to play games of cricket for South Melbourne, the suburb in which he was temporarily living, and to umpire senior games of football at the ground near the lake. The last of the large sheaf of letters he wrote to newspapers in the course of his sporting life was an argumentative defence of his own umpiring. It was a Saturday football match between Albert Park and Carlton, and was ended early by the onrush of darkness.

We have an insight into Wills' last days, because they were reconstructed by a psychiatrist, Greg de Moore. On the morning of Saturday, 1 May 1880, Wills was admitted to the Melbourne Hospital in Lonsdale Street; his hand was trembling, he was suffering from hallucinations, and he was becoming violent. That same afternoon he escaped from the hospital and paid his fare to travel in the slow horse-drawn coach to his home in Heidelberg, close to the Old England Hotel. On the following day he snatched a pair of scissors and stabbed himself to death. He was aged forty-four.

He was buried on the hill top at Heidelberg, overlooking that green valley which, eight years later, Streeton and Roberts and the painters of the Heidelberg School would depict in summer colours. A third generation Australian – then a rarity – he had often expressed in football and cricket a version of the national feeling which these artists were to express with paint, and he had been quietly proud that the football game he did so much to shape was often called 'the national game'. Indeed, one of Streeton's famous paintings depicts a football match in a park. Painted in 1889, and clearly depicting the Australian brand of football, it is labelled 'The National Game'.

Tom's grave, eventually falling into neglect, was restored in modern times by the Melbourne Cricket Club and by public subscription. At the foot of the grave the text 'O Lord God Thou Knowest' was inscribed in subtle reference to the disturbed mind and emotions of his last year. His exploits on the green grass of the Yarra Park were elegantly praised in bold gold letters:

FOUNDER OF AUSTRALIAN FOOTBALL
AND CHAMPION CRICKETER OF HIS TIME

The day of his birth – and death too – was carved on the grey marble slab on his grave, but the reference to his achievements in football was not quite right.

Should the ghost of Tom Wills ever visit the Yarra Park he would be intrigued to see the huge stadium enclosing the ground on which he had often played cricket, and delighted to know that football is now played there almost as much as cricket. Several hundred yards to the north he would be cheered, or sobered, to see a hotel still standing on the site of Bryant's Hotel, where a football

Portrait of T W Wills.
'He very sensibly advised us to work out a game of our own'
– H C A Harrison, reminiscing about T W Wills in his autobiography,
The Story of an Athlete, *1923.*

was provided in 1858 for the first footballers and where a year later, in one of the hotel's rooms, Wills chaired the meeting which drafted the very first rules of a game that was already different from every other kind of football. The ghost of Tom Wills would also be stirred to see, outside the stadium, the sloping ground – still unfenced – where he umpired and played many of the early football matches; and his eyes would dart from the avenues of elms which now cross that first football ground to the ancient redgum trees with the Aboriginal scars on the white trunks and the now feeble branches into which he had sometimes kicked a football in those first years of the national game.

Acknowledgements and Sources

The National Australian Football Council, eager to know how Australian football began and curious about the prevailing view that it was an offshoot of Gaelic football, commissioned the original edition of this book. The Commonwealth Bank financed the research and some of the publishing expenses, especially the gathering of illustrations. The general manager of the National Australian Football Council, E W Biggs, and Dr Colin Davey were strong supporters of the project. Dr Robert Hess wrote for that Council a fine draft report on the opening years of football. I also thank those who read chapters of the manuscript and offered comments or pointed to further evidence. I especially thank Dr Ian F Jobling of the University of Queensland, Don Gibb and Ian Meikle of the Rusden Campus of Victoria College, Professor John Molony of the Australian National University, and the Melbourne Cricket Club's honorary librarian, Rex Harcourt, and his colleague Norman Sowden.

The finding of illustrations, and the research on Chapter 7 – football outside Victoria – was mainly the work of Rob Hess: it was he who discovered that football as a regular sport commenced much earlier in Hobart than was previously realised. I pay tribute to his research skills. I am also grateful to Horrie Webber who gave me accounts of various matches reported in Melbourne newspapers in the 1860s, as well as his own shrewd interpretation of those reports. He also explained to me how the manufacture of footballs in England moved from the farmyard or cottage to the precision of city factories.

I relied much on the newspaper reports of early football matches.

Often they are brief and hard to interpret. And yet they often tell us more than the official rules, which were few and not always clear. There is no alternative but to read about the early games and try to deduce from the flimsiest of clues how football was played. I am sure that with ingenuity later generations will find out much more than we know about the way in which football was usually played in 1858, 1868 and 1878.

I gained much from reading descriptions of early football matches in Melbourne, especially in *Bell's Life in Victoria*, and *The Argus* and *The Australasian* of Melbourne. Another vital source is the shilling magazine, *The Footballer: An Annual Record of Football in Victoria and the Australian Colonies*, edited by Thomas Power of the Carlton Football Club and published by Henriques & Co. of Melbourne, from 1875 onwards.

Of the writings on the early history of Australian football, several are invaluable. Gavan Daws, while an undergraduate at Melbourne University in 1954, wrote a talented research essay on the first half-dozen years of football in Victoria. Called 'The Origins of Australian Rules Football' and subsequently quoted by many historians, it is housed in the library of the History Department, Medley Building, University of Melbourne. W F Mandle wrote a pathfinding article for *Historical Studies*, April 1973, on 'Games people played: cricket and football in England & Victoria in the late nineteenth century'. It is still an outstanding contribution. Ian Turner did more than anybody in Melbourne in the 1970s to quicken interest in the history of football but he died before he could do full justice to his knowledge. His article 'Work and Play in Victorian Victoria' is in the *Victorian Historical Journal* of February 1978. His book was completed by Leonie Sandercock after his death and published in their joint names as *Up Where Cazaly? The Greatest Australian Game* (Granada, 1981). C C Mulle's *History of Australian Rules Football 1858 to 1958* (Horticultural Press, Carlton, 1959) was a brave early work.

An important source for the late 1850s and the 1860s is A Mancini and G M Hibbins, *Running with the Ball: Football's Foster Father* (Lynedoch Publications, 1987). Besides reprinting with painstaking editorial notes the autobiography of H C A Harrison, it includes a valuable preface of fifty pages on early steps in the growth of the game. The book included new material, especially on the late 1850s. Rob Hess completed in 1987 a typescript containing valuable material on the opening years of football and the cultural background in England and Australia. Entitled 'The Origins of Australian Rules Football', it is housed at the National Australian Football Council in Jolimont, Victoria.

Some early accounts of football matches are printed word for word in Garrie Hutchinson's fascinating *The Great Australian Book of Football Stories* (Currey O'Neil, 1983). A mine of information is in Graeme Atkinson's *Everything You've Ever Wanted to Know About Australian Rules Football* ... (Five Mile Press, 1982).

Thomas Wills, a strong sponsor and player of Australian football, deserves a biography, though whether there is enough material for a book I cannot tell. His cricketing episode with the Aboriginals is covered by D J Mulvaney in *Cricket Walkabout: The Australian Aboriginal Cricketers on Tour 1867–68* (Melbourne University Press, 1967). An enlarged and revised edition was recently published in 1988 by Macmillan, with Rex Harcourt as joint author. A long chronicle of Tom Wills' sporting career is in *The Australasian*, 8 May 1868. Wills' term as a Richmond cricketer is described in Frank Tyson's *The History of the Richmond Cricket Club* (East Melbourne, 1987).

On schools' football, and the background to the schools, useful sources include J B Cooper, *The History of St Kilda* (Melbourne, 1931) for the local grammar school; Mancini and Hibbins, *Running with the Ball*, ch. 2; P W Musgrove, 'From Brown to Bunter' in *Melbourne Studies in Education 1982* (Melbourne University Press, 1983) pp. 190–4; I V Hansen, *Nor Free Nor Secular* (Oxford University Press, 1971) ch. 1; and R Goodman, *The Church in Victoria during the Episcopate of the Right Reverend Charles Perry* (Seeley, London, 1892) pp. 306–8, where Brumby's career is outlined.

My observation on the dry winter in Melbourne in 1858 came from an analysis of Melbourne's monthly rainfall, as set out in *Results of Rainfall Observations Made in Victoria During 1840–1910* (Commonwealth Bureau of Meteorology, Melbourne, 1911) p. xvi. The state of the surface and the position of the gum trees on the football field in the Richmond Paddock are mentioned in frequent newspaper descriptions of football matches. Harrison's letter of complaint about the trees, written to the Lord

Mayor on 22 June 1868, is in the Melbourne City Council file, VPRS 3181, Unit 733, in the Public Records Office of Victoria at Laverton. For the East Melbourne ground the best source is A E Clarke's *East Melbourne Cricket Club: Its History 1860 to 1910: Jubilee Year* (Geo. Robertson, Melbourne, 1910) and for the Melbourne Cricket Ground it is Keith Dunstan's *The Paddock that Grew* (Cassell, 1962).

Researchers will find stimulus in the papers given to the Sporting Traditions Conference by B O'Dwyer on 'The Shaping of Victorian Rules Football' (1987) and E Grow on 'Nineteenth Century Football and the Melbourne Press' (1986).

On early football, played outside Melbourne and Geelong, an indispensable source is the 1982 typescript compiled by Wayne Hankin who reproduces the newspaper accounts of decade after decade of football in Ballarat. Entitled 'Football in Ballarat', it is housed in the Melbourne Cricket Club library. Dr Peter Yule, the historian of Warrnambool, kindly gave me *Examiner* accounts of matches played in 1861 and 1868 in southwestern Victoria. On football in Bendigo, I am indebted to Mr C J Michelsen, and to R J Burton and Michele Matthews of the Bendigo City municipality. Some of the early matches between metropolitan clubs and provincial and upcountry teams were reported in the weekly *Australasian*.

On the rise of football outside Victoria, possibly the best single source of information is the annual *Footballer*, first published in 1875. So far as I can judge, it has rarely been used by historians of football. On the rise of Australian football in New Zealand, South Australia and New South Wales in the late 1870s and early 1880s, the *Footballer* contains valuable detail. *The Mercury* supplied evidence on football in Hobart in the years 1866–1871, *The Cornwall Chronicle* on football in Launceston in 1875–1877, *The South Australian Register* on Adelaide football in the months April, May and June of 1860, 1861 and 1862.

Books covering the rise of football outside Victoria include Bernard Whimpress, *The South Australian Football Story* (Adelaide, 1983); Ken Pinchin, *A Century of Tasmanian Football 1879–1979* (Launceston, 1979); and G Christian, J Lee and B Messenger, *The Footballers: A History of Football in Western Australia* (Perth, 1985). R E N Twopeny, a promoter and player of football in South Australia in the 1870s, eulogises Australian football in his *Town Life in Australia* (Penguin Books, 1973, pp. 206–9) originally published in 1883. G Davison discusses Twopeny's life and briefly his football career in *Historical Studies*, October 1974. A paper by M P Sharp, 'Australian football in Sydney before 1914', was published in *Sporting Tradition: The Journal of the Australian Society for Sports History*, vol. 4, Nov. 1987. *The Oxford Companion to Sports and Games*, p. 894, makes the claim that Rugby began in New Zealand at the South Island town of Nelson, where Australian football already had a precarious footing. The rise of football outside Victoria is wide open to research.

On the history of other codes of football I have consulted a miscellany of books and articles. Successive editions of *Encyclopaedia Britannica*, especially from 1909–11, are valuable on the history of the American, Association (soccer) and Rugby codes of football. *The Oxford Companion to Sports and Games*, edited by John Arlott (Oxford University Press, 1975) offers in its 1,143 pages much about the various codes of football. English football in the 1840s and 1850s and the shaping of the rules is discussed in Percy M Young, *A History of British Football* (Arrow Books, 1973), especially chapters 7 and 8. England's influence on the development of sports is analysed cogently in Claudio Veliz, 'A World Made in England' in *Quadrant*, no. 187, March 1983, pp. 8–19. A stimulating article on American football is 'Football in America: A Study in Culture Diffusion', by David Riesman and Reuel Denney, *American Quarterly*, 1951, pp. 309–25.

There is an official history of the Gaelic Athletic Association, Marcus de Burca's *The GAA: A History* (published by Cumann Lutchleas Gael, Dublin, 1980). W F Mandle discusses the rise of the Gaelic game in the 1880s and 1890s in a chapter of a book of which he was co-editor along with O MacDonough and Pauric Travers, *Irish Culture and Popular Nationalism, 1750–1950* (Macmillan, London, 1983). John Hutchinson discusses the Gaelic Athletic Association in *The Dynamics of Cultural Nationalism* (Allen & Unwin, London, 1987) and he notes on p. 290 its 'antagonism to British sports and those who played them'. The popularity of hurling in Irish districts in Victoria, and its survival as a competitor of football in wintertime, can be gleaned from *The Footballer* of 1877 when reporting on Kyneton, and of 1881 when reporting on Warrnambool district. The Gaelic rules of 1889, included in this book, come from the booklet, *Gaelic Athletic Association: Constitution and Rules – Official Copy, 1889* (J Macnamara, steam printer, Limerick). A diagram of field placements in the Gaelic game is in the same booklet.

On Aboriginal football I consulted N W Thomas, *Natives of Australia* (Constable, 1906) pp. 138–9 and R Brough Smyth, *The Aborigines of Victoria* (Govt Printer, 1878, vol. 1, p. 176).

The Melbourne Cricket Club deserves praise for building up a fine library on the history of sport: I used it often and always with pleasure.

G B, 1990

Sources for the Second Edition
For the discovery that additional football matches were played on the premier cricket ground in the years 1859–69, see Alf Batchelder, 'The First Football Matches on the Melbourne Cricket Ground', *The Yorker*, published by Melbourne Cricket Club Library, no. 18, July 1998. For the summary of the 1881 season and the rough and ready way in which a premiership was unofficially awarded, see Pindar's essay in Thomas P Power, ed., *The Footballer: An Annual Record of Football in Victoria*, Melbourne, 1882. For a summary of Thurgood's background and career, see the article 'Thurgood', by John H Reeves, in *The Australian Dictionary of Biography*, vol. 12. (Melbourne University Press, 1990).

In the last ten years many useful books have appeared on the history of Australian football. I gained new information or insights from Robert Pascoe, *The Winter Game: Over 100 Years of Australian Football* (Mandarin, 1996); the book edited by Rob Hess and Bob Stewart, *More Than a Game: An Unauthorised History of Australian Rules Football* (Melbourne University Press, 1998), in which Chapter 2 by Robin Grow and Chapter 3 by Rob Hess, covering football in the years 1877 to 1914, are relevant to my work; Richard Stremski's *Kill for Collingwood* (Allen & Unwin, 1986); and the massive compendium edited by John Ross and Garrie Hutchinson, *100 Years of Australian Football* (Penguin Books, 1996) including an essay by Gillian Hibbins on the British background of the early Melbourne shapers of the game.

On the Gaelic and Aboriginal games and the associated theories, I am also indebted to two new works. The *1999 AFL Heroes: Twelve of Our Deadly Brothers* (ATSIC and the AFL, 1999) is a calendar and booklet with a brief essay outlining the theory that Aborigines exercised a strong influence on the origins of the game. The essay is entitled 'Aussie Rules: Our Claim to the Game'. A book that shows in massive detail the successive rules of the two main games of the Gaelic Athletic Association is Joseph F Lennon, *Towards a Philosophy for Legislation in Gaelic Games* (Northern Recreation Consultants, Gormanstown, Ireland, 1997). The title printed on the cover is 'The Playing Rules of Football and Hurling 1885–1995'. Kindly provided by the author, this massive compilation is the source of the 1884 Gaelic rules set out in Appendix Two.

On football in 1896 and 1897, when the rules were about to change substantially and the new League was emerging, I used the following Melbourne newspapers at the State Library of Victoria: *The Weekly Times*, *The Argus* and *The Age*.

I thank Pearl Longden for typing the manuscript, Thomas Deverall for the design of this edition, and Sophy Williams and Chris Feik for supervising this project.

G B, March 2003

Sources for the Third Edition

In the Preface, the new assessments of the theory that the game was Aboriginal in origin have been made by Greg de Moore, *Tom Wills: His Spectacular Rise and Tragic Fall* (Allen & Unwin, 2008, especially page 284) and by Gillian Hibbins, *Sport and Racing in Colonial Melbourne. The Cousins and Me: Colden Harrison, Tom Wills and William Hammersley* (Lynedoch Publications, 2007, especially page 404). In Chapter 11, the psychiatrist who reconstructed Wills' last days is Greg de Moore. On Aborigines playing casually in country football – but not senior football – in the 1860s, I am grateful to Roy Hay of Geelong for new information.

G B, June 2010

Early Rules of Football

In bringing together formal rules of Australian football during key years of the game's infancy, there are clear benefits. We can easily see how often the rules were substantially altered. We also see that many important matters were not mentioned in the rules.

These rules should not be interpreted too literally. Some rules were not as rigorously enforced as others, especially in the era when the two captains had to agree on which specific infringement should be penalised during the course of a match. In the early era several unwritten rules were influential. The unwritten rules or conventions were more numerous than the written rules, though not quite so important in their total effect on the game.

The rules printed below do not embody all the changes in rules in the game's early years. No written rules for the opening year of regular football, 1858, have yet been found. The rules of May 1859 and May 1860 are set out in full but other alterations and experiments came and went in the space of that intervening year; and some of the 1860 changes were challenged during that year. The important rewriting of the rules in 1866 embodied some changes that had arrived earlier. Likewise, certain rules were altered before the major review of the rules undertaken in 1874.

This is the first time that most of these rules have been reprinted since the nineteenth century. The first two sets of rules have been kindly made available by the Melbourne Cricket Club; they are in handwriting. The 1884 Gaelic rules and the first nationwide Australian rules of 1906 have been added to this edition.

Rules of the Melbourne Football Club, May 1859

§

I

The distance between the Goals and the Goal Posts shall be decided upon by the Captains of the sides playing.

II

The Captains on each side shall toss for choice of Goal; the side losing the toss has the Kick off from the centre point between the Goals.

III

A Goal must be Kicked fairly between the posts, without touching either of them, or a portion of the person of any player on either side.

IV

The game shall be played within a space of not more than 200 yards wide, the same to be measured equally on each side of a line drawn through the centres of the two Goals; and two posts to be call the 'Kick Off' posts shall be erected at a distance of 20 yards on each side of the Goal posts at both ends, and in a straight line with them.

V

In case the Ball is kicked behind Goal, any one of the side behind whose Goal it is kicked may bring it 20 yards in front of any portion of the space between the 'Kick off' posts, and shall kick it as nearly as possible in a line with the opposite Goal.

VI

Any player catching the Ball *directly* from the foot may call 'mark'. He then has a free kick; no player from the opposite side being allowed to come *inside* the spot marked.

VII

Tripping and pushing are both allowed (but no hacking) when any player is in rapid motion or in possession of the Ball, except in the case provided for in Rule VI.

VII

The Ball may be taken in hand *only* when caught from the foot, or on the hop. In no case shall it be *lifted* from the ground.

IX

When a Ball goes out of bounds (the same being indicated by a row of posts) it shall be brought back to the point where it crossed the boundary-line, and thrown in at right angles with that line.

X

The Ball, while *in play*, may under no circumstances be thrown.

Melbourne: Rules of Football
§

Agreed to at a meeting of clubs held on May 28th 1860.

I

The distance between the Goals and the Goal posts shall be decided upon by the Captains of the sides Playing.

II

The Captains on each side shall toss for choice of goal; the side losing the toss has the kick-off from the centre point between the Goals.

III

A Goal must be kicked fairly between the posts without touching either of them, or any portion of the person of one of the opposite side. In case of the Ball being forced between the Goal Posts in a scrimmage, a Goal shall be awarded.

IV

The Game shall be played within a space of not more than 200 yards wide, the same to be measured equally on each side of a line drawn through the centres of the two Goals; and two posts, to be called the 'Kick off' posts, shall be erected at a distance of 20 yards on each side of the Goal Posts at both ends, and in a straight line with them.

V

In case the Ball is kicked behind Goal, any one of the side behind whose Goal it is kicked may bring it 20 yards in front of any portion of the space between the 'Kick off' posts, and shall kick it as nearly as possible in a line with the opposite Goal.

VI

Any Player catching the Ball *directly* from the foot may call 'mark'. He then has a free kick; no player from the opposite side being allowed to come *inside* the spot marked.

VII

Tripping, holding and hacking are strictly prohibited. Pushing with the hands or body is allowed when any Player is in rapid motion, or in possession of the Ball, except in the case provided for in Rule VI.

VIII

The Ball may not be lifted from the ground under any circumstances, or taken in hand except as provided for in Rule VI (catch from the foot) or when on the first hop. It shall not be run with in any case.

IX

When a Ball goes out of bounds (the same being indicated by a row of posts) it shall be brought back to the point where it Crossed the boundary-line, and thrown in at right angles with that line.

V

The Ball, while *in Play*, may under no circumstances be thrown.

XI

In case of deliberate infringement of any of the above Rules by either side, the Captain of the opposite side may claim that any one of his party may have a free kick from the place where the breach of Rules was made; the two Captains in all cases, save where Umpires are appointed, to be the sole judges of infringements.

Victorian Rules, 1866

§

Drafted by delegates of the Carlton, Melbourne, Royal Park and South Yarra clubs at the Freemasons' Hotel, Melbourne, 8 May 1866.

1. The distance between the goals shall not be more than 200 yards; and the width of playing space, to be measured equally on each side of a line drawn through the centre of the goals, not more than 150 yards. The goal posts shall be seven yards apart, of unlimited height.
2. The captains of each side shall toss for choice of goal; the side losing the toss, or a goal, has a kick-off from the centre point between the goals. After a goal is kicked the sides shall change ends.
3. A goal must be kicked fairly between the posts without touching either of them, or any portion of the person of one of the opposite side. In case

of the ball being forced (except with the hand or arms) between the goal posts in a scrummage, a goal shall be awarded.

4. Two posts, to be called the 'kick-off' posts, shall be erected at a distance of 20 yards on each side of the goal posts, and in a straight line with them.

5. In case the ball is kicked behind Goal, any one of the side behind whose Goal it is kicked may bring it 20 yards in front of any portion of the space between the 'kick-off' posts, and shall kick it towards the opposite Goal.

6. Any Player catching the Ball directly from the foot or leg may call 'Mark'; he then has a free kick from any spot in a line with his mark and the centre of his opponent's goal posts; no player being allowed to come inside the spot marked, or within five yards in any other direction.

7. Tripping and hacking are strictly prohibited. Pushing with the hands or body is allowed when any player is in rapid motion. Holding is only allowed while a player has the ball in hand, except in the case provided in Rule 6.

8. The ball may be taken in hand at any time, but not carried further than is necessary for a kick, and no player shall run with the ball unless he strikes it against the ground in every five or six yards.

9. When a ball goes out of bounds (the same being indicated by a row of posts), it shall be brought back to the point where it crossed the boundary-line, and thrown in at right angles with that line.

10. The ball, while in play, may, under no circumstances, be thrown.

11. In case of deliberate infringement of any of the above rules the captain of the opposite side may claim that any one of his party may have a free-kick from the place where the breach of rule was made.

12. Before the commencement of a match each side shall appoint an umpire, and they shall be the sole judges of goals and breaches of rules. The nearest umpire shall be appealed to in every case of dispute.

Victorian Rules of Football, 1874

§

Revised at a meeting held at Nissen's Café, Melbourne on 12 May 1874, when delegates attended from the Albert Park, Carlton, Geelong, Melbourne, North Melbourne, and St Kilda clubs.

1. The distance between the Goals shall not be more than 200 yards; and the width of playing space (to be measured equally on each side of the line drawn through the centres of the Goals) not more than 150 yards. The Goal Posts shall be seven yards apart, of unlimited height.

2. The Captains on each side shall toss for choice of Goal, the side losing the toss, or a Goal, has the kick off from the centre point between the Goals. When half the time arranged for play has expired, the sides shall change ends, and the ball be thrown in the air by the Umpire in the centre of the ground.

3. A Goal must be kicked by one of the side playing for the Goal between the posts, without touching either of them or any player after being kicked.

4. Two posts, to be called the 'kick-off' posts, shall be erected at a distance of 20 yards on each side of the Goal Posts, and in a straight line with them.

5. In case the ball is kicked behind Goal, within the 'kick-off' posts, any one of the side behind whose Goal it is kicked may bring it 20 yards in front of any portion of the space between the 'kick-off' posts, and shall kick it towards the opposite Goal.

6. Any player catching the Ball directly from the foot or leg, on or below the knee of another Player, may call 'Mark'; he then has a free kick from any spot in a line with his mark and the centre of his opponent's Goal Posts; no player being allowed to come inside the spot marked, or within five yards in any other direction.

7. The Ball may be taken in hand at any time, but not carried further than is necessary for a kick, and no player shall run with the Ball unless he strikes it against the ground in every five or six yards. In the event of a player, with the Ball in hand, trying to pass an adversary and being held by him, he shall at once drop the Ball, which shall not be again taken in hand by any player till after it has been kicked.

8. Tripping, Hacking and Rabbiting are prohibited. Pushing with the hands or body is allowed only when any player is in rapid motion. Holding is allowed while a player has the Ball in hand, except in the cases provided for in rules 5 and 6.

9. When the Ball goes out of Bounds (the same being indicated by a row

of posts), it shall be brought back to the point where it crossed the Boundary-line, and thrown in at right angles with that line, but shall not be playable until after it touches the ground within Bounds.

10. The Ball, while in play, may under no circumstances be thrown.

11. In case of infringement of any of the above Rules, any player of the opposite side may claim that any one of his party may have a free kick from the place where the breach of Rule was made. The Umpire's decision shall in every case be final, and the Clubs disputing the same shall lose the match.

12. Before the commencement of a match each side shall appoint an Umpire, and they shall be the sole Judges of Goals and of cases of the ball going behind Goal. A Field Umpire shall also be appointed, who shall decide all other matters, and may appeal to the Goal Umpire.

13. No player shall play with more than one Club during one season. For the purposes of this rule, schools be not considered clubs.

Definitions:

— A drop kick or drop is made by letting the Ball drop from your hands on to the ground, and kicking it the very instant it rises.

— A place kick or place is kicking the Ball after it has been placed on the ground.

— A punt consists in letting the Ball fall from your hands, and kicking it before it touches the ground.

— A scrummage commences when the Ball is on the ground, and all who have closed round on their respective sides begin kicking at it.

— Rabbiting is one player stooping down so as to cause another to fall by placing his body below the other's hips.

First Rules of the Victorian Football Association, 1877

§

1. The distance between the goals should not be more than 200 yards, and the width of playing space to be measured equally on each side of a line drawn through the centre of the goals not more than 150 yards. The goal posts shall be seven yards apart; of not less than 12ft in height. The ball to be used shall be the No. 2 size Rugby (26in in circumference).

2. The captains of each side shall toss for choice of goal. The side losing the toss or goal has the kick-off from the centre-point between the goal. When half the time arranged for play has expired, the players shall change ends, and the ball be thrown in the air by the field umpire in the centre of the ground.

3. A goal must be kicked by one of the side playing for goal between the posts, without touching either of them (flags excepted), or any player after being kicked. Should any of the spectators standing between the goal-posts interfere with or stop the progress of the ball going through, a goal shall be scored.

4. Two posts, to be called the 'kick-off posts', shall be erected at a distance of twenty yards on each side of the goal-posts in a straight line with them.

5. In case the ball is kicked behind goal by one of the opposite side within the kick-off posts, any one of the side behind whose goal it is kicked may bring it ten yards in front of any portion of the space between the kick-off posts, and shall kick it towards the opposite goal.

6. Any player catching the ball directly from the foot or leg on or below the knee of another player may call 'mark'. He then has a free kick from any spot behind and in a line with his mark and the centre of his opponents' goal-posts, no player being allowed to come inside the spot marked, or within five yards in any other direction.

7. The ball may be taken in hand at any time, but not carried further than is necessary for a kick, unless the player strikes it against the ground every five or six yards. In the event of a player with the ball in hand trying to pass an adversary, and being held by him, he must at once drop the ball.

8. Tripping, hacking, rabbiting, and slinging are prohibited; pushing with the hands or body is allowed only when a player is in rapid motion within five or six yards of the ball. Holding a player is allowed only while such player has the ball in hand, except in cases provided for in Rules 5, 6 and 7.

9. When the ball goes out of bounds it shall be brought back to the spot where it crossed the boundary line, and thrown in by the umpire at right angles with that line, but shall not be playable until after it touches the ground within bounds.

10. The ball while in play may, under no circumstances, be thrown or handed to a player.

11. In case of infringement of any of the above rules, any player of the opposite side may claim a free kick from the place where the breach of the rule was made, the player nearest the place of infringement being the only one entitled to the kick.

12. Before the commencement of a match, each side shall appoint an umpire who shall be the sole judge of goals and of cases of the ball going behind goal. A field umpire shall also be appointed, who shall decide in all other matters, and may appeal to the goal umpire.

13. The field umpire on being appealed to may either award a 'free-kick', call 'play on', or stop the play and throw the ball in the air, and stop all attempts at scrimmages. In every case his decision shall be final, and the club disputing same shall lose the match. But in the event of an umpire refusing to decide upon any matter in dispute, clubs may, according to Rule 8 of the Association, appeal to that body, whose decision shall be final.

14. No one wearing projecting nails, iron plates, or gutta percha on any part of his boots or shoes shall be allowed to play in a match.

15. No player shall play with more than one club during one season, except he permanently change his residence from town to country, or vice versa. For the purpose of this rule, schools or universities shall not be considered clubs. In the event of a club disbanding, its members may be at liberty to play with any other club, with the consent of the Association.

16. None of the above laws shall be altered or rescinded, nor shall any rule be added during a season, nor shall any rule be repealed, altered, amended, or adopted without the concurrence of a majority of the Association at a meeting specially called for that purpose.

South Australian Rules, 1877

§

1. The distance between the Goals shall not be more than 200 yards and not less than 180 yards; and the width of playing space (to be measured equally on each side of the line drawn through the centres of the Goals) not more than 150 yards and not less than 120 yards. The Goal posts shall be seven yards apart, of unlimited height.

2. The Captains on each side shall toss for choice of Goal; the side losing the toss or a Goal, has the kick-off from the centre point between the Goals. When half the time arranged for play has expired, the sides shall change ends, and the ball be thrown in the air by the Umpire in the centre of the ground.

3. A Goal must be kicked by one of the side playing for the Goal between the posts, without touching either of them or any player after being kicked.

4. Two posts, to be called the 'kick-off' posts, shall be erected at a distance of 20 yards on each side of the Goal Posts, and in a straight line with them.

5. In case the ball is kicked behind the Goal, within the 'kick-off' posts, any one of the side behind whose goal it is kicked may bring it 20 yards in front of any portion of the space between the 'kick-off' posts, and shall kick it towards the opposite Goal.

6. Any player catching the Ball directly from the foot or leg, on or below the knee of another player may call 'Mark'; he then has a free-kick from any spot in a line with his mark and the centre of his opponent's Goal Posts; no player being allowed to come inside the spot marked, or within five yards in any other direction.

7. The Ball may be taken in hand any time, but not carried further than is necessary for a kick, and no player shall run with the Ball unless he strikes it against the ground in every five or six yards. In the event of a player, with the Ball in hand, trying to pass an adversary and being held by him, he shall at once drop the Ball.

8. Tripping, Hacking and Rabbiting are prohibited. Pushing with the hands or body is allowed only when a player is in rapid motion. Holding is allowed while a player has the Ball in hand, except in the cases provided for in rules 5 and 6.

9. When the Ball goes out of bounds (the same being indicated by a row of posts), it shall be brought back to the point where it crossed the Boundary-line, and thrown in at right angles with that line, but shall not be playable until after it touch the ground within bounds.

10. The Ball, while in play, may under no circumstances be thrown.

11. In case of infringement of any of the above Rules, any player of the opposite side may claim that any one of his party may have a free kick from

the place where the breach of Rule was made. The Umpire's decision shall in every case be final, and the Clubs disputing the same shall lose the match.

12. Before the commencement of a match each side shall appoint an Umpire, and they shall be the sole Judges of Goals and of cases of the ball going behind Goal. A Field Umpire shall also be appointed, who shall decide all other matters, and may appeal to the Goal Umpire.

13. When any club shall send a challenge to another to play a match, it shall be understood that each team shall consist of twenty players unless it is otherwise arranged, and in the event of one side arriving on the ground with a less number the opposite side shall not be obliged to reduce the number of its players.

14. The Ball to be used shall be the 'Rugby' or Oval Ball.

The First Rules of Gaelic Football, 1884
§

1. There shall not be less than fourteen or more than twenty-one players aside.

2. There shall be two umpires and a referee. Where the umpires disagree the referee's decision shall be final.

3. The ground shall be at least 120 yards long by 80 in breadth, and properly marked by boundary lines. Boundary lines must be at least five yards from fences.

4. The goal posts shall stand at each end in centre of the goal line. They shall be 15 feet apart, with a cross-bar 8 feet from the ground.

5. The captains of each team shall toss for choice of sides before commencing play, and the players shall stand in two ranks opposite each other until the ball is thrown up, each man holding the hand of one of the other side.

6. Pushing or tripping from behind, holding from behind, or butting with the head, shall be deemed foul, and the players so offending shall be ordered to stand aside, and may not afterwards take part in the match, nor can his side substitute another man.

7. The time of actual play shall be one hour. Sides to be changed only at half time.

8. The match shall be decided by the greater number of goals. If no goal be kicked the match shall be deemed a draw. A goal is when the ball is kicked through the goal posts under the cross-bar.

9. When the ball is kicked over the side line it shall be thrown back by a player of the opposite side to him who kicked it over. If kicked over the goal line by a player whose goal line it is, it shall be thrown back in any direction by a player of the other side. If kicked over the goal line by a player of the other side, the goal keeper whose line it crosses shall have a free kick. No player of the other side to approach nearer 25 yards of him till the ball is kicked.

10. The umpires and referee shall have during the match full power to disqualify any player, or order him to stand aside and discontinue play for any act which they may consider unfair, as set out in Rule 6.

Rules of Gaelic Football, 1889

§

1. The ground for full teams (21 a side) shall be 196 yards long by 140 yards broad, or as near that size as can be got. The ground must be properly marked by boundary lines. Boundary lines to be at least five yards from the fences. Note. – There is no objection to a larger ground, but no ground should be less than 140 yards long by 84 yards broad.

2. There shall not be less than 14, or more than 21 players a-side in regular matches.

3. There shall be two umpires and a referee. Where the umpires disagree the referee's decision shall be final. There shall also be a goal umpire at each end of the ground to watch for goals and points. The referee shall keep the time, and throw up the ball at the commencement of each half time.

4. The goal posts shall stand at each end in centre of goal line. They shall be 21 feet apart with a cross-bar eight feet from the ground. Besides the goal posts, there shall be two upright posts standing in each goal line 21 feet from the goal posts. A goal is won when the ball is driven between the goal posts and under the cross-bar. A point is counted when the ball is driven over the cross-bar, or over the goal line within 21 feet of either goal posts.

5. The captains of the teams shall toss for choice of sides before commencing play, and the players shall stand in two ranks opposite each other

in the centre of the field until the ball is thrown up, each holding the hand of one of the other side.

6. Pushing from behind, butting with the head, tripping and holding, shall be deemed foul, and the player so offending shall be ordered to stand aside for such time as the referee may think fit, and his side cannot substitute another man. The referee may also allow a free kick if he sees reason for it. If a player be hurt and unable to play through any breach of this rule, the referee shall allow his side to take in a man in his place.

7. The time of actual play shall be one hour (unless otherwise arranged), sides to be changed only at half time.

8. When a player drives the ball over the side line it shall be thrown back from the point where it first crossed the line by a player on the opposite side. It may be thrown in any direction, but the thrower must not play it himself until it has been touched by some other player. Neither goal nor point can be scored from a throw in from the side lines, unless the ball be struck by some player after the throw in, and before it crosses the goal line. When the ball is driven over the goal line the goal-keeper shall have a free kick from goal; no player on the opposite side to approach nearer than the 21-yards line till the ball is kicked. No player of the kicker's side to be further out from his own goal line than the centre of the ground until the ball is kicked. If a ball that otherwise would not have crossed the line be driven over the cross-bar, or over any part of the goal line outside the goal posts by a player whose goal line it is, the opposite side shall have a free kick 40 yards out from the goal post.

9. The match shall be decided by the greater number of goals; when no goal is made, or when the goals are even, it shall be decided by the greater number of points.

10. The ball may be struck with the hand. It may be caught when off the ground, and the player so catching it may kick it any way he pleases, but must not carry or throw it. Note: There is nothing in this rule to prevent the player throwing the ball a little in front to allow himself more freedom in kicking it.

11. Where the rules are broken the referee may allow a free kick if he thinks fit. In all free kicks the ball must be kicked from the ground. No player on the opposite side to approach nearer than 14 yards until the ball

is kicked; but if the free kick is allowed nearer than 14 yards off the goal line, the opposite players need not stand behind the line.

12. If the ball strikes a bystander near the side-line, except the referee or umpire, it shall be considered out of play, and must be thrown in as directed in Rule 8. If it occurs at the goal line it also shall be considered out of play and must be kicked from the goal. In the latter case, the referee may allow a point or goal if he considers that the ball would have passed through the goal or point space, but for being stopped.

13. The referee shall have, during the match, full power to disqualify any player, or order him to stand aside and discontinue play, for any act he may consider unfair, as set out in Rule 6, or for vicious play.

14. No nails or iron tips allowed on the boots. Strips of leather fastened on the soles will prevent slipping.

15. The dress for football will be kneebreeches and stocking and shoes or boots.

N.B.: The Rules should be read carefully. The referee of a match should see they are observed to the letter.

The annexed page represents a field of play, with boundary lines, and both teams placed. The figures X representing one team, and the figures O representing the other.

```
            |  H  |
         O  O  O
            X
      O   O   O   O
            X
     XO  XO  XO  XO
     XO  XO  XO  XO
     XO  XO  XO  XO
            O
         X  X  X  X
            O
            X  X  X
            |  H  |
```

During play the teams should keep as nearly as possible in this order. The goal and point-keepers and the four backs should keep firmly in their places, and mind their opponents' forwards, for the rest, every man should mind a man.

Australasian Rules of Football, 1906
§

Drafted at the inaugural meeting of the new football council set up to guide the game in Australia and New Zealand:

1. The distance between the goal posts shall not be more than 200 yards, nor less than 150 yards, and the width of the playing space not more than 150 yards, nor less than 100 yards, to be measured equally on each side of a line drawn through the centre of the goals. The goal posts shall be seven yards apart, of not less than twenty feet in height. Two posts shall be placed at a distance of seven yards, one on each side of the goal posts, and in a straight line with them. The intervening line between such posts shall be called the goal line. The ball to be used shall be not less than $23\,1/2$ nor more than $24\,1/2$ inches in circumference laterally, and not less than $29\,1/2$ nor more than $30\,1/2$ inches longitudinally. The ball to be approved by the field umpire.

2. Matches shall be played with not more than eighteen a side unless where handicaps are conceded. Any team detected during the progress of the game playing more than the number arranged for shall have all the points kicked prior to the detection of the same annulled. The field umpire shall have power at the request of either captain to stop the game and call the players into line at any time for the purpose of counting them. Previous to calling the players into line the field umpire shall notify the time-keepers, who shall make an allowance for the time so taken. In the event of a club commencing play with less than the number arranged for, that club shall be allowed to complete its number at any stage of the game.

3. The captain of each side shall toss for choice of goal. The players shall then take their proper positions on the field, and the game shall be commenced by the field umpire bouncing the ball in the centre of the ground.

When a goal has been obtained, the players shall again take their positions as above, and the ball shall be bounced in the centre.

4. All matches throughout the season shall be played twenty-five minutes each quarter. When one-fourth, one-half, and three-quarters of the time arranged for play have expired, the players shall change ends, and the ball shall be bounced in the centre of the ground as in Law 3. At half-time the players may leave the ground for not more than fifteen minutes. Each club shall appoint a time-keeper whose duty it shall be to keep time, and ring a bell approved of by the controlling body, at the times indicated above. At the first sound of the bell the ball shall be dead, but in the event of a player having marked a ball before the bell has rung, he shall be allowed his kick, and should he obtain a goal or a behind from it, it shall be reckoned, provided no breach of the laws have taken place. A goal or behind obtained from a ball in transit before the bell has rung shall be reckoned. Should the ball be touched after the bell has rung it shall be dead.

5. A goal shall be won when the ball is kicked between the goal posts without touching either of them or any player after being kicked. A behind shall be won when the ball passes between the goal posts after being touched by any player or touches either of the goal posts, or is kicked or forced between the behind post and goal post. Should the ball touch a behind post it shall be out of bounds.

6. The side kicking the greatest number of points shall win the match. A goal shall count six points and a behind one point.

7. When the ball goes out of bounds, it shall be brought back to the spot where it crossed the boundary line, and be there thrown in by the umpire towards the centre of the playing space. Immediately the ball leaves the umpire's hands it shall be in play. Should the ball drop out of bounds from a kick off, a free kick shall be given to the opposite side at the spot where the ball went out of bounds. In case the ball is kicked behind the goal line by one of the opposite side (except when a goal is kicked, in which case the ball is bounced in the centre of the ground), any one of the side behind whose goal is kicked shall kick it off from within any part of the space to be indicated by two lines running parallel in a straight line from the goal posts for a distance of ten yards, and a horizontal line at the end of the said distance, joining the two parallel lines. Such lines be marked white.

Should the ball be kicked off beyond such white lines the ball shall be bounced on the white lines at the spot nearest where such infringement took place. No player of the opposing side shall be allowed to come within ten yards of the kick-off space when the ball is being kicked off from behind.

8. Any player catching the ball directly from a kick of another player not less than ten yards distant shall be allowed a kick in any direction from any spot behind where he caught the ball, no player being allowed to come over that spot, or within ten yards in any other direction. In kicking for goal the player must kick over his mark. Should a goal be obtained from a free kick or mark, it shall be reckoned, notwithstanding any infringement of the above law by an opposing player.

9. Should a player wilfully waste time the field umpire shall instruct the time-keepers to add such time on, and besides award a free kick to the opposing player nearest to the spot where the offence takes place. The offending player or players shall be reported to the controlling body, which shall deal with the matter. Should a player unduly interfere with a man while kicking for goal, he shall be reported to the controlling body.

10. The ball may be taken in hand at any time, but not carried further than is necessary for a kick, unless the player strikes it against the ground at least once in every ten yards. In the event of a player, with the ball in hand, trying to pass an adversary, and being held by him, he must at once drop the ball. While being held if the player does not drop the ball a free kick shall be given to the man who holds him. If the player be deliberately held back or thrown after he has dropped the ball he shall be awarded a free kick.

11. If any player, when the ball is in play, wilfully kick or force it out of bounds, the umpire shall give a free kick to the nearest player of the opposing team from the spot where the ball went out of bounds.

12. The ball while in play shall under no circumstances be thrown or handed to a player. A free kick shall be given against the player infringing this law to the nearest opposing player.

13. Tripping, hacking, rabbiting, slinging, striking a player with either fist or elbow, throwing a player after he has made a mark when the ball is out of play, or catching hold of a player below the knee, are prohibited. Charging a player when he is standing still or when in the air for a mark

is prohibited. Pushing a player from behind or while he is in the air is prohibited under any circumstances. A free kick shall be given against the player infringing the law.

14. The controlling body shall appoint for each match a field umpire who shall have full control of the play, and shall inflict penalties in accordance with the laws. In cases of doubt and in scrimmages he shall bounce the ball where the occurrence took place. A player disputing the decision of an umpire, or unduly interfering with or assaulting, or using abusive, threatening, or insulting language towards him during the progress of the game, or within or without the enclosure on the day of the match, shall be dealt with as the controlling body may think fit. A player assaulting another player, or using abusive, threatening, or insulting language, or otherwise misconducting himself during the progress of the game, or within the enclosure on the day of the match, shall be reported by the umpire to and dealt with as the controlling body may think fit.

15. The field umpire shall, prior to, and may at any time before the conclusion of the match, examine the boots of the players, and no one wearing projecting nails or iron plates shall be allowed to play until a change be made to the satisfaction of the umpire.

16. Two goal umpires shall be appointed for each match. They shall be sole judges of goals and behinds, and their decision shall be final, except in cases where the ball has become dead, either by ringing of the bell, or decision of the field umpire. Goals shall be indicated by two flags, and a behind by one flag. The goal umpire must, before raising his flag or flags to register a goal or behind, ascertain from the field umpire whether the ball had not been touched or any infringement of the laws had taken place. A goal or behind given in accordance with the above cannot be annulled.

17. The goal umpires shall keep a record of all goals and behinds kicked in any match, and furnish a report to the Secretary of the controlling body within three days.

18. The controlling body may disqualify players for any term who have been reported for breaches of the laws.

19. Should the Field Umpire appointed for a match before or during the progress of a game become incapable through sickness or accident to perform his duties, a substitute shall be appointed by mutual arrangement

between the Captains of the opposing sides, failing which any delegate or delegates present shall decide in the matter.

'Good bye – till next season': the end of the 25th football season (**The Australasian Sketcher,** *21 October 1882*).

Index

Page numbers in italic refer to illustrations. As noted on page 32 teams from Collingwood and Richmond appeared in the 1860s but had no connection with the present clubs, founded in 1892 and 1885 respectively. References to the present clubs have been distinguished by adding the foundation date within parentheses.

14th Regiment
  in Hobart 141
  in Melbourne 83-4
    v Albert Park (1869) 84-5
    v Melbourne (1869) 85
  in Perth 141-2
18th Regiment
  crowd control 86-7
  v Carlton (1870) 87

Abbotsford Football Club 110
Aborigines, influence on Australian football 203-5
Acraman, John 136
Adelaide, football in 1860s 134-8
Adelaide Football Club 134, *136*, 145
  and formulation of rules 137-8
  and foundation of SAFA 145
  v Port Adelaide (1875) 138
  v St Kilda (1877) 146-7
Adelaide Oval 138
Adelphian Football Club 109
admission charges 101, 103, 160
  introduction 112-13
Albert Ground 32

Albert Park 109
Albert Park Football Club 82, 118
  and foundation of VFA 129
  and new rules (1874) 125
  v 14th Regiment (1869) 84-5
  v Hobson's Bay Railway 77
  v Melbourne (1870) 78-9
  see also South Melbourne Football Club
Albert Park/North Melbourne combined team 128
Albion Imperials Football Club 120
Albury 170
American football (gridiron) 2, 197-9
appeals to the umpire 59
Association football *see* soccer
Assumption College, Kilmore 188
attendances 38, 41, 81, *83*, 107-8, 157-8, 164
  in Adelaide 146, 153
  at Albert Park v Carlton (1870) 86-7
  Carlton v Melbourne games 112
  charges *see* admission charges
  compared with soccer in UK 108
  by women *86*, 174

by soldiers 86-7
in Sydney 151
in Tasmania 155-6
Australian football
 and Gaelic football 193-6
 influences 43-5
  Aborigines 203-5
  cricket 186, 199-200
  Irish 187-97
 in New Zealand 142-3
 rules 46-9, 53-64, 125-7, 169-71, 172-3
  differing interpretations 93-4
  influence of Harrison 68, 70, 71-2
  see also football, rules; also specific issues, e.g. marking
 size of grounds 13, 44, 46, 50-1
 see also football
Australian Rules Football see Australian football
Avoca 114
Ayers, Henry 134-5, 146

Baker, C. 124
ball
 bouncing 74-5
 dimensions 116
 manufacture 66-7, 116
 shape of 46, 64-7
Ballarat 36-8, 91-4, 158-9
 combined team v VFL (1897) 172
Ballarat Athletic Club 36
Ballarat Football Club 37, 42, 118, 128
 drops out of senior football 158-9
 and foundation of VFA 130
 v Geelong
  (1862) 37-8
  (1863) 62-3
  (1871) 93-4
  (1872) 96
 v Melbourne (1871) 79-80
 v Norwood (1880) 153
 v Redan (1871) 92
Ballarat Imperials Football Club 120
Bankers Football Club 145
Barclay, George 135-6
barracking 87-9, 175
 origin of term 88-9
Barwon Football Club 118, 124-5, 128

and foundation of VFA 130
v Carlton (1877) 119
Batman's Hill 11
Beechworth Football Club 130
behind posts, forerunners 56, 58
behinds 56, 124, 169-70, 171
Bell's Life in Victoria
 announcement of football match (1858) 23-4
 on *Tom Brown's School Days* 29
 Wills's letter 19-22
Bendigo 35-6
Bendigo Football Club, v Sandhurst (1883), trophy *43*
bookmakers 163
boundary umpires 179
Boyle and Scott (ball manufacturers) 116
Bracken, L. 125
Bracken, W. 119, 120
Break O'Day Football Club 139, 140
Brickwood's Academy 5
Broken Hill 182
Bromby, John E. 12-13, 14, 25
Brunswick Football Club 109, 170
Bryant, James ('Jerry') 23-4, 26, 55
Budd, Henry H. 67

Caledonian Society, challenge cup 55
caps 42
Carlton Football Club 128, 166
 in 1877-88 seasons 160
 admission charges 112
 attendances 112
 drawn games 124
 drop kick competition (1877) 117-18
 foundation 3, 32
 and foundation of VFA 129
 and foundation of VFL 168
 grounds 111-12
 and match-fixing 163
 and new rules (1874) 125
 players 60, *72*, 118
 and shape of ball 67
 v 18th Regiment (1870) 87
 v Barwon (1877) 119
 v East Melbourne (1876) 125
 v Essendon (1893) 167
 v Fitzroy (1897) 171

Index

v Melbourne
  (1871) 80
  (1876) 112, 125
  (1877) 113-14
  (1880) *99*
  (1881) *76*
  attendances 107-8
  v Norwood (1880) 153
  v South Melbourne (1910) 183
  v Waratah RFC (1877) 151-2
Carlton Imperial Football Club 111, 128
Castlemaine Football Club 130
centre bounces 179-80
charging 60, 126-7, 170
cigarette cards *162*
Clarke, J.E. 75-6
Clarke, *Sir* William 130
club colours 42-3, 110-11
club loyalty 31
Clyde Hotel (Carlton) 110
Coleraine 114
Collingwood Football Club 3, 32, 110, 124, 129
Collingwood Football Club (1892) 166, 173
  and foundation of VFL 168
  ladies grandstand 174
  and match-fixing 163
  v Melbourne (1896) 177
  v St Kilda (1897) 172
  v South Adelaide (1897) 182
  v South Melbourne (1896) 174
colours *see* club colours
Comet Football Club 109
Condon, — (Collingwood captain) 181
Conway, Jack 60
Cosby, *Ensign* — 86
Coulthard, George *119*, 152
country football 34-40, 90-5, 114, 158-9
Coverdale, Myles 140
Crapp, H. 'Ivo' 181
cricket, influence on Australian football 186, 199-200
cricket grounds
  as venues for football 51-2, 114
    Adelaide Oval 138
    MCG 52, 101, 113-14

Cricketer's Guide, The 46
Cullinlaringo station, Qld 208
Cusack, Michael 193

defensive spirit 122-3
depression, impact on football 164
Dobson, Henry 139
dodgers 78
Dooley, Tim 88
drawn games
  (1880) 124
  (1896) 167-8
drop kicks 117
Dunedin 142-3
duration *see* playing time

East Melbourne cricket ground 102-3
East Melbourne Football Club 124, 125, 128, 157
Eighteenth Regiment *see* 18th Regiment
Emerald Hill football team 32
Essendon Football Club 3, 32, 129
  in 1881 season 160
  in 1891-4 seasons 165-6
  colours 110
  drawn games 124
  at East Melbourne 103
  and foundation of VFL 168
  and player payments 163
  v Carlton (1893) 167
  v Royal Park (1862) 41
Excelsior Football Club 109

Faraday Union Football Club 109
Fawkner Park 26-7
Fitzroy Football Club 32, 110-11, 157, 166
  and foundation of VFL 168
  v Carlton (1897) 171
  v St Kilda (1897) 173
followers (position) 121-2
football
  as character training 21, 22, 29, 97
  check in popularity 41-2
  conflict between different codes 133
  earliest matches 11-12, 23-7, *23*
  early clubs 31
  in early schools 12-19
  first recorded match in Australia 188

popular support 12, 98, 103-4, 132, 174-5
  see also attendances; barracking
relative antiquity of codes 2-3
rules 24, 25-6, 27-8
  in South Australia, early days 134-8
  in Sydney 89
  in Tasmania, early days 138-41
  see also Australian football; also names of other codes, *e.g.* Gaelic football
Footballer, The 54
  playing positions 58
Footscray Football Club 157, 170
  drawn games (1896) 167
  not invited to join VFL 168
Fourteenth Regiment *see* 14th Regiment
Forrester, Chubby 86
Freeman, 'Billy' 77
Fremantle Football Club 166
Friendly Societies' Gardens 99

Gaelic Athletic Association 189, 193
Gaelic football 2, 192-6
  re-invention 193
  rules 192-3
Geelong 32-4
  early football 12
Geelong Football Club 33-4, 42, 118, 128
  in 1877-88 seasons 160
  in 1881 season 159
  in Adelaide (1879) 152
  attendances 107, 108
  colours 42-3
  drawn games 124
    (1896) 167
  foundation 3
  and foundation of VFA 130
  and foundation of VFL 168
  Harrison as a player 33-4, 38, 71
  and new rules (1874) 125
  v Ballarat 37-8
    (1863) 62-3
    (1871) 93-4
    (1872) 96
  v Barwon (1876) 124-5
  v Geelong Imperial (1876) 124
  v Melbourne
    (1861) 71
    (1862) 54
    (1863) 55
    (1880) *178*
  v Norwood (1880) 153
  Wills and 97
  Wills family members as players 209
Geelong Imperial Football Club 124, 128
Glenferrie Oval 112
goal sneaks 115-16, 123-4
goal square 56-7
goal umpires 178
goals
  scoring 53
    1874 rule changes 127, 128
    by deflection off a tree 53-4
  disputes 54, 85, 124-5
  easier 122
goldfields 34-8, 40
Gordon, Adam Lindsay 210
Gorman, Tom 60
Grace, W.G. 103
gridiron *see* American football (gridiron)
grounds
  dimensions 13, 44, 46, 50-1, 112
    problem for umpires 176-7
  shape 49-50, 114-15
Grubb, H. 139

hacking 59-60
Hamilton 91
Hammersley, William J. 47, 60
Harrison, H.C.A. 55, 60, 68-73, 82, 102, 205
  as a player 72-3, 77
    for Geelong 33-4., 38, 71
    for Melbourne 33, 71, 78-80, 85
    for Richmond 33
  on Ensign Cosby incident 85-6
  and football in Adelaide 137
  and football in Geelong 33-4
  portraits 69, *205*
  relationship to Wills 33, 68-9, 70
  as rule-maker 68, 70, 71-2
  Story of an Athlete 205
  on trees in Richmond Paddock 105
  and Victorian Football Association 130

Index

Hawthorn Football Club 129
  colours 110
Heathcote 40
high marks 119-20
  Aboriginal influence 203, 204
  hazardous 120
Hobart Town Football Club 138-9
  v New Town (1866) 139
Hobson's Bay Railway team 77
Hotham Football Club 109, 118, 124, 129
  and foundation of VFA 130
  in Tasmania (1881) 155
  v Norwood (1880) 153
Hotham Union Football Club 109
Hotham United Football Club *see* Hotham Football Club
Hughes, Thomas 29

Inglewood Football Club 130
Inglewood (town) 114
inter-colonial matches
  Australian football 152, 153-4
    and foundation of VFA 130, 131
    see also entries under Victoria
  cricket 9, 133

Jacomb, Newton 61
James, G.L., *Shall I try Australia?* 87-8
Jenkins, Stitt 33
Jolimont Football Club 109

Kangaroo Flat ground 90
Kelland, W.G. 117
Kelly, Pat 84, 88
Kennedy, George D. 145
Kensington Football Club 137-8
  and foundation of SAFA 145
Kent County Cricket Club 6
kick-off posts 56, *58*
kicking 116, 117-18, 167
Kilmore 114
Kingston, Charles Cameron 137

Launceston Football Club 140-1
Lee, Dick 124, 165
Little, John 36
little kicks *see* little marks
little marks 99, 118-19, 169, 170

Macadam, John 17, 102
Madeline Street Reserve 112
marking 51, 64, 73
  see also high marks; little marks
Marshall, George 66
Marshall, Theodore 75-7
Maryborough 40
match-fixing 163
matches
  duration 18, 54, 55-6, 63, 91
      South Australia 135
Melbourne City Football Club 109
Melbourne Cricket Club 23
  and early promotion of football 26, 49
  Wills and 8-9, 20, 26
Melbourne Cricket Ground 85
  1860s 100-1
  (1881) *158*
  availability for football 52, 101, 113-14
  parkland, appearance in 1850s 1-2
  reversible grandstand 114
    after fire (1994) 95
Melbourne Football Club 33, 60, 109, 124, 128
  attendances 107-8, 112
  colours 43
  foundation 3, 26, 32
  and foundation of VFA 130
  and foundation of VFL 168
  Harrison as player 33, 71, 78-80, 85
  and rules 37, 46
    new rules (1874) 125
  in Sydney (1881) 154
  v 14th Regiment (1869) 85
  v Albert Park (1870) 78
  v Ballarat (1871) 79-80
  v Carlton
    (1871) 80
    (1876) 112, 125
    (1877) 113-14
    (1880) *99*
    (1881) 76
  v Collingwood (1896) 177
  v East Melbourne (1876) 125
  v Geelong
    (1861) 71
    (1862) 54

(1863) 55
(1880) *178*
v Norwood (1880) 153
v Richmond (1860) 104
v Royal Park (1865) 75-6
v SA combined team (1877) 146
v St Kilda (1859) 104
v Sandhurst (1872) 90
v South Melbourne (1897) 182
v South Yarra
(1858) 27
(1859) 52
v University (1862) 55
v Victorian FC (Adelaide) (1877) 146
Melbourne Grammar School 12-13, 14, 25-6, 27
v St Kilda Grammar School (1858) 14
v Scotch College (1858) 15-18
commemorative plaque *19*
shape of ball 65
umpires 17, 58
Metropolitan Football Club *see* Melbourne Football Club
Miller, Henry 102
Mills, John 120-1
Morrison, Alexander 14-15
Mullen, C.C. 32
Munro, Charles J. 142
Mynn, Alfred 6

New South Wales v Victoria (1881) 154
New Town Football Club 138
v Break O'Day (1871) 140
v Hobart Town (1866) 139
New Zealand, Australian football in 142-3
Newing, W. 151
Nissen's Café 125
North Melbourne Football Club 130, 170, 173
and new rules (1874) 125
not invited to join VFL 168
see also Albert Park/North Melbourne combined team; Hotham Football Club
Northcott, William C. 13-14
Norwood Football Club, in Victoria 153

Noyes, A.W. 84
NSW v Victoria (cricket, 1858) 9
Nudd, H. 118

O'Dodd, J. 139
offside rule 46, 53, 63-4, 123, 177
Old Etonians 148
overhead marks *see* high marks
own goals 128

Parade Hotel 23, 47
payments to players *see* player payments
Pearce, James *133*
Perth, football in 141-2, 164
player payments 160-3
playing positions 58, 115-16
playing time 18, 39, 54, 55-6, 63, 91
in South Australia 135
Police Paddock 100
popular support 12, 98, 103-4, 174-5
temporary decline (1863) 41-2
see also attendances; barracking
Port Adelaide Football Club 3, 137-8, 144
and foundation of SAFA 145
v Adelaide (1875) 138
Port Fairy 91, 114
Port Melbourne Football Club 110, 157, 170, 173
drawn games (1896) 167
not invited to join VFL 168
players on strike 162
positions on the field *see* playing positions
Powlett football team 109
Prahran Football Club 32, 157
and match-fixing 163
Prince Alfred College (Adelaide) 145
Princes Park 168
Punt Road Oval 100
pushing in the back 60-1, 172

Queensland
Australian football in 148-9, 155
team (1888) *154*

rabbiting 126
Redan Football Club 92
Richmond Cricket Club 9

Index

Richmond Football Club 32, 33, 109
  v Melbourne (1860) 104
Richmond Football Club (1885)
  joins VFA 157
  and match fixing 163
  not invited to join VFL 168, 170
Richmond Paddock 23, 46, 54, 55
  appearance in 1860s 106
  see also Yarra Park
Richmond Standard Football Club 109
Rising Sun Football Club 109
Rosalind Park, Bendigo 35
rough play 45, 48, 59-60, 61, 78-80, 126, 172
  in American football 198
  in Ballarat 92, 94
  see also violence, on the field
Royal Park 106, 109-10, 111
Royal Park Football Club 32
  v Essendon (1862) 40
  v Melbourne (1865) 75-6
Rugby League football 2
Rugby School 2, 5-7, 28
  see also Tom Brown's School Days
Rugby Union football 2
  in Sydney 149, 149-51
rules *see* Australian football, rules; football, rules
running play 64, 73-6

St Arnaud 114
St Kilda Alma Football Club 109
St Kilda Football Club 3, 25-6, 32, 109, 128
  and foundation of VFA 130
  and foundation of VFL 169
  and new rules (1874) 125
  rejoins VFA 157
  team sent to Adelaide (1877) 200
  v Adelaide (1877) 146-7
  v Collingwood (1897) 172
  v Fitzroy (1897) 173
  v Melbourne (1859) 104
  v South Australian Natives (1877) 147
St Kilda Grammar School 13-14
  v Melbourne Grammar School (1858) 14
St Patrick's College, Ballarat 188

St Patrick's College, Melbourne 190
Sale Football Club 118
Sandhurst Football Club
  foundation 35
  v Bendigo (1883), trophy 43
  v Melbourne (1872) 90
  v South Yarra (1872) 90
  v Volunteers (1861) 35-6
Sandridge Alma Football Club
  see Port Melbourne Football Club
Sands & McDougall football team 109
Savigny, W.H. 140
Scotch College 14-18
  v Melbourne Grammar School (1858) 15-18
  commemorative plaque 19
  shape of ball 65
  umpires 17, 58
scrummages 61-2, 64, 122, 126, 201
  goals scored by 53
sending-off rule 184, 185-6
  in Gaelic football 184-5
Shall I try Australia? (James) 87-8
Smith, Thomas Henry 47, 190
soccer 2
South Adelaide Football Club 144
  and foundation of SAFA 145
  v Collingwood (1897) 182
South Australia
  Australian football in 143-8
  football in 1860s 134-8
  v Victoria
    (1879) 127, 152
    (1880) 153
South Australian Football Association 145
South Australian Natives 147
South Fremantle Football Club *see* Fremantle Football Club
South Melbourne Football Club 109, 118, 129, 152
  in 1877-88 seasons 160
  in 1881 season 159
  attendances 108
  drawn games 124
  and foundation of VFL 168
  v Carlton (1910) 183
  v Collingwood (1896) 174
  v Melbourne (1897) 182

v Norwood (1880) 153
see also Emerald Hill
South Melbourne ground 80
South Melbourne Imperial Football Club 109
South Park Football Club 109, 145
South Williamstown Football Club 157
South Yarra Football Club 32, 110
   Presentation Challenge Cup *80*
   v Melbourne
     (1858) 27
     (1859) 52
   v Sandhurst (1872) 90
South Yarra (suburb) 26-7
Southern Rugby Football Union 149
spectators, encroachment on arena 103-4, 108, 128
Spence, J.B. 136
Stawell 114
Story of an Athlete (Harrison) 205
Stowell Football Club 139
Stratford Football Club 118
Streeton, Arthur 100
suspensions 180, 181
Swan, E. 139
Sydney, Australian football in 148-52

tackling 125-6
Tasmania
   Australian football in 155-6
   football in 1860s 138-41
teams, number of players 169, 172, 177
Thompson, James B. 35, 45, 47
throwing in 57, 121, *185*
throwing the ball up 121
Thurgood, Albert 164-7
   kicking ability 165, 167
timekeepers 179
Tom Brown's School Days 28-30
Topping, George 183
Town life in Australia (Twopeny) 148
trees
   within playing arena 16, 17, *23*, 50-1, 52, 104-6
     goals scored by deflection from 53-4
tripping 45, 59, 61

Twopeny, Richard E.N. 145, 146, 147-8
Town life in Australia 148

Ulbrick, J. 117
umpires 46-7, 48, 58-9, 176-86
   captains as 58-9, 61
   disputed decisions 85
     South Australia 138
     see also goals, scoring, disputes
   evolving role 177-80
   Melbourne GS v Scotch College (1858) 17
   payment 178, 179
   violence against 181, 182-3
University Football Club 32
   drops out of senior football 111
   joins VFA 157
   v Melbourne (1862) 55

Vaucluse Football Club 109
Victoria
   Australian football
     v New South Wales (1881) 154
     v South Australia
       (1879) 127, 152
       (1880) 153
   cricket
     v NSW (1858) 9
Victoria Parade Football Club 109
Victoria United Football Club 109
Victorian Football Association
   foundation 129-31
   and inter-colonial matches 131, 150-1
   membership 129-30, 157
   organizes fixtures 160
   payment of umpires 178
   and player payments 161, 162-3
   rule changes (1897) 169-70, 172-3
Victorian Football Club (Adelaide) 144-5
   colours 144
   and foundation of SAFA 145
   v Melbourne (1877) 146
   in Victoria (1878) 152
Victorian Football League 160
   combined team v Ballarat (1897) 172
   foundation 168-9
Victorian Gymnastic Games 12

Victorian Railways football team 109
violence
  against umpires 181, 182-3
  on the field 180, 183
Volunteers v Sandhurst (1861) 35-6

Waratah Rugby Union Football Club 151-2
Wardill, Dick 174
warehousmen's football team 32
Warrnambool 38-40, 91
Warwick Football Club 109
Way, Samuel 145
Were, J.B. 102
West Melbourne Football Club 124, 129, 157
Western Australia 141-2
  spread of Australian football 164
Williamstown Football Club 129, 170
  colours 110
  drawn games (1896) 167
  joins VFA 157
  not invited to join VFL 168
Wills, Edward 4
Wills, Emily 69
Wills, Horatio Spencer 4, 6, 208
Wills, Thomas Wentworth 101
  ancestry 3-4
  childhood 4-5
  coach of Aboriginal cricket team 204, 209
  and football in Geelong 32-3, 33-4, 97
  and formulation of rules 47
  on hacking 60
  influence on Australian football 3, 26, 206-9, 211-12
  as innovator 207
  later life 210-12
  letter to *Bell's Life* 19-22, 25
  personality and appearance 6, 8, 22
  portraits 4, *212*
  relationship to Harrison 68-9, 70
  relationship with Aborigines 5, 204
  at Rugby School 5-7
  sporting prowess 5-10
  umpire for Melbourne Grammar 17
Woodville Football Club 144
  and foundation of SAFA 145

Wray, Thomas 49
Wright, G. 139

Yarra Park 16-17, 23, 27, 52, 98-103, 109-10
Young Victorians Football Club 109